CREATING CULTURE, PERFORMING COMMUNITY

This book is a publication of

Indiana University Press
Office of Scholarly Publishing
Herman B Wells Library 350
1320 East 10th Street
Bloomington, Indiana 47405 USA

iupress.org

© 2025 by Mintzi Auanda Martínez-Rivera

All rights reserved

No part of this book may be reproduced or utilized in any form or by any means, electronic or mechanical, including photocopying and recording, or by any information storage and retrieval system, without permission in writing from the publisher.

First Printing 2025

Cataloging information is available from the Library of Congress.

ISBN 978-0-253-07341-9 (hardback)
ISBN 978-0-253-07342-6 (paperback)
ISBN 978-0-253-07344-0 (ebook)
ISBN 978-0-253-07343-3 (web PDF)

TO MY ANCESTORS,
who guide me

TO MY COMMUNITIES,
who support and give me purpose

TO MY FAMILY,
who gives me life and the love that allows me to be

Contents

Acknowledgments ix

Introduction: Getting Married in Angahuan 1

1. Under the Volcano's Shadow: Angahuan and the
   P'urhépecha Area 33

2. Carrying the Uarhota: Courtship Rituals and Youth
   Cultures in Angahuan 61

3. Te Toca: Eloping versus Asking for Marriage 89

4. Creating Culture: Organizing a Tembuchakua 107

   Interlude: Joel and Daniela's P'urhépecha Wedding
   (October 2009) 133

5. Performing Community: Following the Confetti Trail 145

6. Transforming the Tembuchakua 175

   Conclusion: Getting Married in Angahuan, Revisited 203

References 211
Index 225

Acknowledgments

While this book comes out of my dissertation research, I worked on the manuscript for over ten years. The reason it took so long was that I needed to find my voice. I had to find the story that I needed to tell. In that time, a huge community made up of my family, friends, colleagues, and editors aided me in multiple ways, helping me become the scholar and person that I strive to be. While these acknowledgments are not an exhaustive representation of the twenty years I have been working on this project, I do wish to express my gratitude to those who have supported me in the last ten years.

Thank you to the amazing crew at Indiana University Press, especially Allison Chaplin and Sophia Hebert, who have been an incredible and supportive help during the last stages of the writing, production, and publication of this book. Thank you to Pamela S. Rude for her patience while we worked on the book cover. I am also grateful to the two anonymous reviewers who provided insightful and productive feedback, which helped make this manuscript stronger. I am honored and humbled that this book is part of *Underground Cultures*, a series edited by my incredible colega-comadre Solimar Otero. Soli, your support has meant everything to me; thank you for believing in this project and allowing it to be part of your book series.

During the five years that I was part of the Department of Sociology and Anthropology at Providence College, my first tenure-track home, I was fortunate that I had the support and mentorship of an amazing group of colleagues. I am forever grateful to Abigail Brooks, Kara Cebulko, Christopher Chambers, Sophia Edwards, Eric Hirsch, Rahsaan Mahadeo, Brandon Martinez, Jessica Mulligan, Charlotte O'Kelly, Maureen Outlaw, Vanessa M. Sullivan, and Eve

Veliz-Moran. Abigail and Jessica read early drafts of the first chapters and provided the insights that allowed me to start finding my voice. Kara, thank you so much for writing so many letters of recommendation and for your unwavering support. Thank you all for giving me an academic home and allowing me to soar.

The final version of this book was completed at my new academic home, The Ohio State University. I am incredibly honored to be in the company of brilliant and generous colleagues who made my first year there a pleasure. I am especially grateful to the Folklore community: Katie Borland, Merrill Kaplan, Galey Modan, Dorothy Noyes, Amy Shuman, and Jasper Waugh-Quasebarth. I am also grateful to the Latinx Studies / Ethnic Studies community, especially Paloma Martínez-Cruz and Namiko Kunimoto. In the English Department, I have been welcomed by wonderful colleagues, such as Amrita Dhar, Pranav Jani, Beverly Moss, Joe Ponce, Elissa Washuta, and Susan Williams. Susan Williams, Galey Modan, David Brewer, and Clare Simmons, thank you for the last round of comments for the introduction, which you generously gave me during my first annual review.

The bulk of the writing of this book was completed during a 2021–2022 yearlong research leave supported by a six-month Career Enhancement Fellowship (CEF) from the Institute of Citizens and Scholars (formerly known as the Woodrow Wilson Foundation) and a third-year research leave from Providence College. I was fortunate that Luis Urrieta Jr. agreed to be my mentor as part of the CEF program. His insightful and incisive feedback and comments helped me shape the book into what it is today. Even after we finished working as part of the CEF program, I could hear his voice guiding me as I worked on the manuscript. ¡Diosï Meaiamu, Tata Luis!

During the ten years that it took me to finish this book, I worked on other projects that pushed me theoretically and methodologically and as a writer. Coediting with my hermanas-colegas-comadres, Solimar Otero and Rachel Valentina González, was an intellectually joyful challenge. I have grown and become better thanks to you both. Love you!

Starting in 2017, I have been fortunate to be part of a growing P'urhépecha Studies community in the United States. Connecting first with Gabriela Spears-Rico, Luis Urrieta Jr., and Pavel Shlossberg and then welcoming Mario Alberto Gómez Zamora and fabian romero, among a growing number of P'urhépecha and P'urhepechista scholars, has allowed me to further refine my theoretical approaches based on P'urhépecha epistemologies and worldviews. I am grateful to all of you, and I am humbled to be part of our community. Diosï meaiamu uajia.

ACKNOWLEDGMENTS

xi

My academic work is heavily intertwined with my personal life, in the sense that my personal life gives meaning and purpose to my academic work. Without a strong and rich personal life, I would not be able to do what I do. Therefore, I am incredibly grateful to my strong network of friends, who, more than friends, are family.

In Bloomington, Indiana, I am grateful to/for the Latinx Studies community, mainly Arlene Díaz, Silvia Martinez, John Nieto-Phillips, Alberto Varón, and Micaela Richter, who gave me a job and home when I had just finished my PhD. You all helped me transition from graduate school into a faculty role. The Latinx Studies community has all but saved my life; siempre estaré agradecida. Thank you to John H. McDowell, Pat, and Michael, who always had a space for me in their home, for all the cariño and support. Maria Hamilton Abegunde, thank you for your wisdom, poetry, joy, brilliance, and healing hugs. Marvin D. Sterling, thank you for being a dear friend, a fellow nerd, and a dedicated writing partner. I am incredibly grateful for your solidarity and intellectual generosity.

In Providence, Rhode Island, I am grateful for my afternoon walks with Sydney Manley—they kept me sane during the worst of the pandemic. I am also grateful and miss terribly the hugs, meals, and conversations with Chris Chambers and Jacob van den Berg (and SweetPea). I love and cherish you both. En especial estoy agradecida por la amistad, cariño, compañia, y apoyo de Javier Mocarquer. Mil gracias por todas las charlas, comidas, caminatas, y tardes de tertulia. Te amo y extraño, pero sé que nos veremos pronto.

In Columbus, Ohio, I am grateful and fortunate to have a new, yet strong, community/family. Super agradecida por Carlos Rivas and Vanni Castillo, and fabian romero and Kim Saito (and Suki). Transitions are never easy, but I am fortunate to have you in my life. I look forward to many more nights of delicious meals, bowling, and karaoke.

During these ten years, I have also been supported by my chosen family. Eric César Morales, and Sofia McDowell and the superstar Gianni, mil gracias por todas las risas, las vacaciones en Ixtapa, y hasta los pun (dad) jokes. Pablo Martín Dominguez, mi hermano del otro lado del charco, mil gracias por tu apoyo incondicional y conversaciones intelectuales intensas, te amo y extraño. Victor Rodríguez Pereira y Rashid Marcano, gracias por nuestras conversaciones random que a veces terminan siendo profundas. Miguel Díaz Cruz y Gloria Colom Braña, juntos con Danny y Loki, desde los bonobos a los desayunos en medio de la nada en Texas, mil gracias por todas las risas, lágrimas, grabados, y por estar en mi vida. Rachel V. González, Tony, and Martha, my life is better because you are in it. Rachel, in addition to being my conference wife and academic sister, you are one of my intellectual rocks; thank you for being such an inspiration. Johanna Moya-Fábregas, Leah, Yolanda, Sean, Piper, and Niko, thank you so much for giving me a home in Austin, for the laughter, delicious food, and love. Johanna, soy super afortunada, honrada, y feliz de tenerte en mi vida. Caminar la vida contigo en estos veinte años, desde escuela graduada hasta ahora, han sido un privilegio y miles de horas de pavera. Tu forma de ver y enfrentar la vida me inspiran y sirven de guía. Gracias por hacerme la tía de Leah, y por estar en mi vida.

Este libro no hubiera sido posible sin el apoyo de la comunidad y generosidad de Angahuan. Siempre estaré agradecida con Ta Lucas Gómez Bravo (QEPD), mi instructor de P'urhépecha en la Michoacana. Ta Lucas además de iniciarme en la complejidad de la lengua y cultura P'urhépecha, me presentó a la familia de su hermano, a los Gómez Santacruz, con los cuales he vivido en Angahuan desde el 2006. Mi más sincero agradecimiento y amor a todos los Gómez Santacruz: Ta Emiliano, Na Juana, Cayetana, Inés, Tomasa, María de Jesús, Esperanza, Francisco, Eusebio, Cecilia, Zenón y Leticia, a sus parejas y a sus hijés. Su hospitalidad, generosidad, cariño, cuidado, paciencia, y alegría hicieron posible el que yo pudiera hacer esta investigación y completar este libro. Mil gracias por contestar todas mis preguntas y mensajes de texto cuando se me ocurría una cosa mientras escribía el libro. Soy sumamente afortunada de tenerlos en mi vida y que seamos familia. Diosï meiamu uajia.

Además de la familia Gómez Santacruz, varias personas en Angahuan me abrieron sus puertas para compartir y hablar conmigo. Especialmente quiero agradecer a Ta Manuel, Aureliano, Fermín, Tariacuri, Simón, Epifania, Padre Armando, Sandra, y Lucía, quienes siempre sacaban tiempo para hablar conmigo, explicarme cosas y aclarar dudas. Además, quiero agradecer a la familia extendida de los Gómez Santacruz, sus ahijados y demás parientes, por ayudar con este proyecto y darme permiso para documentar bodas, funerales, bautizos, primeras comuniones, y otras festividades. Este trabajo fue colaborativo, en el cual tanto personas conocidas como desconocidas me ayudaron y apoyaron. Siempre estaré endeudada con los comuneros de Angahuan. Solo espero que este trabajo y mi trabajo futuro puedan reflejar la complejidad y riqueza de su cultura y comunidad.

Siempre estaré agradecida y llevaré en mi corazón a mi familia extendida, a los Rivera Rivera (en Puerto Rico), y a los Martínez Chávez, Chávez Guido, y Chávez Castillo (en Michoacán). El apoyo de todos mis tiés, primés, sobrinés, ha sido clave en que tenga una vida llena de alegrias, amor, generosidad, deliciosa comida, y muchas aventuras. En especial estoy sumamente agradecida con los Martínez Chávez y Chávez Guido, quienes me abrieron las puertas y me

ACKNOWLEDGMENTS xiii

apoyaron durante el proceso de investigación y mientras escribía el libro. Miles de gracias a mi media-hermana, Heidi y mi increíble sobrina Ana por todo su cariño y apoyo. Erandi Martínez Muro, gracias por tu alegría, paciencia y todo lo que haces por nosotres. Haces que nuestra casa esté en orden, y que mi papá y mamá estén cuidados y felices.

Mi familia inmediata, mis padres y hermanes, son mi roca y mi razón de ser. Todo lo que he logrado es gracias a ustedes. Mis progenitores, Antonio Martínez Chávez y Carmen Belén Rivera Rivera son un ejemplo de generosidad, amor, dedicación, determinación, alegría, y pasión. El hogar y la familia que ustedes han creado son un ejemplo a seguir, en como dán la bienvenida a gente nueva y los convierten en familia. Mil gracias por siempre tener la puerta abierta para sus hijes, por darme un espacio para escribir y trabajar, por inspirarme, por los besos y abrazos, por secar mis lagrimas y hacerme reir, por las pláticas, por empujarme a ser mejor, por toda la comida deliciosa y el sabrozo mezcal. Citlali, Niraj, Rishi y Keia, gracias por todo su amor, por darme otro hogar, por todas las alegrías, aventuras, por hacer que mi vida sea mejor. Marco Antonio (Toño), Ale, y Luka, mil gracias por su apoyo incondicional, por sus bromas, por apoyar mis embelecos intelectuales, y por su constante amor. Yuiza, Mario, Kairós, y Soma (QEPD), gracias por la compañía mientras escribía el libro. Nuestro grupo de escritura (junto con deliciosas comidas, buen vino, y mezcal) hicieron de este proceso de escritura, uno comunitario y colaborativo. Yuiza, miles de gracias por hacer los mapas y la ayuda con el diseño del libro. Durante mi año sabático en el 2021–2022 Salgari, mi bello, juguetón, y dramático Westie, llegó a mi vida. El ha sido una presencia constante mientras trabajo, dormido a mi lado o a mis pies, forzándome a tomar descansos para jugar con él o sacarlo a caminar. Mil gracias a todes, sin ustedes mi vida no tendría sentido. Los amo al infinito.

Este libro no hubiera sido possible sin mi principal editora, fuente de inspiración, alpha reader, mi brillante hermana, Citlali. En febrero 2022, durante unas vacaciones en Ixtapa, cuando estaba frustrada porque aunque llevaba muchos años/meses trabajando en el libro y seguía sin encontrarle el hilo, sin encontrar mi voz, mientras caminabamos/nadabamos en la piscina del hotel, reorganizamos mi libro y todas las piezas, poco a poco fueron cayendo en su sitio. Citlali, mil gracias por TODO. Yo te amo más.

This book is the result of hard work and love, supported by a vast and wide community. Please accept my apologies if I forgot to acknowledge you. And while many individuals aided in different stages of this research and writing process, the ideas hereby expressed are mine, and I take full responsibility for them.

CREATING CULTURE, PERFORMING COMMUNITY

Fig. 0.1 Pablo and Lisa's wedding. April 19, 2009.

Introduction

Getting Married in Angahuan

We woke up just after six on a cold April morning. As I lay in my warm bed, buried under a pile of wool blankets, I could hear the early sounds of the community, the sounds of different animals waking up—the crow of roosters, hens clucking, cows mooing, dogs barking, and birds singing—buses and trucks going up the road into the Sierra and the sounds of neighbors turning on their radios to kick off the day with music. Minutes before seven, as the sun rose over the mountains and dissipated the morning mist, Na Juana, Ta Emiliano, and I left the house.[1] Everybody else in the house was still fast asleep. We walked briskly toward Na Beatriz and Ta Anselmo's house, which was very close to us. When we arrived, Paulina and Laura (Na Beatriz's oldest daughters) were already up and sweeping the patio. Decorations of white and blue balloons and white cardboard cutouts of doves had been put up last night, and the tables for the feast were in their place along the patio. The parangua (firepit) was lit in the kitchen, and older female relatives were starting the preparations for the different meals of the day. Na Beatriz and Ta Anselmo had already left for the church to make sure everything was ready for the wedding mass. Pablo, the groom, came out of his room. He was wearing new clothes today: a black leather jacket, blue jeans, a button-down shirt, and a pair of black boots. We had come to the house specifically to accompany Pablo to the church. Before we left, Pablo knelt in front of his grandmothers and Na Juana and Ta Emiliano to receive their blessings. Pablo's nervous gaze swept the patio, and Na Juana gently reminded him that it was time to leave. We walked to the church, where Pablo's parents were waiting for us along with the bride, Lisa, her family, and their wedding godparents.[2] Lisa, like Pablo, was also wearing new clothes, but hers were not mestizo. She wore the traditional P'urhépecha female dress: her sïtakua (skirt) was pink, the tangarikua (apron) was green, her saco (outer blouse) was blue, and her kuanindikua (rebozo, or shawl) was a beautiful midnight blue.[3] Padre Armando gave the initial blessing at the church entrance and led the procession toward the altar where the Catholic wedding mass took place. We left the church after the mass, and as soon as Lisa and Pablo walked outside, a wind band, which had arrived during the mass, began to play. Relatives lined up to hug them and offer their blessings and congratulations. Pablo's sisters, Paulina and Laura, and other young female relatives began throwing confetti at the bride and groom and the people gathered around them. As the (un)official wedding photographer, I took requests from relatives wanting pictures with the couple (fig. 0.1). After around twenty minutes of pictures and congratulations, the procession began: Pablo and Lisa at the front, flanked by their wedding godparents, followed by young female relatives throwing confetti. After them, the rest of the wedding party, mainly aunts, uncles, and other older relatives, followed. At the end of the procession was the band, playing music. This was the beginning of a very long and very amazing day.[4]

Pablo and Lisa's wedding was the first I had been invited to after arriving in Angahuan in February 2009. It was, I discovered later, a perfect example of a P'urhépecha wedding in Angahuan, as it had all the characteristic elements of such a ceremony. But it was also a revelatory event for me. My first intention upon coming to Angahuan was to study the practice of reciprocity and the formation of social networks as performed during visitas (visits) and how young people in the community were participating in or challenging those practices. As I found out that day, the tembuchakua (wedding) in Angahuan is the epitome of the practice of visitas, as it is made up of different rituals that move participants throughout the community. Throughout the day of Pablo and Lisa's wedding, the guests moved constantly among the houses of the groom, the bride, and the wedding godparents, performing a myriad of rituals. Ideas of culture and community were visibly created, transformed, reinforced, and performed by the people moving from one place to another throughout the day.

Surrounded by the Sierra P'urhépecha mountains and under the shadow of the Paricutín volcano, Santo Santiago de Angahuan is a small P'urhépecha community of 4,330 inhabitants (according to the 2020 census) in Michoacán, México (fig. 03).[5] Angahuan is located 2,340 meters (7,677 feet) above sea level, making it the highest P'urhépecha settlement. Angahuan is part of the municipality of Uruapan, 35 kilometers southeast of the community. People from nearby cities describe Angahuan as a traditional P'urhépecha community. In Angahuan, P'urhépecha language is the principal mode of communication; most women wear traditional dress; the troje, a type of log cabin, is still visible

INTRODUCTION   3

throughout the town; the community has a strong religious and civil cargo system; and almost every weekend, there are celebrations, rituals, and festivals in the community.[6] However, Angahuan is also filled with trocas (pickup trucks) brought by returning norteños (returning migrants from the USA), people wearing Gap and Abercrombie & Fitch clothes, families gathering at night to watch the most popular TV Azteca or Televisa telenovela, and music from reggaeton, banda, bachata, and norteña groups. Like many other P'urhépecha and Indigenous communities, the people of Angahuan define what it means to be a member of their community and culture.

In the last twenty years, P'urhépecha cultural practices have gone through multiple cultural and structural transformations in Angahuan due to national or global events. In the last fifteen years, the effects of the US-México economic recession, the war on drugs that began in 2006, and the mass deportations of migrant workers in the United States between 2008 and 2012 were deeply felt in Angahuan. As a result, cultural practices transformed to adapt to the current political, economic, and social climate. For example, in the late 1990s, wedding practices in Angahuan changed to incorporate practices that people saw in telenovelas, movies, or nearby communities (discussed in chap. 6). Additionally, wedding practices adapted to the current reality and necessities of the families involved; people transformed the wedding to fit their economic realities. In 2010, families started celebrating a new wedding modality by mixing and choosing from the different rituals performed in the civil and religious weddings to cut costs (before families separated the weddings into two events). As Agustín, a research collaborator, told me in relation to celebrations in the community: "Se está agrandando, pero a la vez se está respetando lo que ya había" ("It is growing, but at the same time, we are respecting what was already there"). As this book explains, rituals in Angahuan have grown and become more elaborate, as exemplified in the tembuchakua, but the core of the rituals is being respected and maintained. Therefore, these transformations were and are made in a distinctly P'urhépecha/Angahuan way that follows the cultural logic of the community.

Through a deep ethnographic account of ritual practices, I analyze the creation, curation, performance, and transformations of wedding rituals in a P'urhépecha community. And while Angahuan has a richly complex cultural calendar filled with rituals relating to the political and religious cargo system, as well as rituals pertaining to life cycles, this book focuses specifically on the tembuchakua, as this wedding ritual serves as a cultural template that influences the way others are organized and performed in the community. By documenting the complex process of organizing and performing wedding rituals, my analysis highlights the conscious and active role of the people of Angahuan in transforming their culture. Moreover, by analyzing Indigenous identity and vernacular cultural practices, and how Angahuan residents are active participants in the transformation of their culture, I challenge the notions that Indigenous people are removed from the contemporary world and that Indigenous cultures cannot change without ceasing to be "authentic/ Indigenous."[7] To challenge these outdated conceptualizations about Indigeneity, this book moves among three interwoven arguments / axes / points of encounter: the creation of culture, the performance of community, and the transformation of cultural practices. As a result, this work showcases how Angahuan people create, curate, and transform their cultural practices. It also argues that, throughout this process, they perform what it means to be an active member of their P'urhépecha community and re/articulate and perform their own identity.

Throughout *Creating Culture, Performing Community*, I pay special attention to young people and their growing and active participation in the negotiation, creation, and performance of cultural practices in Angahuan, especially regarding the wedding ritual. Contrary to arguments contending that young people are forgetting or not engaging with or participating in their culture, my research in Angahuan argues that young people are active cultural participants who contribute to the cultural transformations that enable the continuity of P'urhépecha culture in their community. Specifically, young people transform their cultural practices so that they are relevant to their current situation, make sense to and for their generation, and fulfill their cultural needs. By doing this, young people actively learn and perform how to be a member of their P'urhépecha community.

As I mentioned, when I arrived in Angahuan in 2009 to start my yearlong research stay, I had not intended to research or write about weddings. However, when I left in 2010 and began to organize and code my data, everything pointed toward the wedding. I pivoted my research to follow my data and the story that was in front of me. This project caught me by surprise, and it has been a joy as well as intellectually challenging and rewarding to write about. The process of planning and having a wedding—and of writing and reading this text—may seem linear, but the experiences were far from straightforward. I hope that, despite all the movement and moving parts, this wedding story and how P'urhépecha people in Angahuan create their cultural practices and perform their belonging to their community are apparent and that this book does justice to the complexity and beauty of P'urhépecha vernacular cultural practices.

Fig. 0.2 Chucha and José's wedding. October 2010. Photo provided by the Gómez Santacruz family.

Brief Introduction to the Tembuchakua

In Angahuan, weddings can include up to four distinct events with their accompanying rituals: the Catholic ceremony, the civil ceremony, the P'urhépecha wedding, and casarse de blanco. The religious wedding in Angahuan is called misa kuani, and the civil wedding is called sivil kuambuni. The misa kuani, which is more important than the sivil kuambuni, is composed of the Catholic mass, the P'urhépecha wedding, and, depending on the financial situation or preferences of the bride and groom's families, the casarse de blanco (to marry in white or white wedding) (fig. 0.2). The misa kuani normally last three days (the day before, the day of, and the day after the wedding), and each day has specific rituals. The sivil kuambuni is celebrated in one day, making it less expensive and elaborate than the misa kuani. Casarse de blanco is, literally, "to marry in a white wedding gown" and was inspired by telenovela weddings (see chap. 6). In the space of three to four hours, the casarse de blanco covers all the different rituals of a traditional mestizo Mexican wedding: the waltz, the toast, throwing the bouquet and the garter, and a game of la víbora de la mar.[8]

When planning weddings, Angahuan families take into consideration the community's calendar of celebrations.[9] Weddings are not performed during Lent, from late June to late August, or in November. While the Church does not have an official ban on marriages during Lent, I was told by research collaborators that people in Angahuan do not celebrate misa kuani between Ash Wednesday and Holy Week. This explains why, during the weeks leading up to Lent and immediately after Holy Week, there can be up to eight misa kuani on the same weekend. In addition, Lent comes right after the harvest months of January and February, so most people in the community have enough food for wedding feasts.[10] Misa kuani are also very rare during the summer months (June–August), as those months feature multiple community-wide celebrations: schools celebrate their graduation ceremonies in June, the fiestas patronales in honor of Santo Santiago take place during July, and the fiesta in honor of the Assumption of the Virgin closes the season in August. People usually spend their savings on those events, so most of them cannot organize or participate in a wedding in those three months.[11] Padre Armando, the town's priest, explained to me that people in the community believe that it would be disrespectful to perform a wedding in November, as in that month they celebrate Days of the Dead. Weddings are rarely held on dates that conflict with other celebrations, such as the celebration of the Virgin of Guadalupe (December 12), Christmas, New Year, or Three Kings Day (January 6). However, even during times when weddings are not typically celebrated, wedding-related rituals and cultural practices may still take place (such as elopement, bathing the bride, etc.).

Tembuchakua celebrations are divided among the homes of the groom, bride, and wedding godparents, and guests move through those three houses performing various rituals. Participation in and attendance at a wedding, be it the misa kuani or the sivil kuambuni, depend on a person's relation to the bride, groom, or godparents. During my time with my host family, the misa kuani we participated in most actively and put in the most effort were those in which we were relatives of the groom, as we had more responsibilities. When we were the bride's relatives, Na Juana and Ta Emiliano would go for several hours (depending on how close they were to the bride's family), and my host sisters would also go for only a few hours to help with the cooking and making of ichuskuta (corn tortillas). During a sivil kuambuni, only the closest relatives

INTRODUCTION

attend the festivities, and, like the misa kuani, events are divided by gender and age, and one participates only in those rituals where te toca (when it is your turn—a concept and practice that I discuss in chap. 3). As I spent more time in Angahuan, all these rules became apparent as I performed and participated based on my gender and position within many social networks.

Conceptualizing the Tembuchakua: Analytical and Theoretical Paths

This book may seem like a traditional anthropological text—research in a remote Indigenous community; focus on ritual practices; and engagement with ideas of culture, community, and cultural transformations—however, it seeks to move anthropology and folklore studies in different directions. *Creating Culture, Performing Community* is part of my overarching project of intellectual activism, which seeks to push the disciplines beyond the Western Enlightenment canon. Like my coedited works, *Chiricú Journal* 2017, *Theorizing Folklore from the Margins* 2021, and *Journal of American Folklore* 2022, *Creating Culture, Performing Community* focuses on voices that are normally relegated to the intellectual periphery, voices that are considered providers of data but not creators of knowledge. In this regard, while engaging with traditional areas of research—and similar to the scholarship of Rachel V. González (2019), Solimar Otero (2020), and Roberto Cintli Rodríguez (2014)—*Creating Culture, Performing Community* centers the work of Black, Indigenous, and People of Color (BIPOC) scholars from a hemispheric perspective. To do so, this work engages with decolonial and anticolonial approaches and highlights Critical Native American and Indigenous Studies, Critical (Indigenous) Youth Studies, and the important yet overlooked work of P'urhépecha scholars.

Some scholars think there is only one way to conduct anti-oppressive and decolonial research methods, and if this approach is not used from the beginning, the work cannot be considered anti-oppressive or decolonial. I was one of these scholars. But as I read and understood more about these approaches, I realized that there is no single path that one can take to transform the type of work that we do.[12] For example, while my initial work followed the traditional format of ethnographic research—albeit with some modifications that felt right and necessary—the way I approach my data, whom I choose as my intellectual interlocutors (citation politics), and who inspires my writing and thinking did not follow the Western Enlightenment canon.

In the last decade, decolonial and anticolonial research (see, most recently, Mignolo and Walsh 2018; Rivera Cusicanqui 2014; and Segato 2013) has impacted Latin American studies with a particular focus on transforming research methods and intellectual approaches. Silvia Rivera Cusicanqui's (2014) work, specifically her concept of ch'ixi and how to theorize from and through Aymara worldview and language, has been a great source of inspiration as I develop the concept of te toca. It also informed how I engage with P'urhépecha scholars who theorize P'urhépecha culture and realities from and with their own language and worldview. Mariana Mora's *Kuxlejal Politics* (2017) also serves as an important example of anthropological decolonial research and practices. By analyzing decolonial practices developed by Zapatista communities in Chiapas, México, as well as discussing her own decolonial research methods, Mora provides a rich intellectual path for decolonizing anthropology. Following in Mora's footsteps, I engage with and incorporate decolonial methods and approaches by highlighting my own research methods, which were guided by a "sincere [reciprocal] collaborative approach" (Chávez 2021). Moreover, and to advance decolonial and anticolonial approaches, I merge Critical Native American and Indigenous Studies—such as the works by Deloria (2004), Smith (1999), and Berglund, Johnson, and Lee (2016)—to highlight Native American and Indigenous ways of knowing and knowledge creation.

Building on the work by Ibrahim and Steinberg (2014) and Steinberg and Ibrahim (2015) on Critical Youth Studies, my work centers youth participation as a key component of cultural transformation. The field of Critical Youth Studies is influenced by Critical Race and Ethnic Studies, Critical Native American and Indigenous Studies, and anti-oppressive research methodologies. One of the main propositions of Critical Youth Studies is to do research *with* youth, not about youth, a tenet I follow in general, not just in my work with youth in Angahuan. In addition, Critical Youth Studies conceptualizes youth as cultural agents and active creators of knowledge, a dynamic I see in Angahuan. In addition to incorporating Critical Indigenous Youth Studies into my theoretical frameworks, my work expands the limited body of research centered on youth studies in Latin America. In 2005, Jackson and Warren (2005) advocated for an increase in research on Latin American youth studies, and while some scholars have heeded the call—such as Virtanen (2012) and Magaña (2020)—research on this population is still scarce. Maya Lorena Pérez Ruiz (2008, 2011a, 2011b, 2014, 2015) is one of the few scholars who has focused on Indigenous youth in México, with a special interest in Maya youth. The works of these scholars serve as both foundation and departure as I unpack the different ways in which youth in Angahuan are key forces for cultural transformations in the community.

For the first half of the twentieth century, P'urhépecha research and scholarship in the United States (spearheaded by the Tarasco Project) were popular.[13]

INTRODUCTION

However, by the 1960s and 1970s, P'urhépecha scholarship had dwindled, and currently, only a handful of scholars in the United States are focusing on the P'urhépecha community. In the meantime, P'urhépecha scholarship in México, specifically in Michoacán, has expanded and grown more robust. Starting in 2017, US scholars who conduct research in P'urhépecha communities have cooperated with our counterparts in México, participating in conferences and collaborating in publications. In addition, my colleagues in the United States are publishing works on this community and area of research. I am particularly inspired and honored to work with Luis Urrieta Jr. (2012, 2017), Pavel Shlossberg (2015, 2023), Gabriela Spears-Rico (2015, 2019), fabian romero (2023), and Mario A. Gómez Zamora (2017, n.d.). Our first collaborative project, *Dancing with Life: Recontextualizing Mexican Masks*, was edited by Pavel Shlossberg and published in 2023. *Creating Culture, Performing Community*, therefore, is part of the US P'urhépecha studies revival, and I hope that, by engaging in dialogue with my counterparts in México and the United States, this work will continue to bridge the gap between US scholarship and Mexican and P'urhépecha scholarship.

I do not wish to go into great detail in this book's introduction; however, I do want to highlight some of the ways I encounter and dialogue with and around particular concepts that guide my analysis. Specifically, I explore how ideas of rites of passage, rituals, performance, community/comunalidad, and culture intersect with each other as they pertain to the tembuchakua in Angahuan and ideas of creating culture and performing community.

The wedding ritual in Angahuan is a rite of passage that helps transition newlyweds from individuals into a married couple. However, they are not the only ones taking part in this process. The families of the newlyweds also participate in the different stages of the rite of passage (separation, transition, and reincorporation) but in different ways (van Gennep 1960). In this sense, the tembuchakua is a rite of passage for the newlyweds, their families, and their wedding godparents. During the tembuchakua's three days, the three families (the groom's, bride's, and wedding godparents') must work together to successfully create a new family network. All the participants have different roles to perform during the wedding, and together they create the tembuchakua. In this regard, the tembuchakua both supports and expands ideas of rites of passage, performance, and community.

As previously stated, this book interweaves three arguments / axes / points of encounter: creation of culture, performance of community, and cultural transformations. I understand cultural transformations as the simultaneous process of continuity and change. Rituals, as exemplified in the tembuchakua

Fig. 0.3 Panoramic view of Angahuan. April 2009.

in Angahuan, are a site of cultural continuity, as they embody symbolic cultural knowledge that contributes to the social organization of a community (as discussed in chap. 5), but they also provide the necessary tools for creativity and negotiation to transform their culture by drawing on shared symbols (as discussed in chap. 4). Rituals, in general, are lived cultural experiences and are a reflection of both cultural structures and current cultural transformations. Therefore, the framework that I present in this book, cultural transformation as the simultaneous process/performance of continuity and change, allows me to explore the different ways people in Angahuan make conscious and deliberate decisions on how to curate and create their cultural practices, as well as perform their own ideas of what it means to belong to their community.

Indigenous peoples are still often imagined as static and removed from modernity; if they change, they cease to be "Indigenous/traditional" (Martínez-Rivera

INTRODUCTION 11

2014, 2018). This perspective is prevalent in México to this day. However, if we understand transformation as a simultaneous process of continuity and change, and we reconceptualize Indigenous identity so that transformation is an integral characteristic of being Indigenous, current cultural and political expressions of and by Indigenous people will not be qualified as more or less Indigenous but simply as Indigenous. By proposing alternative approaches to understanding Indigeneity, my work also showcases how people carefully transform their cultural practices and how, by doing so, people rearticulate their own identity. Thus, *Creating Culture, Performing Community* has three main aims: to analyze how people create their own culture; to showcase how cultural practices are performed to reflect ideas of what it means to be a member of a community; and, by exploring the process of cultural transformation, to move beyond limited understandings of Indigenous identity and cultural practices.

Finding Home in Angahuan

Many people were and are confused by my presence in Angahuan. Since I am a person of Puerto Rican and Mexican descent who was born in Chicago but raised in both México and Puerto Rico, people in Angahuan (and in México in general) have a hard time placing me. I am alternatively viewed as an insider and an outsider.[14] I lived in México until I was ten, then moved with my family to Puerto Rico. While in México, we lived in Pátzcuaro—where my dad's family moved before and during the Mexican Revolution—the religious center of the Tarascan (P'urhépecha) Empire before the arrival of the Spaniards.[15] Another factor that perplexes people is that I do not "look Mexican." I have curly black hair and light-colored skin. I am considered tall for a Mexican woman in my home state, and my body type is more typical of someone of Caribbean descent. When I speak Spanish, my accent is neither Mexican nor Puerto Rican, and I can easily switch between cultural and linguistic codes. Furthermore, I was one of the few people in Angahuan to wear glasses, which contributed to marking me as a turisï (non-P'urhépecha). My parents named me Mintzi Auanda del Carmen Beatriz—Mintzi Auanda in honor of my father's heritage and Carmen Beatriz in honor of my mother's heritage. Mintzi and Auanda are P'urhépecha names. Mintzita means "heart," and Auanda means "blue" or "sky."[16] Therefore, my name means "heart of the sky" or "blue heart." When I give my name in Angahuan or other P'urhépecha communities, people believe that I have adopted that name. I often must produce my government-issued ID card, which only partially convinces them. My name, along with these other factors, contributed to a fluctuating perception of me as both an insider and an

Fig. 0.4 Author's first visit to the Paricutín volcano. Circa December 1990. Photo by Antonio Martínez Chávez (author's father), with permission.

outsider. From one minute to the next, I went from being considered a Mexican of P'urhépecha descent to a foreigner from Puerto Rico.

My first memory of Angahuan is from when I was eight (fig. 0.4). Relatives from the United States came to visit us on Christmas in 1990, so we took them to different tourist spots in the area. We visited Angahuan to see the Paricutín, the youngest volcano in the world. I have two memories from the visit. The first is of walking around the high walls of dry lava, gazing into the ruins of San Juan Parangaricutiro's church, and admiring the magnificence and wonder of the Paricutín. The other thing I remember from that trip is being enveloped by a sense of peace, calm, and belonging. I took a small volcanic rock to remember the trip. Eighteen months after visiting the Paricutín, in July 1992, we moved to Puerto Rico. One of the few things I brought to Puerto Rico was the small volcanic rock from Angahuan. At eight years old, I already knew that Angahuan was a special place for me. Many years later, I returned to Angahuan as a graduate student of anthropology and folklore.

I began graduate studies in the Department of Folklore and Ethnomusicology at Indiana University Bloomington in August 2004. Two years later, I added a second PhD program in anthropology. I wanted to conduct research in and around the P'urhépecha region of Michoacán. First, I had to acquire the necessary language skills to conduct my research. Therefore, in the summer of 2005, I returned to Michoacán to study P'urhépecha at the Universidad Michoacana de San Nicolás de Hidalgo in Morelia under the tutelage of Lucas Gómez Bravo (QEPD),[17] a leading P'urhépecha linguist and teacher, and a comunero (community member) of Angahuan. For my master's project, I conducted fieldwork in the community of Nuevo San Juan Parangaricutiro, but I knew I wanted to work in another community for my doctoral research. In 2005, in between taking language classes in Morelia and conducting research in Nuevo San Juan, I visited other P'urhépecha communities in search of a field site.

Angahuan was one of the communities I visited that summer. As I traveled through the Sierra on my way to Angahuan, the sense of calmness and peace that I had felt when I was eight returned. On that day trip to the community, I went to the church and met the priest, Padre Nacho.[18] I told him I was considering conducting fieldwork in Angahuan. He looked at me with a piercing gaze and told me: "Espero que no seas de esos antropólogos que vienen a la comunidad, recogen información y se van para nunca volver" ("I hope you're not like one of those anthropologists who comes to the community, collects data, and never returns").

Startled by his statement, I told him to rest assured that I did not want to be like *those* anthropologists and that I would find ways to reciprocate and work for and in the community. After meeting with Padre Nacho and a walk around the plaza, I returned to Uruapan. When I shared with my uncles my desire to return to Angahuan for the celebration of Santo Santiago, they organized a family trip, as they did not want me to go by myself. During the trip, we stayed for a night in the communal Mirador cabins, attended the pirekua (P'urhépecha song and music) concert on July 23, and saw the uarhukua (P'urhépecha stickball game) tournament, as my cousin's boyfriend (now husband) played for Uruapan's uarhukua team. After the tournament, we enjoyed a delicious dinner in one of the local restaurants, and then we returned to Uruapan.[19] I had an amazing time with my uncles, aunts, great-aunts, and cousins, seeing Angahuan with different eyes, the eyes of a naive and excited young anthropologist and folklorist. That summer, I spent only a few days in Angahuan, but I knew that I had found my place.

When I returned in the summer of 2006 to continue my language training at the Universidad Michoacana with Ta Lucas, I spoke with him about my desire to conduct fieldwork in his community. He approved of the idea and helped organize my visit. He introduced me to his brother's family and arranged for a one-week stay that July. During that week in Angahuan, I taught English at the church in exchange for help with learning P'urhépecha. With the support of the Gómez Santacruz family, I began researching in Angahuan in 2006.

I have lived with the Gómez Santacruz family since the beginning of my research in Angahuan. The family comprises Ta Emiliano Gómez (Ta Lucas's older brother); his wife, Na Juana Santacruz; their ten children—Cayetana (Caye), Inés, Tomasa (Tomi), María de Jesús (Chucha), Esperanza (Pela), Francisco (Pancho), Eusebio (Cheio), Cecilia (Ceci), Zenón (Chinó), and Leticia (Leti)—nine in-laws; and nineteen grandchildren. When I first stayed with the family in 2006, only Inés and Tomi were married, and only Inés had a baby. Little by little, over the course of my multiyear relationship with the family, everybody else got married and started having children.

Although they are not wealthy, Ta Emiliano and Na Juana have provided their children with the best educational opportunities available to them, sending them to study in Morelia, Uruapan, and Cherán. Cayetana finished her bachelor's degree in education and is an elementary school teacher in Angahuan, Esperanza graduated from the Normal Indígena de Cherán and also teaches in the community, and Inés completed her high school degree and is the librarian at the community's public library. The younger children (Francisco, Eusebio, Cecilia, and Leticia) also completed high school. Zenón, the youngest son, just completed his undergraduate education at the Universidad Michoacana and is a certified veterinarian.

Starting with two small trojes, the Gómez Santacruz home compound has been gradually expanded, accommodating the needs of the growing family. At present, the home is made up of several brick structures arranged around an inner courtyard. In addition to the two original trojes (which were the boys' rooms when I lived there in 2009), Ta Emiliano built a large brick structure that served as a small grocery store (in México, an abarrotería), but now they sell animal forage. Behind the store, the family built another large structure (brick walls, small window, concrete floor, and zinc roof) with Cayetana's savings as a teacher. This was the daughters' room, which they shared when I stayed with them. Ta Emiliano and Na Juana have their own room, which doubles as storage space for harvested corn and overflow kitchenware. At the back of the house is a small structure consisting of three walls and a curtain for showering, a laundry area, and an outhouse. In January 2010, at the end of my yearlong stay, Na Juana and Ta Emiliano built a new kitchen next to the daughters' room. Before this, the kitchen was a small, dirt-floor structure made of brick and wood. The new kitchen is made of brick and has a concrete floor, high ceilings, and, most important, is big enough to accommodate multiple tables or paranguecha

INTRODUCTION 15

(firepits) as needed. The main cooking area is still the parangua, as the family prefers the warmth of the firepit on cold nights. In addition to the original structures, Pancho and his family and Chinó have their own trojes.

Behind the house, Na Juana and Ta Emiliano have a small tareta (milpa in Spanish, meaning cornfield), where they plant corn, squash, beans, and other crops. Na Juana also has a small garden where she plants quelites (different types of greens), cilantro, nurite (a plant used for tea that only grows in the Sierra), and other herbs. The family also has a larger tareta higher on the mountain in an area called uauacho, where they plant the bulk of their yearly supply of corn and beans.[20] Ta Emiliano sometimes keeps pigs in the back of the house, which he then sells, trades, or butchers to sell the meat. In 2009, he bought a horse to help with planting and farming tasks, and when he was not using the horse for agricultural tasks, he rented it to local guides to take tourists to the Paricutín.

In Angahuan, I am partially treated as a ward of the Gómez Santacruz family.[21] If somebody in the community wanted to ask a favor of me (to be a godmother at a wedding, take pictures at a birthday, give money to help during a celebration, etc.), they first asked Ta Emiliano or Na Juana for permission to approach me. People were curious about me, so, before asking for a favor, they spoke with them to inquire about my character and whether I would be willing to help, contribute, or participate. In addition, as a de facto member of the Gómez Santacruz household, I was able to—in some cases required to— participate in sociocultural and religious events in the community.

As a member of the Gómez Santacruz household, I had chores. My main task was to wash dishes (something that could take many hours each day). I would also go to the store, run errands, help in the kitchen, occasionally go to the corn mill, and help in the cornfield or avocado orchard. I tried to learn how to make ichuskuta (corn tortillas) by hand, but they came out square no matter how long or hard I tried. After it became obvious that I was a hopeless case, I was relieved of ichuskuta-making duties. However, I did learn to embroider, and, during my time in the community, I embroidered blouses, belts, and even a kuanindikua. Embroidering was a great entryway into the female world. Gossip, stories, and, more relevant for my research, important decisions are discussed while embroidering. Visitors to the house would talk to me about my embroidery, which also helped people relate to me and vice versa. By including me in their chores and daily activities, the Gómez Santacruz family made me feel at home and welcomed.

In addition to negotiating and finding my space in Angahuan, I also had to negotiate constantly among different familial forces. Mainly, I had to negotiate

Fig. 0.5 Author with members of the Gómez Santacruz family. January 2010. Photo taken by my tío Fernando.

with my uncles and aunts who lived in Uruapan. As a young single woman and the daughter of the head of the family (my father), my uncles and aunts felt responsible for protecting me while I was in México. Because of this, I had to negotiate with my relatives so I could visit different communities and travel throughout the state to do my research without the required "protection" (a husband or older male of the family). Aided by my parents' support, and after explaining to my uncles and aunts that this was my work, they were supportive of my research stays in Angahuan, which was crucial to my success. In addition to staying with me in Angahuan during my first visit in July 2005, my uncles and aunts returned to Angahuan to meet my host family in 2009. As I will describe, my family's support and collaboration made a huge impact and difference during my fieldwork.

Hanging Out in Angahuan: Documenting Community Life

This book is based on over twenty-four months (summers 2006, 2007, 2008, 2011, 2016, spring 2018, and February 2009–February 2010) of fieldwork research. I employed a variety of fieldwork research methods, such as conducting

INTRODUCTION

repeated interviews with key research collaborators and documenting (through video and audio recordings and photography) different types of events and celebrations, such as life cycle rituals (births, baptisms, and funerals) and the full social-religious calendar of events. In addition to digital documentation, I kept a detailed diary in which I described my everyday life in the community. I employed semistructured interviews that focused on why people participate in sociocultural events. I participated in the daily routine of the community, paying special attention to rituals and their central role in the sociocultural life of the people of Angahuan. Most of the information in this book, however, is based on the data collected during my 2009–2010 stay, as it was during this time that I documented the tembuchakua as well as other important life cycle rituals. All of the material collected for this research has since been requested and archived by the American Folklife Center of the Library of Congress to create its first collection focusing solely on P'urhépecha culture.[22]

I also conducted archival research at several academic centers in México, including the Universidad Michoacana de San Nicolás de Hidalgo in Morelia, El Colegio de Michoacán in Zamora, and the Centro de Cooperación Regional para la Educación de Adultos en América Latina y el Caribe (CREFAL) in Pátzcuaro. In addition, I consulted researchers from the Centro de Investigaciones y Estudios Superiores en Antropología Social in Guadalajara.[23] I also participated in Kw'aniskuyarhani's bimonthly meetings, which allowed me to meet leading P'urhépecha scholars who aided and supported my project.[24] Meeting with Mexican scholars was crucial for my research for at least two reasons: I wanted my work to be in dialogue with Mexican and, more importantly, P'urhépecha scholarship and scholars, and this exchange helped me contextualize my data within the larger P'urhépecha region.[25]

Between February 2009 and February 2010, I fully participated in and documented four weddings, and I partially participated in several others (e.g., taking soaps to the bride on the eve of her wedding). I attended the weddings that me tocaba (I had to go [to]), took part as expected, and was the (un)official wedding photographer. I also participated in and observed many celebrations, such as the town's fiestas patronales in honor of Santo Santiago Apóstol (July), the fiestas in honor of the Assumption of the Virgin (August), the Three Kings celebration (January), and Holy Week (March–April), to name a few. Moreover, I participated in and documented various life cycle events in the community, such as baptisms, births, birthdays, saints' days, funerals, and graduations. There was a celebration every week, small or large, familial or communal.

Based on this range of experiences, I can confidently state that the wedding is the quintessential cultural and social event in Angahuan. From my observations, the cultural practices of other celebrations come together during weddings. I also noticed how wedding celebrations interact with other cultural practices in the community. The tembuchakua, as it is celebrated and performed in Angahuan, provides a clear view of cultural transformation and can help us understand the creation of culture and the performance of community.

During my time in Angahuan, I found at least two significant ways to reciprocate with the community members: collecting documentation about Angahuan for the archives and documenting events as a photographer. During my third summer in Angahuan, in 2008, Padre Nacho entrusted me with photocopies of articles, books, and news clippings about Angahuan. Some of the articles dated back to the 1940s and the first reports of Paricutín's eruption, and all of the articles were by researchers who had gone to Angahuan and never returned. Padre Nacho was determined to build a comprehensive collection of works published about Angahuan, a task he had been working on for years. Before 2008, he had never mentioned his archive and had even refused to lend me a map of the community. His refusal was understandable. He had previously lent maps and documents to students and researchers, and they were never returned. He lent me the documents on the condition that I make a copy so the church could have one copy to lend and another to keep safe. Taking it a step further, I asked if I could make extra copies for Angahuan's public library and Ta Manuel Sosa's personal collection. Ta Manuel is a research collaborator and fellow anthropologist; he is also a leading communal figure in documenting and cataloging Angahuan's oral histories and cultural practices.[26] Padre Nacho agreed, and I made photocopies for the church, the library, Ta Manuel, and me. Since that summer, whenever I come across a publication about Angahuan, I make copies for the church, the library, and Ta Manuel.

During the summers of 2007 and 2008, I noticed freelance photographers coming to the community during special celebrations, taking pictures, and returning a few days later to sell them. They would go from house to house, looking for the people in the pictures, and selling them for $15 MXN or more per picture (roughly $1.50 USD at the time). Many people would buy the pictures even though they were overpriced (printing pictures in Uruapan might cost between $2 and $4 MXN per picture). When I started taking photographs for my research in 2009, I made copies as gifts. Word spread about my free photographs, and soon, relatives of Na Juana and Ta Emiliano, as well as neighbors, began to request my services. That is how I was able to document both large and small events, from birthday celebrations to weddings. Some of the people who requested my services wanted to pay me, so I asked them to cover the cost of printing. During special celebrations, people would come to me to get their

INTRODUCTION   19

picture taken. In exchange, they would show me around and explain the event to me, introducing me to others so I could document everything and share copies of the photos I took. Several times during my yearlong stay, the Gómez Santacruz family and I attended more than one activity in a day: a wedding and a posada, for example.[27] On those occasions, I ran from house to house, trying to document all the activities at both events. Being a photographer gave me two great opportunities: not only was I able to document many of the traditional practices celebrated in Angahuan during the entire year, but I was also able to reciprocate the favors I received during my time there.

As I found ways to give back and be an active member of the community, I observed events and dynamics that I would not have seen otherwise. Thus my data and experience in Angahuan are heavily influenced by the fact that the community began to consider me a member of the Gómez Santacruz family. This status meant that I had responsibilities and that my actions would impact the family's reputation. I had to be very careful in my behavior to protect them.

During graduate school, I was trained to follow the classical US anthropological model. Research methods, in particular, followed a very traditional and Western male-centered understanding of fieldwork: participant observation, interviews, field notes, research subjects/informants, and so on. One of the main discussion topics in my fieldwork class was the importance of establishing rapport while keeping a distance from the "research subjects." I did not have the intellectual tools at the time to challenge what I was being taught, but I knew that this approach did not resonate with the type of researcher I wanted to be. Unfortunately, it was not until I completed my dissertation research that I discovered anti-oppressive and decolonial research methodologies and learned another way to do ethnographic research.[28] In some ways, I am an autodidact: I had to teach myself about decolonial, subaltern, and anti-oppressive theories and methodologies. In the company of dear friends who also wanted and needed more than what was offered by the Western/Eurocentric/heteropatriarchal canon we had been taught, I started reading Critical Race and Ethnic Studies scholarship and Native American, Latinx, and Critical Youth Studies. These new avenues of activist scholarship from the margins transformed my intellectual paths and goals. However, my research methods during the principal data collection for this project were and are greatly influenced by the traditional way of doing ethnographic fieldwork, although with modifications that aligned with my research ethics.

Because I recognized the colonial limitations of classical fieldwork even before encountering anti-oppressive and decolonial research methods, I knew I could not follow the strict guidelines of conducting research, especially

Fig. 0.6 Author's family with members of Gómez Santacruz family during my father's seventieth birthday celebration in Uruapan. July 2013.

regarding the division between researcher and subjects. Instead, I tried to find ways to participate and reciprocate in the community. I tried to learn to "behave like a relative" (Dass 2021). To do so, I treated people as friends and acquaintances. I shared stories about my family and life because I believed that if I wanted people to share their stories with me, it was only fair that I do the same. I did not want to treat people as "informants," although in some cases, I had to put on my "ethnographer hat" to conduct in-depth interviews. My relationships with some research collaborators were based on friendship, while others were strictly researcher / research participant. Some people saw me as an anthropologist/folklorist, and others regarded me as a member of the Gómez Santacruz family.

INTRODUCTION

I felt it was crucial to my research that my family be involved and meet my host family in Angahuan. This would not only help to strengthen the bonds I was forming with my host family but also distinguish me from the researchers they had encountered in the past, who came to the community, collected data, and left. I also wanted to share my work with my family. My parents and younger sister traveled to Angahuan in July 2009 to meet my host family and stayed in Angahuan for Santo Santiago's celebrations. Since then, my family and my host family have been involved in a reciprocal relationship, regularly attending family celebrations in Angahuan (with the Gómez Santacruz family) or in Uruapan (with the Martínez Chávez family) (fig. 0.6).

As we perform research with and through our bodies, I had to learn how to walk, talk, move, and speak differently during my time in Angahuan. And although my research has been "solitary"—all the data and knowledge have been experienced, processed, constructed, and expressed through my body—my research and learning process have been communal and familial. Indigenous (decolonial) scholars have published works that reflect on how research is ceremony, storytelling, a gift, and kinship, and that knowledge creation is a communal process even if it is experienced through "individual" bodies (Archibal et al. 2019; Chilisa 2012; Kovach 2009, 2010, 2018; romero 2023). The fact that my blood family created kinship with my host family radically transformed my research experience from a solitary endeavor to a communal and familial project. And, as I describe in Martínez-Rivera 2021, this communal research process kept me safe in the conflict zone that Michoacán has become due to the war on drugs.

Conducting Research in a Conflict Zone

In a recent publication (Martínez-Rivera 2021), I detailed the effects and dynamics of conducting research in a conflict zone. While I do not wish to repeat myself, I do want to acknowledge the events taking place while I was in Michoacán and how they affected both my research and the people around me.

Since 2006, Michoacán and other parts of México have been embroiled in a senseless and gruesome war on drugs. While the roots of the conflict, specifically drug production and trafficking in Michoacán, can be traced as far back as the 1930s, the current conflict began in the early 2000s with the election of President Vicente Fox, the candidate of the Partido de Acción Nacional (National Action Party, or PAN), and the laws he presided over, which impacted businesses run by cartels (such as smuggling of Chinese knock-off products). His successor and fellow PANista, President Felipe Calderón, was elected in

July 2006, and in December—two weeks after assuming the presidency—he deployed over twenty thousand military personnel around the country, with over seven thousand operatives sent to Michoacán.[29] Since it began, the war on drugs, per some estimates, has claimed between sixty thousand and four hundred thousand lives in México.[30]

In Michoacán, violence escalated exponentially after military forces were deployed in December 2006. At that time, the two principal narco groups, la Familia Michoacana and the Zetas, were fighting among themselves for control of the state while also battling the military. By 2010, most of the leaders of La Familia had been captured or killed, and by 2011, the remaining members re-formed as Los Caballeros Templarios. By 2013, Los Templarios had gained control over most of the state, and the government (both federal and state) seemed incapable of stopping the violence. As of 2023, Michoacán is home to multiple bigger cartels, mainly Los Templarios, el Cartel Jalisco Nueva Generación, and Los Viagras, and smaller narco groups embroiled in constant fights for territory.

In many ways, Michoacán is a conflict zone. It received a level 4 travel warning (issued to areas designated as war and conflict zones) from the US State Department. Civilians trust neither the government nor government officials. Different groups "patrol" cities, towns, and roads, but nobody knows who they are. Police forces have orchestrated massacres, tampered with evidence, and routinely violated citizens' human rights. Since the war on drugs began, many massacres have taken place, most of them orchestrated by the state government. Some attacks occurred in Apatzingán (eight civilian casualties) and Tanhuato (forty-two civilians and one police officer dead), both in 2015, and in Arantepacua in 2017 (three civilians killed, including a teenager) (Human Rights Watch 2015; Spears-Rico 2019). During the Day of the Dead celebrations in 2021, eleven young men (ranging in age from fifteen to early thirties) who were in their communities gathering materials for Day of the Dead altars were killed in Tarecuato by narco cells (which are smaller groups, not affiliated with the cartels).

Instability and violence in nearby communities quickly impacted the security situation in Angahuan. As drug cells monitored the traffic going up and down the Sierra, putting up blockades, charging for transportation and protection fees, stealing cars, and so on, the road between Uruapan and Angahuan became dangerous. In Angahuan, violence from the war on drugs and economic instability contributed to an increase in tensions, alcoholism, and general violence in the community. Shoot-outs among community members, in part due to alcohol use, increased. In September 2017, for example, after a communal assembly and because of communal political instability from the

INTRODUCTION

increased presence of drug trafficking and other illegal activities in the community, a shoot-out ensued among different community factions. The jefe de tenencia (a communal political official in the community) was arrested and charged with homicide after one comunero was killed and two others were badly injured in the fight.

People in Angahuan have also been killed (most murders are never solved) or "disappeared." In June 2009, César, one of my research collaborators, was brutally killed in a nearby community—he was nineteen years old. The reasons are unknown, and the culprits were never apprehended. Víctor, another research collaborator, disappeared in 2015. His whereabouts are still unknown, but he is presumed dead. Sometime after this disappearance, a former communal leader also disappeared, and he is also presumed dead.

Starting in 2011, different communities in Michoacán, both Indigenous and mestizo, began rising up in arms to defend their lands from large-scale violence and repression at the hands of both the cartels (specifically Los Templarios) and the state. In April 2011, in response to Los Templarios murdering members of its community, the P'urhépecha community of Cherán expelled all representatives of the state government, the police, and anyone not from the community or associated with the cartel. Led by a group of women, the community formed a self-defense movement to protect its land, forest, and people from the cartels and the government, and it formed a government based on el Costumbre.[31]

Following Cherán's movement and expulsion of narco cells and government officials, Los Templarios had to find another forest from which to steal wood. Rumors circulated that the illegal woodcutters were heading to Angahuan. When I arrived in June 2011, the tension in the air was palpable, as Angahuan's comuneros were preparing to protect their forest. As far as I know, the illegal woodcutters never entered Angahuan's forest at that time. However, cartels have slowly infiltrated the community, and since 2018, various narco cells have claimed abandoned houses in the community to use as safe houses and to stash weapons and drugs. People have also found drug laboratories hidden in the Sierra. The state police have tried to arrest the narcos cells, which led to shoot-outs in the community, such as in May 2019 and January 2020. The shoot-out in January 2020 was on the eighth, in the middle of communal celebrations of the kurpiticha (this tradition is discussed in chap. 2 and Martínez-Rivera 2023). The celebrations were halted while everything calmed down, and as soon as the area was somewhat secure, the celebrations continued.

During my research, I sometimes questioned whether it was in my best interest to stay in Angahuan (particularly in 2009–2010). Although I had never been hurt, I had found myself in several unsafe situations. I must admit, however, that I eventually became used to living with this tension and was always aware of my surroundings, to such an extent that I internalized it—violence and the threat of violence became part of everyday life. And because of that, at times, I made decisions to privilege my research over my safety.

As I have gotten older, I choose to privilege my safety and well-being over my research. From July 2017 to August 2018, I lived in Pátzcuaro, México, with my parents. I planned to focus on my publications, conduct research, and apply for academic jobs. However, I was not able to conduct as much fieldwork as I had hoped, as the level of violence was increasing (the presidential and state elections in July 2018 led to increased insecurity and violence throughout the state). Whenever I organized a trip to Angahuan, violence escalated there or in Pátzcuaro or Uruapan, making the trip too dangerous. Similarly, during my fellowship and pretenure research leave (summer 2021–summer 2022), I could not conduct fieldwork because of the COVID-19 pandemic and the rise in violence in the region. But thanks to social media, I have stayed in touch with community members and have been able to enjoy their celebrations, especially weddings, from far away.

Research, especially ethnographic research, is always full of challenges, but it is even more so in a conflict zone. Anti-oppressive research methods and decolonial approaches that I naturally incorporated into my methods allowed me to conduct my research as safely as possible. As described in Martínez-Rivera 2021, I developed multiple strategies and contingencies to safeguard my data, and my broad network in both Angahuan and Uruapan (my host family, acquaintances in Angahuan, and relatives in Uruapan) helped me stay physically and emotionally safe. Ethnographic research is in many ways a lonely endeavor (especially if approached from a white heterosexual colonial model), but it does not have to be that way. As Berry et al. (2017, 560) argue, we must create a furtive anthropology that "centers an embodied [Black feminist analysis and inspired by Indigenous decolonial thinking] analytics." The only way I could do my research and stay safe was with the help and support of my communities.

A Brief Note on Language, Style, and Images

In this book, all P'urhépecha terminology is based on Angahuan's linguistic variant. The P'urhépecha alphabet used is the one developed by the Centro de Investigación de la Cultura P'urhépecha (P'urhépecha Culture Research Center, now renamed CENEsPO, or Centro Nicolaita de Estudio de los Pueblos Originarios) in the Universidad Michoacana de San Nicolás de Hidalgo in Morelia, the variation that Ta Lucas taught me. In the same vein as other

Indigenous and Decolonial scholars, throughout the text I refrained from using italics to mark words and phrases in P'urhépecha and Spanish, and I only provide definitions the first time I use a word or phrase. Moreover, I conjugate both P'urhépecha and Spanish following their own linguistic rules and incorporate them into the text as they would be used by multilingual individuals. This is an invitation to read and engage with this text, and with P'urhépecha language, differently. All Spanish and P'urhépecha translations are mine. All images are mine, except those mentioned that were taken by family members.

A Road Map

This book comprises six chapters in addition to this introduction, a conclusion, and an interlude. The first chapter, "Under the Volcano's Shadow," follows an imaginary walk through the community to provide brief yet crucial background information about the P'urhépecha region and Angahuan, specifically. The second chapter, "Carrying the Uarhota," focuses on social organization, general youth culture, and courtship rituals in Angahuan. The third chapter, "Te Toca," introduces the concept of te toca and its relation to eloping or asking for marriage. This concept of te toca helps center the ideas of creating culture and performing community, as it is a central tenet of P'urhépecha culture. Chapter 4, "Creating Culture," deals with the process of negotiating and organizing the tembuchakua, as well as highlighting the process of creating and curating P'urhépecha vernacular cultural practices. Between chapters 4 and 5, I include an interlude, which is a detailed ethnographic description of a wedding that will be analyzed in the fifth chapter. The interlude invites readers to take a moment to pause and read slowly before continuing their journey. The fifth chapter, "Performing Community," provides a deep analysis of the misa kuani, specifically the P'urhépecha wedding, and provides a model for unpacking the different ritual forms in P'urhépecha culture. Each of these forms performs ideas of community and P'urhépecha values and behaviors. Chapter 6, "Transforming the Tembuchakua," provides descriptions and analysis of four different wedding styles I documented during the 2009–2010 year. At the conclusion of our journey, I provide descriptions of a wedding from 2022 that was shared and documented via Facebook to showcase how wedding practices in Angahuan continue to transform based on the needs and interests of Angahuan's people.

Even though I grew up in Pátzcuaro, I continue to be inspired and challenged by having to constantly relearn something, as every time I return to Angahuan, I learn something new, or I am confronted with the fact that what I thought I knew was incomplete or incorrect, or that the cultural practice has

Fig. 0.7 Ta Lucas Gómez Bravo (QDEP). ¡Presente! April 2009.

INTRODUCTION

changed since my last visit. One of the challenges, frustrations, and joys of writing about cultural practices is that they, like us, are never static. Cultural practices, as an expression of our beingness, are complex and depend on change to survive, grow, and thrive. And while at no point this book aims to present an "authentic" or current view of the P'urhépecha region or Angahuan, I humbly offer the observations, conversations, analysis, and experiences I gathered as I learned what it meant and means to get married in Angahuan.

Notes

1. The designation "Ta" or "Na" in Angahuan's variant of P'urhépecha is equivalent to "tata" or "nana" in other P'urhépecha variants. Ta and Na, or tata and nana, mean señor and señora, or don and doña, and roughly translate to mister and madam and are used to denote respect toward a person. Most names in this book are pseudonyms, except when individuals requested the use of their real name.

2. Wedding godparents, and godparents in general, are part of the four main Catholic sacraments. More on godparenthood in chapter 1.

3. The P'urhépecha female attire, more commonly known in Spanish as rollo, is incredibly distinctive and elaborate, and in Angahuan's variation, it has three layers of clothing. The first layer, the undergarments, is composed of an embroidered blouse, called uanengo, and an embroidered petticoat called tatchukua. The petticoat is held in place by an embroidered belt called jongarikua. The next layer is composed of the sïtakua, a tightly pleated calf-length skirt, held in place by another jongarikua. The sïtakua, and the reason the whole dress is called rollo, is the most distinctive piece of the attire, as pleats create a fanlike texture in the back. The last layer is composed of the saco, an outer blouse, normally made with cloth that has sequins or lace, and the tangarikua, an apron normally decorated with sequins, lace, or embroidery. The last piece, which might be the most important, is the kuanindikua, the rebozo or shawl, which in Angahuan's style tends to be embroidered.

4. This opening vignette was also published in the article "La transformación histórica del *Misa kuani*: un análisis etnohistórico-etnográfico de la boda p'urhépecha desde la *Relación de Michoacán* al presente" (Martínez-Rivera 2020).

5. For many decades, scholars have debated over the original name of the P'urhépecha area and people. For many centuries after the Spanish Conquest, they were called Tarascos/Tarascan, a name given to them by the Spaniards. Michoacán was the name given to the area by the Nahuatl-speaking Aztecs. P'urhépecha was the term used for the working class in the Tarascan empire; today's Indigenous people in the area use this term to describe themselves. Some scholars have retained the term Tarascan to refer to the preconquest Indigenous population and P'urhépecha for the present-day population; I also follow this

practice. More importantly, members of P'urhépecha communities self-identify as P'urhépecha. For a detailed discussion on the terminology Tarascos versus P'urhépecha, see Márquez Joaquín 2007; and Paredes Martínez 2017. See chapter 1 for general information regarding the P'urhépecha region.

6. The cargo system is a system of religious-political-economic organization that influences how the community is socially organized. More details of the cargo system are in chapter 1. A troje is a one-room wooden-plank house built without nails. The roof is made of tejamanil (wooden roofing tiles), the base is stone, and a tapanco (attic) provides storage space.

7. In previous works (Martínez-Rivera 2014, 2018), I historically analyzed the development of the Indigenismo project in México and how during different intellectual waves, scholars and government officials framed Indigenous identity and experience in very limited and limiting ways. While for some people (scholars, government agents, and the Mexican public in general) ideas of Indigenous identity have expanded to include current Indigenous expressions, the reality is that Indigenous identity is still very much framed and imagined as static and tied to the past in order to be "authentic."

8. The víbora de la mar is a traditional children's game from Spain, but it is also popular in México and other countries in Latin America. The game is usually played at weddings throughout México. The bride and groom stand on two chairs and use the bride's veil as a bridge between the chairs. All the young female relatives of the newlyweds hold hands and start running through the venue as the song is played faster. The idea is to break the "snake" and move underneath the bridge created by the newlyweds. Next, the young male relatives do the same. People typically fall or trip while running.

9. I was not told about the rules for when the sivil kuambuni can be celebrated. I assumed that because it is cheaper to celebrate the sivil kuambuni and it does not have the significance of the misa kuani, families can celebrate the sivil kuambuni when it is convenient for them, regardless of the communal calendar of events.

10. In Angahuan, fresh new corn is harvested in September, but most people leave the corn on the stalks until January or February so they dry out and can be used for ichuskuta, tamales, korunda (a type of tamal made with ash), and other dishes that require corn flour.

11. However, in 2016, I did hear about a misa kuani that was celebrated in July, one week before the celebrations of Santo Santiago. Apparently, the bride's family insisted on the date and pressured the groom's family into agreeing. My host family was not invited to the wedding, no nos tocaba, but we heard all the gossip. It seems that the wedding caused a great deal of friction among the families of the groom, bride, and wedding godparents.

12. For example, I have seen scholars state that their research methods are anti-oppressive and decolonial, but their analyses are based on Eurocentric and

INTRODUCTION   29

Western Enlightenment theories. On the other side of the spectrum, some scholars may follow more traditional methods of data collection, but their analyses shift from and beyond the Western canon.

13. The Proyecto Tarasco, or Tarasco Project, was a binational interdisciplinary research project that started in 1930 and lasted till the early 1940s. See Kemper 2011; and Ojeda Dávila 2018.

14. Many BIPOC scholars have conceptualized the sometimes perilous dynamics and situations of doing research at home and being considered an insider or outsider. See Behar 1996; Berry et al. 2017; Martínez-Rivera 2022; Narayan 1993; and Richards-Greeves 2013.

15. My paternal grandfather's family is from Zacapu, a P'urhépecha community considered to be the cradle of the P'urhépecha culture, but they moved to Pátzcuaro when my grandfather was a teen. My grandmother's family was from Santa Clara del Cobre, another P'urhépecha community, but they moved to Pátzcuaro in the 1910s when Santa Clara was burned to the ground during the Mexican Revolution. My father's family considers Pátzcuaro their hometown.

16. See Martínez-Rivera, "The Legend of Mintzita" (forthcoming) for a discussion of the legend of Mintzita and how and why my parents named me Mintzi.

17. QEPD means "Que en paz descanse," "May They/She/He Rest in Peace."

18. Priests are moved every three to six years through different parishes. When I first arrived in Angahuan, Padre Nacho was the priest; he was then replaced with Padre Armando and later with Padre Feliciano.

19. At the time (2005), there were several Angahuan restaurants offering traditional P'urhépecha food. After Mexican cuisine (specifically P'urhépecha cuisine) was added to UNESCO's Intangible Culture Heritage List in 2010, many women in Angahuan have been nationally and internationally recognized for their cooking skills and have opened restaurants offering traditional P'urhépecha food in Angahuan. Lupe, the wife of Agustín, one of my research collaborators, owns a restaurant that has gained regional recognition since it opened in 2021.

20. The family also has an avocado and peach orchard on a neighboring rancho called Las Cocinas. They normally rent the avocado orchard, which brings in a steady income.

21. By the end of my 2010 stay, Na Juana and Ta Emiliano were introducing me to distant relatives as their long-lost daughter. The relatives were incredibly confused until Na Juana and Ta Emiliano, bursting with laughter because of their confused faces, clarified who I was.

22. For more information on the Mintzi Auanda Martínez-Rivera collection, see https://lccn.loc.gov/2016655322.

23. Specifically, I had meetings with Dr. Luis Vázquez León (QEPD), who was always a generous mentor and intellectual guide. Whenever I traveled to

Guadalajara, we met for coffee and tea and discussed the fields of anthropology, Indigenous politics, theory, and praxis. He passed away from cancer in 2021.

24. The Grupo Kw'aniskuyarhani de estudiosos del pueblo P'urhépecha (Kw'anis for short) was founded over twenty-five years ago and is a group composed of scholars (both P'urhépecha and turisï) and community members. They gather every two months in Pátzcuaro to discuss different topics relating to the P'urhépecha community. Their meetings are free and open to the public. Since I started attending their meetings, I have been invited to present my research and serve as a panelist in multiple sessions.

25. See Martínez-Rivera, "Decolonizing (Folklore) Methods" (forthcoming) for a detailed description of this process and its importance to my work.

26. I use the term research collaborator to identify the people who helped me or provided information and knowledge during my time in Angahuan.

27. A posada is a Mexican Catholic Christmas celebration that begins on December 16 and lasts for nine days, until Christmas Eve. During those nine days, people remember the pilgrimage of Joseph and Mary and their search for shelter (posada). Most Mexican communities, including those in the United States, celebrate variants of the posadas (Acosta 2011). In Angahuan, nine houses are chosen, one house for each night, and all the children in the community go to that house to ask for food. The family organizing the posada will prepare food for five hundred to one thousand people, hang piñatas, and give fruit and candy to the children.

28. For a detailed description of this process, see Martínez-Rivera, "Decolonizing (Folklore) Methods" (forthcoming).

29. For a detailed account of the war on drugs and its impacts, please see Astorga 2012; Fuentes Díaz and Paleta Pérez 2015; Gonzalez 2009; Maldonado Aranda 2013; and Martínez-Rivera 2021.

30. These numbers include civilians, members of the military, and narco groups. In June 2021, José Luis Pardo Veiras and Íñigo Arredondo (2021) argued that the death toll was around 350,000, which is the last estimate available. However, based on current reports, during the presidency of Andrés Manuel López Obrador (2018–2024), there were more than 200,000 deaths and 115,000 disappearances; therefore, the estimate that 400,000 people have died or disappeared in México since 2006 is probably lower than the actual numbers (Jiménez 2024).

31. In Martínez-Rivera 2014, I explained that "the concept of 'El Costumbre,' not La Costumbre, refers to the required and practiced way of living in community (Franco Mendoza 1997). Meaning, it is the traditional way in which indigenous communities governed themselves prior to the arrival of the Spaniards. El Costumbre also includes ritual practices and traditional knowledge inherited from the ancestors" (Jacinto Zavala 1995). For more information on Cherán's self-defense movement and its repercussions in the area, please refer to Paleta Peréz and Fuentes Diaz 2013; Ojeda Dávila 2015; and Spears-Rico 2019.

Fig. 1.1 Paricutín volcano. September 2009.

1

Under the Volcano's Shadow

Angahuan and the P'urhépecha Area

Silence is not something you experience in Angahuan. The cool, clean air is filled with an unexpected melody of sounds that reflects the spirit of the community: communal loudspeakers spout music or information;[1] sawmills buzz with hammers and chain saws; cars and trucks huff up and down the Sierra; radios broadcast music from most houses in the community; cohetes (rockets) shoot through the sky;[2] children at play laugh and mothers call them home. Like the plethora of sounds, different smells combine to show the turisï that they are no longer in the city—the aroma of pine trees and cedars, food and firepits; the scents of hens, pigs, and cows; and the smell of recently tilled earth or passing rain envelop the community. Although the noises and smells are intense at first, one grows accustomed to and tunes out the incessant loudspeakers, the constant music, and the pungent smell of farm animals and firepits. These sensory encounters frame the experience of being in Angahuan, as being both firmly in a place in the present while also connecting it to a sense of order, logic, harmony, and memory.

Before I describe Angahuan's wedding rituals, the creation of culture, the performance of community, and cultural transformations, I would like to comment on this chapter. In many ways, this chapter has been the most difficult to write, as I struggled to make it compelling for those not specifically interested in the P'urhépecha region or culture. While I recognize the problematic history of general/classic contextual chapters in ethnographic texts like this one, part of the reason I am protective of this chapter is because communities like Angahuan, which must constantly battle for their political and cultural autonomy, rely on academic publications to support their legal claims. Community

34   CREATING CULTURE, PERFORMING COMMUNITY

members in Angahuan are using my dissertation and other academic works to prepare legal documents and applications to request funding for cultural projects in and for the community. Therefore, although this chapter contextualizes wedding rituals, it is also an act of reciprocity toward Angahuan and a demonstration of my ethical and moral obligation as an academic. The goal of this chapter, as well as the rest of the book, is to be of service to P'urhépecha community members. This first chapter, thus, provides a contextualizing cultural blueprint of the P'urhépecha region in general and Angahuan more specifically. I then briefly discuss several important elements that contribute to the transformation of P'urhépecha culture in the community, such as economic and infrastructure developments, education, migration, and natural disasters. These first contextualizing pieces will gradually reveal the main elements and cultural values that allow for the creation, curation, performance, and transformation of cultural practices as expressed during a wedding in Angahuan.

The structure of this chapter is inspired by my walks through the community. During my stay in Angahuan, and especially on days when I was feeling overwhelmed, lonely, or lost, I would pack my waterproof fieldwork messenger bag with a water bottle, a notebook, an umbrella (if it was the rainy season), my voice recorder, and my camera. I wandered through the community taking pictures and letting my feelings and thoughts settle. Sometimes, my feet would take me to the public library where I would chat for hours with Inés or all the way to the lookout point at the Mirador where I would gaze at the Paricutín. Other times, I ran into friends and research collaborators or met new people. Those walks allowed me to see and learn Angahuan differently than if I had not moved around the area as much as I did. Movement, as we will see, is incredibly important during P'urhépecha rituals and vernacular cultural practices, as one of the ways people express their belonging in the community is through movement. Chapter 5 looks more closely at the importance of movement; in this chapter, the practice of movement/walking serves to help me introduce Angahuan through one of the experiences I enjoyed the most: walking.

From the Japondarhu to the Juatecharhu

When I conduct research in Angahuan, I use Pátzcuaro or Uruapan as my home base. If I travel from Pátzcuaro to Uruapan, I take a bus that crosses the lake region and starts the climb into the Sierra. From Uruapan, another bus takes me to Angahuan. Depending on traffic, the whole trip can take up to two hours, but if I leave from Uruapan, it is less than an hour. Those bus rides allowed me to process the information I had gathered during my previous stay and prepare for whatever new experiences I might encounter. Taking advantage of the travel time, especially at the start of my intellectual journey to conduct research in Michoacán's P'urhépecha area, I familiarized myself with the general history and cultural contextual information regarding my home state and area. And that is where this story begins, albeit in a very brief way.

The state of Michoacán is officially home to five Indigenous groups. The Mazahua and Hñähñu communities are in the eastern part of the state on the border with the states of México and Querétaro. On the coast, there are a handful of Nahua communities. Pirinda communities are near Morelia, the state's capital. The largest Indigenous group is P'urhépecha, who occupy the central area of the state. P'urhépechas built a vast and powerful empire before the Spanish Conquest, and they retain their status as the principal Indigenous group in the region.[3] Depending on the methods used for counting populations, there are currently between 125,000 and 200,000 P'urhépecha people.[4]

At present, the P'urhépecha region is divided into four areas: Eraxamani or Eraxamakua, Cañada de los Once Pueblos, the Eleven Towns Ravine; Japondarhu, Zona Lacustre, the Lake Pátzcuaro area; Tsakapu Tsironderi or Tsakapindu, Ciénaga de Zacapu, the Zacapu area; and Juatecharhu or P'ukumindu, la Sierra, the Sierra. A new area is delimited near Zamora, but it is not yet officially part of the P'urhépecha territory, although communities are currently fighting to be recognized as a distinct region of the P'urhépecha territory. According to the National Commission for the Development of Indigenous People (CDI),[5] of the 113 municipalities in Michoacán, 22 are P'urhépecha, but P'urhépecha speakers are registered in 95 municipalities (Amézcua Luna and Sánchez Díaz 2015). However, according to Kemper and Adkins (2004), and because of large waves of migration, the P'urhépecha area should be reconfigured to include new areas of settlement, such as other parts of México or the areas in the United States where large P'urhépecha communities live.[6]

Most P'urhépecha towns are compact and centered around a main square, a church dedicated to the patron saint of the community, and a chapel dedicated to the Virgin of Immaculate Conception (Roth-Seneff and Kemper 1983). Since the 1930s, roads connect the P'urhépecha area with nearby cities, making the area accessible and bringing in a large volume of traffic. Most P'urhépecha towns have electricity, although most still do not have running water or plumbing systems. Most P'urhépecha communities are rural except for Tzintzuntzan, Cherán, Paracho, and several others. Some of the principal economic endeavors are agriculture (corn, avocado, and other produce), fishing, and hunting.

Another important economic enterprise is the production of arts and crafts. Most P'urhépecha communities specialize in a particular type of art or craft: for instance, in Paracho, they craft guitars; in Santa Clara del Cobre, they forge copper; and in Ocumicho, they are known for their pottery and clay art.

Linguistically, P'urhépecha language has no relationship with neighboring Mesoamerican languages; P'urhépecha is an isolate. After the Spanish Conquest, P'urhépecha language was one of the first Mesoamerican languages to acquire an alphabet and to be documented. In the mid-sixteenth-century, Fray Maturino Gilberti ([1559] 1997, [1558] 2004) wrote the first alphabet and the first text using P'urhépecha. Since then, scholars have carefully documented the development of P'urhépecha language and created different alphabets.[7] According to the CDI (Comisión para el Desarrollo de los Pueblos Indígenas [National Commission for the Development of Indigenous People]), P'urhépecha language has three linguistic variants: the area around Lake Pátzcuaro, the area of the Ravine, and the Sierra (Amézcua Luna and Sánchez Díaz 2015). All variants of P'urhépecha are mutually intelligible (Roth-Seneff and Kemper 1983). When I began studying Angahuan's linguistic variant with Ta Lucas Gómez Bravo (QEPD) at the Universidad Michoacana, he told me that Angahuan's variant is considered the most difficult. One of the differences is that some verbs and nouns leave out the r while others add an rr (e.g., most P'urhépecha communities say parakata for butterfly, while in Angahuan, it is pronounced parrakata).

P'urhépecha communities have a rich array of expressive cultural practices, such as different musical genres (brass bands, string music, orchestras), dances, rituals and festivals, food, material culture, traditional games, and oral narratives.[8] As a result of P'urhépecha people's rich, expressive cultural practices, Michoacán has been considered and promoted as one of México's main tourist destinations since the beginning of the twentieth century at both national and international levels. Michoacán is home to two World Heritage Sites (Morelia's Historic Center and the Monarch Butterfly Biosphere Reserve); eight Pueblos Mágicos (Magical Towns); three archaeological sites: Tzintzuntzan, Ihuatzio, and Tingambato; the Tianguis Artesanal de Semana Santa in the city of Uruapan; and ecological routes like the Ruta de Don Vasco (Zúñiga Bravo 2019).[9] In 2010, the United Nations Educational, Scientific and Cultural Organization (UNESCO) included P'urhépecha food (as representative of Mexican cuisine) and P'urhépecha music (specifically the pirekua) on its Intangible Cultural Heritage List.[10] Some P'urhépecha cultural practices have even gone global, such as the Danza de los Viejitos (Dance of the Old Men) or the celebrations for Days of the Dead (Hellier-Tinoco 2011; Spears-Rico 2015).

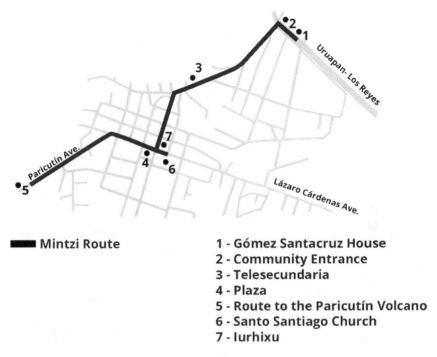

Fig. 1.2 Map of my walk through Angahuan. Map prepared by Yuiza Martínez-Rivera.

Walking and Learning about and with Angahuan

After leaving Uruapan, the way to Angahuan is quite beautiful. The road is flanked by mountains covered in avocado orchards and fragrant pine and cedar forests; the scent of these trees accompanies one throughout the trip. Because Angahuan is in the middle of the Sierra, as one travels toward the community, there is an increase in elevation. As the temperature cools, the scent of pine and cedar intensifies.

Angahuan is surrounded and protected by four mountains and Volcán Paricutín (fig. 1.1). Each mountain has a story. Some are female, and some are male. The two main mountains in the community are Arhakata Juata and Sukuarani Juata (fig. 1.3). In the late afternoon, as the sun goes down, these two peaks are dressed in red, gold, and crimson. They offer warmth and protection to Angahuan. In a region destroyed by deforestation and changes in the use of soil, the forests on both mountains are, surprisingly, almost intact. Ta Manuel Sosa, one of my main research collaborators, told me that many years ago, after

Fig. 1.3 Principal mountains in Angahuan. November 2009.

Paricutín's eruption destroyed the forests and mountains, Angahuan's Cabildo de Ancianos (Council of Elders) decreed that the community must protect Arhakata Juata and Sukuarani Juata because the mountains had protected them from the volcano's destructive forces. Since then, Angahuan's inhabitants have worked hard to take care of their mountains; if any comunero cuts wood in these mountains, they are arrested and taken to jail in Uruapan.[11]

The Gómez Santacruz house faces the main entrance to the community, just in front of the main road. The bus stop for Uruapan and other communities is located several houses down from the Gómez Santacruz household, which was perfect for me, as I normally traveled carrying bags full of groceries and food. I would leave for my walks after completing my chores—helping clean the house, doing dishes, and checking for any other tasks (such as helping in the cornfields, shelling corn, or helping a relative). I normally left at noon and returned home before dinner so I could help in the kitchen (dinnertime was between 3:00 p.m. and 4:00 p.m.). On the way back home, I would stop at one of the many small grocery stores to buy fruit or anything needed for dinner.

As soon as I walked out the door, I would cross the busy road filled with cars and buses going up and down the Sierra and head toward the main plaza. Two main roads lead into the community: the first has a gas station owned and operated by a group of comuneros. The second road serves as the main entrance to the community through which political guests and religious processions enter. This main entrance features a huge metal archway decorated with colorful plastic garlands or punched paper; these decorations are changed depending on the season and communal events.

Angahuan is a precolonial community, and one can still find preconquest structures and artifacts in the area.[12] According to the community's oral histories, some of the first settlers in what is now Angahuan were migrants from the Aztec Empire. They fled the empire because they were tired of suffering the Aztecs' abuse and asked the Tarascan lords for permission to settle in their lands (Soto Bravo 1982, 42). They traveled to Tzintzuntzan, the Tarascan Empire's capital, to ask the caltzontzin (ruler) if they could establish a home in his territory. However, they were informed that the caltzontzin was not in the city; he was in the town of Sirosto, a settlement in the Sierra. Once the migrants found him, the caltzontzin granted them permission to settle in his empire, specifically in the area where they had met.

Led by Don Antonio de Carvajal, the first Spaniards arrived in Angahuan in 1523. Carvajal was tasked with surveying the recently conquered region.[13] The convent in Angahuan was built in 1527 and completed in 1570, the same year construction of the church, which is dedicated to Santo Santiago, began (Soto Bravo 1982, 45–46; Toussaint 1945–1946, 80). At present, the convent (Iurhixu in P'urhépecha) is a Catholic school. It is, after the church, the community's second-most important religious center.

According to historical documents, Angahuan was never a large settlement. In the seventeenth century, there were 75 taxpaying inhabitants. By 1822, the number of community members had grown to 217, and the principal economic enterprise was the production of tejamanil (a type of wooden thatch) (Soto Bravo 1982, 47–49). During the Mexican Revolution (1910–1920), most of Angahuan's inhabitants hid in the mountains to escape from the armies pillaging and killing their way through the Sierra. According to oral histories documented by Valente Soto Bravo (1982), Angahuan was burned to the ground by a Villista army in 1918. The only structures to survive were the convent and the church, both of which were left in ruins (Soto Bravo 1982, 49). The community

Fig. 1.4 Church of Santo Santiago. Angahuan 2009.

Fig. 1.5 Detail of church's archway. Angahuan 2009.

was destroyed again during the Cristero revolts (1926–1929), but the people of Angahuan rebuilt the town once more.

Not long after the Mexican Revolution and the Cristero revolts, another harrowing event rocked the foundations of the community. In early February 1943, a series of powerful earthquakes announced the birth of the Paricutín volcano. The eruptions began on February 20. In a few months, the volcano rose to 3,170 meters (10,440 feet). Over the next several years, it destroyed the towns of Paricutín (from which the volcano got its name) and San Juan Parangaricutiro.[14] Because Angahuan is located on a plateau that overlooks the valley where the volcano emerged, the lava never reached the town, although the ashes did enough damage: forests were destroyed, soil was rendered sterile, and farmers were forced to sell their stock or move the animals to neighboring towns to save them. Paricutín's eruption interrupted the cultural, social, and economic life in the surrounding area.

In the late 2000s, Angahuan's comuneros built a pedestrian walkway connecting the community's entrance to the main plaza. This walkway begins under the entrance archway and is made of volcanic stone. I used this walkway every time I walked to the plaza, and from there, I would see the Volcán Paricutín looming over and guarding Angahuan.

The volcano brought with it an unexpected source of income: tourism. Scholars, researchers, and scientists from all over the world who wanted to document the volcano's evolution traveled to Angahuan. Paricutín was the first volcano to form in nearly 150 years, giving scientists the unique opportunity to document its entire life cycle, from birth to inactivity. During the years that the Paricutín was active, the government built roads to help scientists and tourists reach the community and installed water and electricity in the center of the community. Paricutín has been dormant since its last eruption in 1952, but tourism is still one of Angahuan's main sources of income, as researchers continued to travel to the area to document the impact of the volcano (Eggler 1948; Gaillard 2007; Nolan 1979; Reed 1970; Works and Hadley 2000).

As the land recuperated from the havoc wrought by the Paricutín, the population of Angahuan grew. Since the 1980s, the number of inhabitants has almost tripled, from 1,977 in 1980 to 5,773 in 2010. During my walks, the ongoing expansion of the community was visible in the many houses being built or expanded to accommodate growing families.

Today, Angahuan has electricity, telephone and cell phone service, and running water. Some homes have satellite TV and internet, although internet cafés are still common in the community, as most people do not own computers. Most homes still do not have indoor plumbing, so people collect water in

42   CREATING CULTURE, PERFORMING COMMUNITY

cisterns and large containers for household use. There are sewers in the town's center near the church, but most homes have either septic tanks or outhouses. Most roads are unpaved dirt, although the main roads that surround the plaza and take tourists to the Paricutín are made of cobblestone or concrete.

As I walked on the volcanic stone walkway on my way to the plaza, I would pass in front of one of the middle schools. This telesecundaria (distance-learning middle school, where classes are broadcast via satellite) was the first middle school built in Angahuan. It is composed of multiple single-floor brick structures (the classrooms) and features a large patio with an open basketball court. This middle school, due to its proximity to the jaripeo (rodeo) arena, normally serves as a dancing area during community jaripeos (more on this in chap. 2). Community members take care of the facilities, and mothers take turns preparing lunches for the students.

Education has been a transformative force in the community. Until the 1980s, Angahuan only had two elementary schools. Since then, educational opportunities in Angahuan have increased, partially aided by the state's push for Indigenous education (Soto Bravo 1982).[15] At present, Angahuan has three elementary schools. Two of the schools are public and promote bilingual education (Spanish-P'urhépecha), and the third is a private Catholic school. The Catholic school, called Sor Juana Inés de la Cruz, is in the convent. The community also has a kindergarten, a day care center, a telesecundaria, and a new technical middle school (secundaria técnica), which opened in the fall of 2009.[16] Thanks to the initiative of several community members, the community's first high school, which is part of the Colegio de Bachilleres system, opened in 2006. In 2009, eighteen students graduated from the first class of the Colegio de Bachilleres, one of which was Pancho (fig. 1.6). The whole community joined in the celebration of this achievement. Before the local middle and high schools opened, children who wanted to continue their studies beyond primary school had to attend government-funded boarding schools in Uruapan, Morelia, or other parts of the state or country.

Despite considerable educational hurdles, some young Angahuan residents have managed to pursue higher education and obtain undergraduate and professional degrees. During my 2009–2010 research stay, the most popular field of study for community members was education, especially at the Normal Indígena de Cherán, a pedagogical university in the P'urhépecha community of Cherán that specializes in Indigenous bilingual education. Because admission to the Normal is limited, many aspiring teachers pursue their studies in the nearby city of Uruapan. A few, mainly young men, have been able to study at the Universidad Michoacana de San Nicolás de Hidalgo in Morelia, the state-run

Fig. 1.6 Pancho's high school graduation as part of the first graduating class of the Colegio de Bachilleres in Angahuan. June 2009.

university, which, in addition to being nearly free, is the best university in the state.[17]

As I neared the plaza and areas of dense housing concentration, I could hear the many sawmills and woodworking shops. Occasionally during my walks, I would go into the various shops, which are divided based on products (food, clothing, butcher, etc.) if I needed something.

While subsistence farming is a crucial component of communal and family life, the people of Angahuan rely on three main sources of income: remittances from migrant relatives, tourism, and woodworking.[18] Migration has been a source of cultural, social, economic, and gender transformations in the community.[19] Angahuan has seen a steady flow of circular migration in the last twenty years (Kearney 1986). July, for instance, is when many young men return to celebrate the Santo Santiago festivities in their community. And while Angahuan does have a fair number of migrant workers in the United States, this proportion is not as large as other Indigenous communities in the area. Migrants from

44   CREATING CULTURE, PERFORMING COMMUNITY

the community have usually settled in Pennsylvania, Virginia, and Southern California, with newer migration waves to Oregon and Washington State. In 2009, many men returned to Angahuan because of the combined impact of a large-scale wave of deportations and the decreased opportunities caused by the US economic recession.[20] Crossing the border, additionally, has become more difficult, and many migrants are afraid to travel to Angahuan because they do not know if they will be able to return to the US. During my time in Angahuan (2009–2010), I heard of many young men who had been considering "going to the other side," but they changed their plans when relatives and acquaintances living in the United States recounted how difficult the situation was.[21] I also witnessed the magnitude of the impact of dwindling remittances in those years.

I have always liked Angahuan's plaza. It is not large, but it is always full of life. Following the colonial architectural plan, the plaza is surrounded by the main religious buildings (the church of Santo Santiago and the Iurhixu) as well as political buildings (communal government offices, police station, and small holding cells), a primary school, and the public library. The medical clinic moved several blocks away from the plaza into a bigger space. The recently renovated plaza has a small concrete pergola that serves as a stage during cultural and political events. It also has small, fenced gardens, metal benches, and a large space in the middle that serves as the dancing floor during communal celebrations.

Tourism is the second-most significant source of income for the community. From the plaza, I observed how Angahuan's roads and facilities have changed to accommodate the cars and buses that bring tourists to the community. From the plaza, I had a couple of options: I could go right and follow the road to the Volcán Paricutín, or I could go left, toward the church. For this imaginary walk, I decided to go right first.

Angahuan is part of the ecotourism trail and the Ruta de Don Vasco, two of the principal touristic routes organized by the state government.[22] The main attraction in the community is, of course, the volcano. There is a hotel near the town's main plaza, and two facilities offer cabin rentals, one of which is in the Mirador, a lookout point for the volcano. This area is a communal enterprise and exists for the benefit of Angahuan's people. From the Mirador, one can travel to the volcano on foot or by horse.

The primary way local people make money in the tourism industry is by renting horses and/or guiding tourists to the ruins of San Juan Parangaricutiro's old church or to the Paricutín.[23] Men of all ages work as tour guides. Women own and operate restaurants and food stalls near the ruins of the church or in Angahuan, near the road to the volcano. Several women from Angahuan are nationally, and even internationally, recognized as traditional chefs, and their homes or small restaurants are filled with tourists and government officials. Angahuan is also well known for its embroidered kuanindikua and uanengo, and some of Angahuan's more well-known artists are invited to national exhibitions to showcase their work. The community also has a Casa de las Artesanías (House of Folk Arts) and a Casa del Turista (Tourist Center) where women sell kuanindikuecha (plural for kuanindikua) and local folk art.[24]

If one goes left after reaching the plaza, one encounters the church and Iurhixu (fig. 1.4). Both structures are known for their colonial architecture and masonry work. Works published by famed art historians Manuel Toussaint (1945–1946) and Francisco José Rhode (1946) helped establish Angahuan as a key destination for scholars and others interested in vernacular architecture as the church's entrance is a clear example of Mudejar art (fig. 1.5).[25] Both religious centers are always beautifully decorated, which heightens their appeal.

As I left the church and Iurhixu to return to the plaza, I closed my eyes and listened to the community. Amid the sound of music and children playing at the school, one of the most distinct sounds from the Sierra is the sound of woodworking, the third most important and oldest economic enterprise in the community. Angahuan has been known for its woodwork and its elaboration of tejamanil since at least the nineteenth century (Soto Bravo 1982, 48). However, the Paricutín's eruption caused the death of the communal forest, which left local artisans without a source for raw materials. While the forests regenerated, a new form of woodworking developed: building wooden boxes for the transportation of locally cultivated fruits and vegetables (mostly avocado since Michoacán is the largest avocado producer in the world). As a research collaborator told me, since the late 1970s and through the first years of the new millennium, Angahuan has never been quiet. At any point of the day or night, you can hear the hammers of men of all ages working diligently to build wooden boxes. Some families have their own sawmills where they prepare the different parts of the boxes, then they hire other families or young men to assemble them at the sawmill or at home.[26] Box assemblers are mainly young men, from ten years old to late twenties. This box-building economic enterprise is also dwindling, as many of the packaging and transportation companies in the area, mainly US-based businesses, have started to invest in plastic containers that, unlike wooden crates, can be reused. Instead of mass-producing wooden crates, some sawmills are manufacturing wood panels, which unfortunately consumes much more wood and trees. When I returned to the community in 2018, I was informed that comuneros are cutting wood in the communal reserves, and bald spots were visible on the Arhakata Juata and Sukuarani Juata.

At the time of my main research stay, another important source of wood-related income was the astilladora comunal, the communal woodchipper.[27] In addition to providing stable work, the profits of the astilladora fund many infrastructural projects, such as buying or repairing water pumps, fixing streets, and helping to maintain the church. The astilladora is also a site of conflict, as comuneros argue over who has the right to work there, how the money is distributed, and who oversees the enterprise. Because of internal strife and mismanagement, the astilladora was closed in 2017, and an important source of employment and income for the community disappeared. As a result, a new generation of young men are migrating (both in México and to the US) in search of jobs and better economic opportunities.[28]

A small but growing economic source is the use of microcredits or microloans by different women's groups in the community. The most common enterprise is seamstress workshops where women make clothes or kuanindikuecha. Agatha Hummel, a fellow anthropologist who conducted research in Angahuan from 2007 to 2012, told me in a 2009 personal communication that power relations and gender roles in the community are shifting since women are the principal beneficiaries of many of the state-run welfare programs and microcredits. For example, one of my host sisters, Chucha, is in charge of a group of women weavers who are producing and selling kuanindikuecha.

Other sources of household income include different state-run welfare programs, such as Beca Oportunidades, offered by the Department of Social Development (SEDESOL). Because many of the state-run welfare programs are organized and distributed through the school system, school attendance has increased, and so has the number of available educational opportunities in the community. In other words, families will have more resources if their children are at school rather than working the land or assembling boxes.

Still at the plaza, I reflected on the importance of this landmark. In many ways, the plaza is the heart of the community, where cultural, political, social, and religious events take place, and where the community gathers to organize culturally and politically around its two systems. Angahuan's two community-wide sociopolitical organization systems are the religious cargo and the political or civil cargo. Both systems have a role in the planning and distribution of labor and economic responsibilities in the community.[29] In Angahuan, religious cargos are considered the more important of the two, as participating couples who assume the most important cargos can become part of the Council of Elders.[30] Political cargos, while less important in terms of communal positions of power, are held only by men and respond to external and municipal authorities (although, as I mention shortly, this changed in 2021). Members of each cargo system work closely with one another to make sure that celebrations and rituals are organized and performed and to ensure the general well-being of the community. Some P'urhépecha communities have a stronger civil cargo system than a religious one, and vice versa. In Angahuan, both cargo systems remain strong and important.

In 2009, the civil cargo system was composed of four branches, the Comisariado de Bienes Comunales (Commissioner of Communal Property), the Consejo de Vigilancia (Security Council), the Jefe de Tenencia (Chief of Tenancy), and the Juez (Judge).[31] The Comisariado de Bienes Comunales has a president, secretary, and treasurer; the Consejo de Vigilancia has a president and two secretaries; the Jefe de Tenencia has a president and secretary; and the Juez has two judges. Each role, except for that of the judges, has a substitute or helper. The Jefe de Tenencia and the Comisariado de Bienes Comunales are considered the most important cargos because they help organize the principal celebrations in the community, such as the celebrations of Santo Santiago, and oversee the community's budget. For the fiestas of Santo Santiago, they hire musical bands for the dances and help cover most of the expenses of the celebrations not related to the church. They are also in charge of construction and economic development in the community.

The religious cargo system is closely affiliated with the Catholic Church and has more influence on the community than the civil cargo system. It is the main way the community organizes itself, and it influences both adults and younger people. The cargueros (the couple that holds a cargo) are divided into three main groups: the Church cargueros, the Iurhixo cargueros, and the Saints' cargueros.[32] By participating in the religious cargo system and by assuming all of the different types of cargos—or at least the majority of them—one can become a t'arhepencha (a member of the Council of Elders).[33] As of 2009, there were twenty-nine couples in the Council of Elders (although some of the men were recently widowed) and eight widows.[34] Neither the church nor the priest is involved in the selection of the cargueros, but the parish keeps a record of them, the Cabildo de Ancianos, as well as the belongings and religious images in the possession of the cargueros.[35]

In any given year, there are over fifty-two cargueros (twenty-two couples and eight single men and women). Cargos are divided into two types: major and minor.[36] Based on Ta Manuel and Amalia's (Padre Armando's assistant in 2009–2010) explanations, the order that one must follow to ascend the cargo system is not necessarily fixed.[37] Some couples first decide they want to be mayordomos or anchitakua, stewards and helpers of the principal cargueros of the church and Iurhixo, respectively. Others may first request the cargo of

48   CREATING CULTURE, PERFORMING COMMUNITY

either the Virgin of Guadalupe or the Assumption of the Virgin. Later, one may become either a Pitapi or a Viscal, which are minor cargos in the church. The couple may choose or request other positions either in the church (as Regidor or Kambiti) or in the Iurhixo (as Kengi or Karari). The position of Alcalde is the most important cargo: this couple oversees all others, assists the priest, and helps the Cabildo de Ancianos choose new cargueros. The Alcalde is a five-year cargo: two years as Alcalde in the church and one in the Iurhixo as Priosti; the Alcalde rest for one year between cargos. The other cargos last for a year that begins on the first day of the New Year. On December 8 of each year, the cargueros of the Iurhixu change, but this is not official until the midnight mass on New Year's Eve. After a couple has fulfilled most of their cargos and held the most important ones, such as Alcalde, the couple becomes a t'arhepencha and part of the Council of Elders.

The cargo of the Resurrection—for young single men and women—is the most sought after, and therefore many families request the cargo years before the young person in question is old enough to participate. If the intended person cannot hold the position when it is their turn, their family might negotiate the substitution of another child in the family. Something like this happened to my host family. The cargo of the Resurrection was intended for the oldest daughter, Cayetana, but when it was her turn, she did not accept it, and it went to one of her younger sisters, Chucha. This was a great honor, and many relatives gave Chucha gifts, mainly traditional clothing such as tangarikua, jonguarikua (embroidered belts), or sïtakua to wear during the races of the saints (an event I explain in chap. 2).

In recent years, however, the religious and political organizations in Angahuan have changed. Because of state repression, general violence at the hand of the narcos, and government abandonment during the COVID-19 pandemic, and supported by Cherán and the autodefensas movements in mestizo communities (as described in the intro.), Angahuan and other Indigenous communities are currently advocating for their autonomy and rights of self-determination.[38] The P'urhépecha communities of Nurio, Tanaco, Pichátaro, San Felipe de los Herreros, Arantepacua, Nahuatzen, Comachuen, Urapicho, and Pomacuarán have fought, or are fighting, for their autonomy through legal means or social movements (Ruiz 2020). These communities and others that are either advocating for their autonomy or in the process of their reivindicación étnica (ethnic revindication) are being supported by the Consejo Supremo Indígena de Michoacán (Supreme Indigenous Council of Michoacán).

In a May 2021 communal assembly, the people of Angahuan voted to fight for their autonomy through legal means. This meant that Angahuan would receive their communal budget directly from the state government instead of Uruapan (their cabecera municipal, or head municipality).[39] On April 22, 2022, as part of Angahuan's move toward autonomy, the political cargo system was reconfigured. The position of Jefe de Tenencia disappeared, and the Consejo de Gobierno Comunal (Communal Government Council) was founded. This cargo is composed of a council president (with their substitute) and two representatives from each neighborhood (Angahuan has seven neighborhoods). Additionally, there are different commissions on communal justice; treasury; education and sports; public maintenance and sanitation; natural resources and environmental affairs; communication, health, and family affairs; and tourism and culture. The council and the various commissions are evenly represented by people of different genders, educational background, and ages.

Stopping for a Chat

My walks through Angahuan always taught me something new, especially regarding communal expectations and sociocultural ways of organizing spaces and events based on gender and social roles and networks. Sometimes, after reaching the plaza or finishing errands, I would head to the public library where Inés works. Angahuan's public library is on a corner in front of the main plaza. It is on the second floor of a small brick building, and its walls are surrounded by metal bookshelves filled with educational books, encyclopedias, and other basic textbooks. The main floor of the library is filled with eight child-size tables and chairs, and in a corner, near the entrance, is Inés's desk. During my visits, I would help her with her chores or just sit down and chat. Sometimes, I would ask her questions and or seek clarifications on events and cultural practices I had witnessed or participated in. Those informal conversations with Inés and other friends and research collaborators provided many details about the intricacies of P'urhépecha culture in Angahuan.

One of the areas that I wanted to understand was gender constructions because their impact on cultural events was so evident to me. In many respects, Angahuan and many other P'urhépecha communities, favor a binary model of gender division.[40] This, however, is a result of colonialism and Judeo-Christian ideologies imposed by the Catholic Church.[41] While gender dynamics among current P'urhépecha communities are complex and may sometimes seem to follow European patriarchal, heteronormative, and male-female binary notions of gender, in many ways, P'urhépecha culture still retains ideas of gender complementarity and gender parallelism.[42] These dynamics are especially visible during rituals and ceremonies and in the ways communities organize sociopolitically.[43]

As I documented in Angahuan, gender dynamics as well as social divisions are key components for the organization, performance, and creation of expressive cultural practices. But, as I illustrate throughout the book, while tasks are divided based on gender, the tasks assigned to each gender are not influenced by ideas of prestige, meaning that some tasks are more important than others. All tasks are necessary and vital for the successful performance of rituals, celebrations, and general events in the community. In addition, both men and women in Angahuan can hold positions of power (become cargueros and join the Council of Elders) if they are in a heterosexual, recognized marriage. Women and men (notwithstanding their relationship status) can become a Diosïri Uandarhi, a wise person who speaks of God and imparts knowledge during rituals.[44] As I witnessed multiple times, important decisions are made collaboratively between men and women, even if it may *seem* like men make them. In recent years, due to migration, women (in Angahuan and other P'urhépecha communities) have gained more political and economic power to make community-wide decisions.

Sometimes, during my walks, instead of heading toward the public library, I would visit Ta Manuel. Ta Manuel's home is between the library and Angahuan's government offices. Whenever I visited, I would stay in the living room, a spacious room filled with beautiful wood bookshelves brimming with books and Ta Manuel's research materials. I normally sat on one of the many couches, while Ta Manuel sat facing me. During our chats, I would ask for help understanding some of the dynamics or events I witnessed. For example, I asked Ta Manuel to clarify the kinship system, specifically the compadrazgo system.[45] Angahuan has a strong kinship system that includes relationships based on consanguinity, fictive kinship (influenced by the compadrazgo system), and social networks based on sociocultural and political ways of organizing (Foster [1967] 1988; Govers 2006; Kemper 1979; Mintz and Wolf 1950). Compadrazgo is a "system of ritualized personal relations established between two sets of individuals: the child (ahijado) and his godparents (padrinos) and the parents and godparents (compadres), with the latter ties taking precedence over those between child and godparents" (Kemper 1979, 38). Compadrazgo privileges both horizontal and vertical relationships: horizontal in the sense that the compadres are believed to be social equals and vertical in the sense that the relationship is normally formed between people of different social strata (i.e., between elites and "commoners") (Govers 2006; Mintz and Wolf 1950). The Catholic Church plays a central role in the compadrazgo system. There are four different types of godparents based on the different Catholic sacraments: baptism, confirmation, first communion, and wedding. In Angahuan, godparents are usually chosen from people who are not part of the close family, which expands the godchild's social networks. Before the compadrazgo, the relationships among the godchildren, the child's parents, and the godparents are often minimal or even nonexistent. Once entering a compadrazgo relationship, confianza may grow and flourish.[46]

Scholars of the compadrazgo system in México highlight the importance of the relationship between the godparents and the parents of the godchild, meaning the relationship between the compadres (Govers 2006; Kemper 1979; Mintz and Wolf 1950). In contrast to other cultures in México, in which the relationship between the compadres is more important than the relationship between the godparents and the godchild (Govers 2006), in Angahuan, the relationships between compadres (except for christening compadres) are not as socially relevant. The relationship between godparents and godchildren is much more important than the relationships between compadres. For kinship ties to be successful, however, godparents and godchildren must work to maintain their relationships so there are enough people to help and support them during moments of need (be those celebrations or tragedies).

Godparents have different responsibilities throughout the godchild's life. In Angahuan, wedding and baptism godparents must be married couples. First communion and confirmation godparents do not need to be married couples and, in some cases, can even be single women and men. In July 2011, Cecilia, one of the younger daughters of my host family, at sixteen became the first communion godmother to a young girl who lived nearby. José, Chucha's husband, became the first communion godparent to a young boy, but Chucha was not asked to be godmother. As both examples illustrate, the godparents can be married or single, young, or old, based on the degree of responsibility of the compadrazgo.

Wedding godparents are the most important of all the different types of godparents. They have more responsibilities throughout their godchildren's lives. Unlike other godparents, they are no longer considered fictive kin and are treated like consanguine kin. This means that in Angahuan, the offspring of wedding godchildren become the grandchildren of the godparents: children use the term tata or nana ("grandfather" and "grandmother," respectively) to refer to the wedding godparents of their parents. Moreover, the godchildren become cousins to the godparents' children, and the godchildren's children consider the godparents' children aunts and uncles. Wedding godparents are present throughout the different life stages of their godchildren and their offspring. When a daughter of the godchildren is "stolen," the groom-to-be's family must ask the wedding godparents and the godparents' children for forgiveness (basically, the groom-to-be's family must ask forgiveness from the bride-to-be's parents' wedding godparents)—a dynamic I discuss in chapter 3.

As my host sisters explained to me, the wedding godchildren have an immense responsibility to their wedding godparents. Every time the godparents have an event (whether for a festive or tragic occasion), the wedding godchildren *must* help them in any way they can. Likewise, the wedding godchildren *must* assist their wedding godparents during the planting and harvest seasons. The godchildren are not always notified that they must help their wedding godparents; they simply *know* that they must help (basically, te toca, a practice that is explained in chap. 3). As Inés and Gume (Inés's husband) explained to me, they can say no to their parents when they ask for help, but they cannot refuse their wedding godparents. While most people in the community follow these unwritten rules quite closely, there may be exceptional cases in which the godchildren do not get along with their wedding godparents, which breaks the cycle of mutual help.

In addition to godparents associated with religious occasions, another form of godparenting has emerged in the community that is promoted by the education system: graduation godparents. Together with graduation celebrations, graduation godparents have assumed a small but significant role in Angahuan. Graduation godparents do not need to be a married couple. In some cases, graduates might ask friends, siblings, or other relatives to be their godparents. A graduate and their family can also choose to have a single person be their graduation godparent instead of a couple. The graduation godparents help finance the celebration, and they provide gifts for the graduating student. They are not expected to have any other responsibilities besides their gifts and participation during the graduation. But in cases in which there is a certain degree of confianza between the child and the graduation godparent, the graduation godparent might participate in other important events of their godchild's life.

Relationships in Angahuan are flexible and contextual, and they vary according to the degree of confianza. Even among first-degree cousins or siblings, if there is no confianza, the degree of mutual help is low. Throughout their life, an individual in Angahuan will participate in many different social networks to varying degrees. Therefore, social networks allow for the organization of rituals and celebrations in the community, as people know that they must act according to their position in particular social networks. This allows for better flow in celebrations, as the organizers do not have to instruct helpers and participants on what to do because people expect others to know how to behave and act based on their socially assigned roles. These dynamics will become evident in later chapters.

Home, after a Walk

On my walks back to the Gómez Santacruz home, I could see and feel how Arhakata Juata and Sukuarani Juata became bigger, guarding and protecting the community. Sometimes, I could see the incoming storm clouds as they came down the mountains, and I would have to run if I wanted to avoid getting soaked (I was not always successful). Those walks helped ground me, especially as I sometimes felt like a sponge, soaking up so much that I could not take in anything more. This sometimes made me grumpy, and I think everybody in the house appreciated it when I went for my walks, as I came back calmer and happier.

When one is actively conducting fieldwork and absorbing so much information, the data can become muddled and overwhelming. I hope this metaphorical walk with me made my process easier to understand than the learning methods behind it. This very brief introduction to the P'urhépecha area, Angahuan, and the current events that affect people in Michoacán starts our journey to understanding wedding practices in Angahuan. This introduction does not seek to be exhaustive, as research about, among, and with P'urhépecha communities is lengthy and rich. But I hope it intrigued the reader and helped contextualize this rich area and people, as I go on to discuss youth cultural practices and courtship rituals in Angahuan.

Notes

1. The loudspeakers are used for sending greetings, calling for help during an emergency, and announcing products; sometimes, mothers use them to call their children home. Families operate the loudspeakers and charge people a small fee to transmit or make announcements.

2. Cohetes sound like fireworks, but they lack the sparkles and light. They are used to announce a procession or celebration (religious or tied to life cycle rituals) or to mourn the death of a young one. Their loud noise can be heard throughout the community and helps people find where events are taking place or what is going on.

3. Because of space limitations and to keep this section brief, I will not recount Michoacán's history of conquest and colonization. For those interested, please see Warren 1984 and Paredes Martínez 2017.

4. For the 2000 census, the National Commission for the Development of the Indigenous Population or CDI developed the concept of Población Indígena Estimada (Estimated Indigenous Population, or PIE). The significance of this became apparent in the inclusion of a new set of questions in the census: "Do you

consider yourself Indigenous?" or "Do you not consider yourself Indigenous?" (Kemper and Adkins 2004, 237). This auto-identification was labeled pertenencia indígena, or an Indigenous claim. Persons who did not speak an Indigenous language but self-identified as Indigenous were counted as such in the new census. As a result of the creation of the PIE concept and its application at the municipal level, almost a third of the country's municipalities were legally defined as "Indigenous" (Kemper and Adkins 2004, 238). The perceived number of Indigenous peoples in the country doubled.

5. The CDI was formed from the reconfiguration of the Instituto Nacional Indigenista (INI) during Vicente Fox's presidency (2000–2006). In 2018, when President Andrés Manuel López Obrador came into power, the CDI was again rearranged and transformed into the Instituto Nacional de los Pueblos Indígenas (INPI).

6. For information regarding research on P'urhépecha migration to the United States, please see Leco Tomás 2017; Schütze 2014; and Velasco Ortiz and Olavarria 2014.

7. For a description of the development of P'urhépecha language scholarship, see Gómez Bravo, Pérez González, and Rojas Hernández 2001 and Medina Pérez 2006. For a detailed linguistic analysis of P'urhépecha language, see Chamoreau 2009 and Monzón García 2004.

8. For an in-depth documentation of P'urhépecha cultural calendar of events, see Ojeda Dávila 2006.

9. The Annual Holy Week's Traditional Arts Fair is considered one of the biggest arts fairs in Latin America, drawing over twelve hundred artisans from the region. For a critical and in-depth look at this event and its relationship to nation building, art, communication, commodification, and consumerism, please see Shlossberg 2015.

10. The inclusion of P'urhépecha food and music into UNESCO's Intangible Cultural Heritage List has created a lot of friction among communities and between P'urhépecha leaders and the state government. For an example of these discussions, especially relating to the pirekua, see Márquez Joaquín 2014 and Flores Mercado 2017, 2020.

11. Unfortunately, as I witnessed in 2018, this has changed in recent years. With the increase in violence and economic and social insecurity in the area, woodcutters from Angahuan and other communities are illegally cutting trees from both mountains.

12. Ta Manuel, in collaboration with community leaders, state organizations, and volunteers, created the Museo Comunitario Kutsïkua Arhákucha, which is cataloging, archiving, and preserving Angahuan's material and immaterial vernacular cultural resources and information.

13. According to Warren (1984, 73), the visit by Carvajal was of "fundamental importance for the early history of the Spanish occupation of Michoacán, since it

UNDER THE VOLCANO'S SHADOW   55

formed the basis for the distribution of the encomiendas." While Carvajal's original document has been lost, parts of it were preserved in lawsuits over the encomiendas. Carvajal was around Uruapan from December 22 to December 24 of 1523, and, although his stay was brief, he surveyed all the major towns in the area, along with the smaller localities subjected to each town (1984, 75). According to the Carvajal documents, Angahuan (or Anguagua or Anguangan) was subject to Uruapan, and its principal mountains were Ichaquiato and Chapata. In addition, there were only ten houses counted by the representatives of the caltzontzin, but according to Carvajal's count, there were fifty-five.

14. For more information on the Paricutín's birth and the destruction of the towns of Paricutín and San Juan Parangaricutiro, see Eggler 1948; Foshag and Gonzalez 1956; Gutierrez 1974–1975; Mendoza Valentín 1994, 1995, n.d.; Nolan 1979; Plá 1988, 1989; Reed 1970; and Trask 1943.

15. At the onset of Indigenous education programs in the 1930s and 1940s, Indigenous education mainly referred to the teaching of the national curriculum in Indigenous languages. However, throughout the decades, Indigenous education has changed to not only refer to the education in Indigenous language but also teach children through an Indigenous lens.

16. The day care center, unfortunately, was only open for a couple of years.

17. The fact that it has been mainly young men who have been able to study in Morelia or farther away from the community is tied to strict gender dynamics in the community; families are reluctant to allow young women to leave the house before they are married. Yet, in some cases, families have supported the education of their young women and have allowed them to move to Morelia, Cherán, or other places to attain higher education. However, this is the exception, not the norm.

18. Most families in Angahuan are subsistence farmers and rely on their yearly crops of corn, beans, squash, greens, and other agricultural products to complement their diets. Some families have small avocado and peach orchards and receive some profits either for the selling of product or for renting the land. However, very few families rely on farming as their main source of income.

19. Reciprocity plays a key role in keeping alive the connection between migrants and their Angahuan-based family and friends. Objects such as recordings of celebrations, music, movies, clothes, and so forth are constantly moving back and forth across the border. If someone is going to Angahuan, it is common for other migrants to send presents back to town with them. Likewise, if someone is leaving for the US, they are loaded with presents for the people who are away from the community. With these seemingly small and simple gestures, a large network based on reciprocity, mutual help, and camaraderie is built and fed, keeping the community members of Angahuan united.

56 CREATING CULTURE, PERFORMING COMMUNITY

20. This return could explain in part the population increase between 2005 (4,330) and 2010 (5,773).

21. In January 2013, I returned briefly to Angahuan and was informed that of the ten men who left for the border, only one was able to cross—an effect of the huge waves of deportations and increased border security during Obama's presidency. During the Trump administration, migration became even more perilous.

22. For more information on the Ruta de Don Vasco, see Zúñiga-Bravo 2019.

23. The remains of San Juan's church are visible through the lava. Through the years, the church's remains have become a site for religious pilgrimages and tourism.

24. For more information on the rebozo industry in Angahuan, see Ramirez Garayzar 2014.

25. Mudejar art is a style of ornamentation that combined Christian and Islamic aesthetics and was developed in the Iberian Peninsula between the thirteenth and sixteenth centuries. México is home to fewer than five examples of Mudejar art, and the church in Angahuan is one of those examples.

26. When Pancho, Cheio, and Chino were in school, they worked on building boxes in the afternoons, on weekends, and during vacations. Sometimes they went to people's sawmills; other times, the materials were brought to the house where they worked to assemble the boxes.

27. In 1989, a private company built the astilladora on Angahuan's communal land. By 1991, the astilladora was expropriated by a group of comuneros, and, after a legal battle, the astilladora became property of Angahuan. For more detailed information about the creation and political ramifications of the astilladora, both inside Angahuan and in the region, see Roth-Seneff and Sosa 2003.

28. While some young women have migrated (either to the US or inside México) in search of better job opportunities, those are the exception, not the norm.

29. The cargo system is hailed as a remnant (albeit hybrid) of the type of social and political organization that existed before the Spanish conquest. During one of the many waves of Indigenismo revisionism in México, the cargo system was considered to be the marker of Indigenous identity (Bonfil Batalla [1987] 2005). Some scholars argued that even in cases where acculturation was almost complete, the strength of the cargo system reflected the strong roots of Indigenous ancestry (Bishop 1977).

30. In some cultures in México, religious cargos are solely held by men; in others, the cargos may be held by either a man or a woman (Mathews 1985). However, even in cases where women can be cargueras, a man must be listed as the official carguero (1985, 290). In Angahuan, the couple is listed as cargueros, and both must participate equally and fulfill all the responsibilities of the cargo.

UNDER THE VOLCANO'S SHADOW

31. For more information on the responsibilities and obligations of the different officials in the political cargo system, please refer to the *Estatuto Comunal Comunidad P'urhépecha de Angahuan* (Comunidad de Angahuan 1999). However, and as I describe later in this chapter, in 2021, people in Angahuan voted in favor of requesting their fiscal autonomy from Uruapan. Because of this vote in favor of autonomy, Angahuan's political structure has changed.

32. Ta Manuel informed me that years ago, Angahuan had four different cargos for saints: the Assumption of the Virgin, the Virgin of Guadalupe, the Holy Cross, and Santo Santiago. The Holy Cross, which was celebrated on May 3, has disappeared completely, while the cargo for Santo Santiago has been divided between the cargueros of the church and the political cargos, mainly between the Jefe de Tenencia and the Comisariado de Bienes Comunales.

33. For a detailed study of the religious cargo system in a P'urhépecha community, see Padilla Pineda 2000.

34. For some reason, the church's list of Cabildo members separates widows but not widowers.

35. The church records date back to 1920.

36. During her tenure as assistant to Padre Nacho (2002?–2008), Luisa compiled a document with information about the responsibilities of each carguero. She interviewed members of the Cabildo de Ancianos and the current cargueros. She told me that her information was incomplete and that further research was needed, but she did not have the time to do so. The document she prepared is presented to the cargueros each year at the beginning of their tenure so they can use it as a guide. I was given a copy in 2009, and I am not sure if it has been updated or if it is still given to the cargueros.

37. Ta Manuel has received many requests from people in the community to research exactly how the religious cargo system is supposed to work, as many people have conflicting notions about how to ascend through the ranks.

38. The level of state violence increased during the government of Silvano Aureoles Conejo (2015–2021). Moreover, during this time, the level of narco violence, corruption, and general impunity increased, so much so that in 2019, the level of violence broke the previous record established in 2012.

39. Part of the reason why communities ask for their autonomy is that most head municipalities tend to take money away from Indigenous and rural communities, which means that Indigenous and rural communities do not receive their full budget. By requesting their autonomy and receiving their budget directly, Indigenous communities have access to more economic resources.

40. While other P'urhépecha communities may be more accepting of LGBTQ+ individuals, in Angahuan, unfortunately, there are much stigma and violence against members of this community. Many live as single people, not

58 CREATING CULTURE, PERFORMING COMMUNITY

fully expressing who they are, move away from the community, or decide to form a heterosexual relationship to be accepted into the community.

41. Before the arrival of the Spanish, Tarascan culture, like other First Nations throughout the continent, had a fluid and diverse understanding and expression of gender that did not conform to European male-female binary constructions. For a detailed and critical analysis of gender construction in the Tarascan Empire before and after the conquest, see Santana 2019 and Tortorici 2007.

42. Scholars John Monaghan and Susan Kellogg proposed the concepts of gender complementarity and gender parallelism to explain gender dynamics before the arrival of the Europeans. Gender complementarity refers to how different genders complemented each other in ways that "were harmonizing instead of oppositional" (Santana 2019, 8–9), whereas gender parallelism "describes the existence of 'parallel lines of authority and institutionalized positions of leadership held by women and men' which often existed amongst urbanized Indigenous states such as the Mexica, Inka, and Tarascans" (Santana 2019, 9). As Santana (2019, 5) explores in his dissertation "Indigenous Masculinities and the Tarascan Borderlands in Sixteenth-Century Michoacán," "During the sixteenth century, the Tarascan borderlands were sites where Indigenous hypermasculinities were constructed, reimagined, and performed in ways that were often superficial and reflected the contemporary political moments in which they were produced"—meaning, during the conquest and first decades of colonialism. Santana (2019) argues that it was during this period that Tarascans' and, later, P'urhépecha's reputations as patriarchal, heteronormative, and male-female binary cultures were crafted. And while European patriarchal notions did influence gender constructions, performance, and representations, these perceptions and stereotypes are further complicated by the fact that women held, and hold, positions of power in Tarascan and in current P'urhépecha society.

43. While more research is needed to fully understand the complex gender dynamics among current P'urhépecha communities, I do not wish to present the P'urhépecha community as a gender-egalitarian society, as scholars and activists have highlighted the level of violence against women, children, and members of the LGBTQ+ community. Poet and activist Guadalupe Hernández Dimas (2004; Hernández Dimas and Sereno 2005) has dedicated her career to fighting for P'urhépecha women's rights, and the Parakata-Tzintzun Working Group (established in 2021 in the United States), composed of queer scholars, activists, and poets, seeks to highlight and celebrate queer P'urhépecha experiences. At present, Mario A. Gómez Zamora (PhD student at the University of California, Santa Cruz) is conducting research among queer P'urhépecha in Michoacán and the United States. Their research will provide new terminology

and conceptualizations of gender constructions in P'urhépecha communities and cultures.

44. I elaborate on the Diosïri Uandari in chapter 5.

45. I also had many conversations regarding the compadrazgo system with my host family.

46. While confianza can be translated as trust, it is much more than *just* trust.

Fig. 2.1 Young men with their kanakuecha. August 2009.

2

Carrying the Uarhota

Courtship Rituals and Youth Cultures in Angahuan

In August 2009, I went to the capitanes' (the principal cargueros) house to help out during the celebration of the Assumption of the Virgin. As I always did while in Angahuan, I was staying with the Gómez Santacruz family, and one of their oldest daughters, Tomi (who was related by marriage to the capitanes), asked me if I wanted to help and document the three days of rituals and celebrations.[1] I readily accepted the invitation and went with Tomi on August 15 and 16.[2] Before the festivities, two other daughters of my host family, Chucha and Pela, explained some of the main events as they related to youth cultural practices. Among the many ritual practices and events of the three days, I was especially curious to see the kanakua (a bread crown decorated with flowers). My interest in the kanakua grew when I saw three kanakuecha (plural for kanakua) in Chucha and Pela's room, and they told me the stories of how and when they received them.[3] The gifting of the kanakua during the celebrations of the Assumption of the Virgin occurs on the morning of August 16. As it was explained to me, young men and boys spend the night of the fifteenth in the mountains "capturing" bulls, which are then used for the jaripeo (rodeo) on the sixteenth.[4] Early in the morning of the sixteenth, the hunters come down from the mountain and take the bulls to the cargueros' homes, where the cargueros' young female relatives serve the hunters lunch and later reward them with the kanakuecha. The young men then gift the kanakua to their girlfriends or prospective girlfriends as a token of their affection and commitment.

As I walked to the house of the capitanes on the morning of the sixteenth, I saw many groups of young men leading bulls, safely tied by the horns with long ropes. The screams and laughter of the young hunters as they provoked the bulls into running furiously could be heard throughout the community. To avoid being trampled by running bulls and young men, passersby had to quickly get out of the way. As soon as I arrived at the house of the capitanes, I walked to the kitchen area where a large group of women were already hard at work. Some of them recognized me from the day before and greeted me. The house was packed with people, mainly women, helping the capitanes get ready for the day's events. The house was divided into makeshift work areas. The principal cooking area was near the kitchen at the back of the house where a group of older women (the capitanes' mothers, godmothers, and other older relatives) oversaw the workflow of the day. Three paranguecha (firepits) were already lit, and most of the ingredients for the many dishes that had to be prepared were safely stored. All along the wall of the patio, a mountain of firewood was neatly arranged in piles. In a room in front of the house, which was open to the street, the image of the Virgin was stunningly dressed and decorated, and rested in a beautiful flower-covered altar. The street was closed and covered with a huge plastic tarp. Under the tarp, many tables were set and ready to receive the guests and participants of the day's rituals.

That day, we had to prepare nakatamales for the jaripeo.[5] Before starting our work, we were offered breakfast (bread with kamata—atole in Spanish, a warm drink thickened with corn flour), and each woman was given a small plastic bucket containing a large ball of nixtamal (corn dough). Over twenty women worked with the dough, while a group of older women prepared the atapakua (P'urhépecha beef mole). We had to make over a thousand nakatamales for the jaripeo. We each chose a place and sat on small chairs arranged in circles. Each woman had their bucket with nixtamal on one side, and in the middle of the circle was a bucket with wet corn husks and another empty basket into which we placed the nixtamal-filled corn husks. The work was hard and time-consuming, as we manually spread a thin layer of dough into each corn leaf. The thinner and more even, the better. Little by little, and accompanied by lively conversations, we made enough nakatamales for the jaripeo. There was enough nixtamal left over for us to prepare nakatamales for each woman to take home.

As we worked on the nakatamales, a group of young men arrived with the bulls for the capitanes. The capitanes' young female relatives served them lunch and then presented the kanakua. The young men—who ranged in age from early teens to late twenties—waited anxiously for their kanakuecha. David, a friend of my host sisters and a research collaborator, was part of the group. I asked him if I could take pictures when they received their kanakua. David consulted with the group's leader, and they allowed me to take pictures (fig. 2.1). The young women and men shyly laughed when they exchanged the kanakua. Once the young men received their kanakua, they retired to their respective homes; they had not slept the night before, and I could see that some were falling asleep where they stood. Before leaving, David offered me his kanakua and told me that since he did not have a girlfriend, I might as well have it. I was touched by his kind gesture and readily accepted the gift. As soon as I reentered the capitanes' house, most of the women stared at me and laughed and started asking who had given me the kanakua and what it meant. That afternoon, as I returned home with my kanakua and my bucket filled with nakatamales, people in the street stared at me, not because I was a stranger but because of the kanakua. As soon as I arrived home, everybody in my host family questioned me about the kanakua and later began teasing me about it. For a long time, David and I were teased about the kanakua because, even though it was a lighthearted gesture, for Angahuans, the gift carried multiple meanings and implications.[6]

This experience showed me how certain gifts, objects, and ritual practices are signifiers for either availability or commitment to a relationship among young people in Angahuan. Within the annual ritual and celebration cycle in the community, youth and young adults have different events or spaces in which they can participate and signal that they are in a relationship or looking for one. This chapter, thus, provides a general overview of youth culture and courtship rituals in Angahuan. I first describe social stratification and kinship dynamics to illustrate the spaces that young people occupy in the community. Next, I analyze youth culture and rites of passage in Angahuan. I then focus on some of the most important courtship rituals and practices in the community.

Before I continue, I would like to briefly describe my approach to youth studies and youth cultural practices. First, the term *young adult* in this book is not a local term but one I use to describe the population I interviewed and befriended in the community during my 2009–2010 research stay. I conducted interviews with people from eighteen through late thirties. Most of my research collaborators were in their twenties. Some were married; others were single. I use the terms *youth* and *young adults* interchangeably.[7] Second, since the inception of both anthropology and folklore, children and youth cultural practices have been a central focus of research, especially those tied to rites of passage, specifically from childhood to adulthood (van Gennep 1960; Malinowski [1922] 1953; Mead 1928; Sutton-Smith 1999; Turner [1969] 1977, 1982; Virtanen 2012). According to Bucholtz (2002, 525), initial research on youth focused on youth from the perspective of adulthood, thereby framing it as a "biological and psychological stage in human development" instead of as a cultural category.[8] During this first wave of research on youth, scholars focused on practices associated with life stages such as rites of passage, sexuality, and

64   CREATING CULTURE, PERFORMING COMMUNITY

courtship rituals (Bucholtz 2002, 525). However, recent research frames youth as "a context-renewing and a context-creating sign whereby social relations are both (and often simultaneous[ly]) reproduced and contested" (Bucholtz 2002, 528). In addition, the role of youth, as a cultural category, locates young people as cultural agents (Bucholtz 2002, 526). Contrary to other categories, such as *adolescent,* which highlights the process of change from child into adult, the category of *youth* emphasizes "the here-and-now of young people's experience, the social and cultural practices through which they shape their world" (Bucholtz 2002, 532).

According to Cara Heaven and Matthew Tubridy (2003, 149), youths are more "susceptible to foreign cultural practices" than older generations and "are seen as the part of society that is most likely to engage in a process of cultural borrowing that is disruptive of the reproduction of traditional cultural practices, from modes of dress to language, aesthetic and ideologies." However, even if youths are borrowing from foreign cultural practices, they may be adapting or hybridizing those elements to their local culture. As Joe Grixti (2006, 1907) analyzed in Malta, while "young people everywhere increasingly appear to share similar tastes in style of dress and entertainment, there are still significant regional, ethnic and cultural differences in the way they use and appropriate the media technologies and global images at their disposal." Grixti (2006) and Heaven and Tubridy (2003) also argue that while some elders may frown on technology and its impact on local culture, young people are interested in preserving their traditions and cultural practices, "y se muestran dispuestos a aprender a utilizar las herramientas de comunicación necesarias para cumplir ese cometido" (and they are willing to learn to use the necessary communication tools in order to reach their goal) (Rincón García 2007, 129). In the case of Angahuan, young people are not only learning to use new technologies but also customizing them to fit their needs and cultural practices.[9] They are customizing technology, and, at the same time, they are customizing their own culture, adapting it to meet their own needs.[10]

Critical Youth Studies, as articulated and spearheaded by Awad Ibrahim and Shirley R. Steinberg (2014) and Shirley R. Steinberg and Awad Ibrahim (2015), combines Critical Race and Ethnic Studies, Gender Studies, Critical Indigenous Studies, and anti-oppressive research methodologies. In their two edited volumes, they propose a model and approach to youth studies that highlights and centers youths' ways of doing and being. They (as well as the contributors to their edited volumes) argue that research *with* (not about) youth must be an act of radical love, must be based on social justice, and must recognize and respect youth and their cultural creations (Ibrahim and Steinberg 2014). In this

CARRYING THE UARHOTA

regard, they define youth "as action; as a performative category; as an identity that is both produced through and is producing our bodies and sense of self; as an agentive, ambiguous, fluid, shifting, multiple, complex, stylized, and forever becoming category" (Ibrahim 2014, xvi). Moreover, youth, as defined by Maurice Rafael Magaña (2020, 13), "is an overtly political and self-ascribed identity." These approaches to Critical Youth Studies heavily influence my approach, as I have seen and documented how youth and young adults in Angahuan are active cultural agents in the creation and performance of cultural practices in Angahuan.

This chapter takes us to the next step in our journey to understand marriage rituals in Angahuan, highlighting how young people are active participants who contribute to the cultural transformations that allow for the continuity of their P'urhépecha culture. Moreover, by showcasing how young people participate in and perform rituals that are aimed at them, we begin to understand how culture is created and community is performed in Angahuan.

Growing Up in Angahuan

While living with the Gómez Santacruz family, I learned that, during celebrations, people must act according to their social position within the particular social network they belong to, regardless of economic status.[11] For instance, Tomás, a young musician and teacher, shared with me that he has found himself in uncomfortable situations at friends' weddings. When I first interviewed him in 2009, Tomás was in a difficult position: he was young and single but held a relatively high social position for his age group. He is the youngest child in his home, and there is a large age difference between his older siblings and himself, so some of his nephews and nieces are his age; instead of relating to him as an uncle, they often behave more like friends or cousins. At the wedding of one of his closest friends who was also a nephew, Tomás was participating with his age group, although he belonged to a higher social group. The groom's parents told Tomás that he should not be serving alcohol (in the part of the celebration in which he was participating, young people serve alcohol to the older generation) but rather accompanying them and drinking alcohol. The groom's parents scolded him for not behaving according to his social position. After this, and other similar situations in weddings and celebrations of his close friends and relatives, Tomás decided to stop attending celebrations where it was not appropriate for him to participate with his age group.[12] As Tomás found out the hard way, in Angahuan, age and social position do not go hand in hand, so you must participate in celebrations according to your position in a social network.

66 CREATING CULTURE, PERFORMING COMMUNITY

In P'urhépecha culture, different terms are used to demarcate the life stages of an individual, and each stage has different responsibilities and expectations. Babies are called charhaku until they are one or two years of age (although I heard my host sisters call their children this term at the ages six or seven). Roughly after two years of age, a male child is called tataka sapichu, and a female child is called nanaka sapichu.[13] A male child between seven and fourteen (just before puberty) is called tataka, and a female child is called nanaka. A bachelor over the age of fourteen is called a tumbí, and a young bachelorette is called iurhítskiri. Once a young man and young woman are married, they are called achati and uarhiti, respectively. When they reach old age and have acquired a relative position of respect, a man is called t'arhépiti, and a woman is called kutsïmiti.[14]

Becoming an adult in Angahuan is a long and multifaceted process. A person becomes an adult after they are married and have celebrated their misa kuani. Then married couples must assume certain responsibilities, such as becoming godparents or participating in the cargo system.[15] If a person does not get married, they are called tumbí k'eri: "big/old young man" or iurhítskiri k'eri: "big/old young woman." A tumbí k'eri or iurhítskiri k'eri cannot participate in certain ritual events, as it would not be appropriate based on their age and social status. For example, a tumbí k'eri who is in his forties would not be able to join the young hunters who go for bulls for the jaripeo because they are too old, but they cannot also join the older men in their particular ritual activities because they do not have the status of being married.

In Angahuan, depending on one's position in a social network and their age / social group, one has certain roles in celebrations. For example, during posadas or levantamientos or during the events commemorating the Day of the Dead, nanakas and tatakas may go from house to house asking for food.[16] They are allowed to run around, and, in some cases, they are expected to play pranks. As illustrated by this chapter's opening vignette, the young female relatives (iurhítskiriecha, plural for iurhítskiri) of the capitanes are in charge of feeding and presenting the kanakua to the young men, or tumbiecha (plural for tumbí). Also, as described in that same vignette, labor was divided based on an individual's position within a social network (older female relatives oversaw preparing the atapakua while the younger women were tasked with the more labor-intensive work of preparing the corn husks for the nakatamales). In this regard, as age, responsibility, and respectability increase, one can only attend those celebrations where te toca and participate in them based on one's age group and position in one's social network.[17] This way, labor, expectations, and knowledge are shared, taught, learned, and performed as one grows up in Angahuan.

Angahuan's Youth Culture and Rites of Passage

Youth culture in Angahuan is diverse and rich. The community boasts cholos, goths, punks, emos, rockeros, banda, norteños, and everything in between. Since 2007, Angahuan has had access to cell phone service (Telcel, the largest cell phone provider in México installed a cell tower on a nearby mountain), and most young people own cell phones. Internet access is still somewhat limited, but in 2009, at least two internet shops began providing service, and increasing numbers of young people use email and social media (Facebook, Instagram, WhatsApp, etc.) on their cell phones.[18] During my time in Angahuan in 2009–2010, young people hung out in the plaza or played basketball, football (soccer), or uarhukua (P'urhépecha stickball game) in the sports center near my host family's home. Some of my research collaborators and acquaintances traveled to Uruapan to spend the day in the city. Others traveled to other parts of the state or country for music concerts. Some formed rock bands or played traditional P'urhépecha music (pirekua). A group of young men organized pirekua concerts as well as reggae, ska, and punk concerts in the main plaza. They do, and did, all these things in a distinctly P'urhépecha/Angahuan way.

In terms of rites of passage from childhood into adulthood, the P'urhépecha community of Carapan is known for the celebration of the Ch'anantskua, or "the game of maturity/adulthood" (Cárdenas Fernández 2006; Cerano 1999). During this fiesta, young men and women must prove to the community that they are ready for marriage. According to Cárdenas Fernández (2006) and Cerano (1999), men must prove that they know how to work the land, cut wood, and drink, and that they can defend their manhood by participating in mock fights. Young men must collect money to hire a brass band for the four days of the fiesta, thus proving that they are financially capable. Young women, on the other hand, must demonstrate that they can do housework, mainly cooking and embroidery. At the end of the fiesta, many young couples elope. In Angahuan, people celebrate Ch'anantskua as part of Carnival, which occurs just before Ash Wednesday and the start of Lent, but the meaning is different from Carapan's celebration. During the Ch'anantskua in Angahuan, young people (both single and married) play tricks on one another, mainly throwing water, flour, and sometimes colored paint.

In other communities, such as Nurío, and to some degree in Angahuan, migration has become an important rite of passage for young males (Bello Maldonado 2008). Migration allows young men to acquire different skill sets that will aid them in their transition into married life. Young migrant men tend to work for many years in the US and save money to buy property, build their

Fig. 2.2 Cargueras de la Resurreccion during the Uiítakua. April 2009.

Fig. 2.3 Cargueros de la Resurrección during the Uiítakua. April 2009.

home, or start a small business back in their community. In Angahuan, I heard of several young men who worked in the US and returned after saving enough money to get married.

According to my research collaborators, Angahuan does not have any specific coming-of-age rituals or puberty rites of passage for either gender. They could not explain why. And while the tembuchakua does serve as a form of a rite of passage, marking the transition from tumbí and iurhístkiri into achati and uarhiti, as mentioned previously, the process of becoming and being considered a full adult also depends on the couple's participation in the wider social networks in the community (such as the compadrazgo and cargo systems). On the other hand, in Angahuan, I documented multiple courtship rituals, which I will discuss next, that do have a coming-of-age element.

Courtship Rituals in Angahuan

According to early P'urhépecha scholarship, courtship rituals were usually performed near bodies of water like the river or the town's fountain (León [1889] 1982; Lumholtz 1904; Beals [1945] 1992; Foster [1967] 1988; Mendieta y Núñez 1940). Young people would meet when young women filled containers with water for their family's use. But after the construction of water systems in most P'urhépecha communities, young women no longer needed to fetch water, so other forms of courtship rituals took their place.

In Angahuan, I observed both public and private types of courtship. Public courtship events are those in which the couples are put on display in the community. These may be further divided into two sets of practices: practices that are by and for youths and young adults and practices that are part of a larger event (i.e., performed during a celebration organized by the cargueros). Private courtship relates to all the small practices that are not part of the community's annual cycle of events; in many cases, the courtship takes place around the young woman's home. Each type of courtship ritual has its own style and set of expectations. Of the two, the most important are public courtships: the young people are not only putting themselves on display for all the community to see but are also actively participating in the creation of their cultural practices and performing what it means to be a member of their community.

As mentioned in chapter 1, one of the most sought-after religious cargo positions is the Cargo de la Resurrección. This cargo is held each year by four young men and four young women. The men oversee the image of San Juan Evangelista (Saint John), and the women supervise the image of María Magdalena (Mary Magdalene). Throughout the year, and based on the guidebook

70   CREATING CULTURE, PERFORMING COMMUNITY

prepared in the community's church, the young men and women must go to the Iurhixu every Sunday to sweep the floor, take flowers to the images, and make sure the images are taken care of. The most important part of their cargo, and the reason this cargo is so coveted, is that on Easter Sunday and Easter Monday, the young people participate in the Uíítakua, the Carreras de Santos (the saints' races) (figs. 2.2 and 2.3). The races re-create the moment when Mary Magdalene and Saint John saw Jesus Christ resurrected and ran to inform his mother, the Virgin Mary. The images of Saint John and Mary Magdalene are beautifully decorated and covered with flowers for the event. A path from the Iurhixu to the church is made with sand and flanked by tree branches decorated with ribbons. The image of Resurrected Jesus Christ is in the Iurhixu, and the image of his mother, the Virgin Mary, is in the church. The cargueros, carrying the images, run from the church to the Iurhixu, from mother to son. The church's bells signal when the cargueros must start running from one site to the other. Those who attend the races, especially young women and girls, throw confetti at the images and the cargueros. They throw so much confetti that by the end of the event, the ground, the images, and the cargueros are completely covered in it. Chucha, one of my host sisters, participated in the Cargo de la Resurrección when she was a teenager and told me that throughout the year, the cargueros receive gifts from their relatives, usually clothes, so they can wear new outfits during the various rituals taking place during Holy Week. Participating in this cargo signals not only that the young men and women are respectable people (i.e., they are virgins and good Catholics) but also that they participate in the community and their families are respectable (if this were not the case, they would not have received the cargo). This cargo is one of the most visible and respected positions for youth in the community.

During the fiesta cycle, youths and young adults also participate in the pastorelas and the kurpiti, traditional dances celebrated during Christmastime.[19] The pastorelas are performed on December 24, 25, and 26, and only single women (from different age groups) can take part.[20] The kurpiti is performed from January 6 to 8, and only single young men (regardless of age) may participate. Despite its seven barrios (Guadalupe, San Juan, Calvario, Capilla, San José, Santo Santiago, and Cristo Rey), Angahuan maintains a ritual and cultural distinction between the barrio de arriba (north neighborhood) and the barrio de abajo (south neighborhood). For many celebrations, including the pastorelas and the kurpiti, participants are grouped by these two barrios.[21] Each barrio must collect enough money to hire a wind band or orchestra that will accompany the dancers for the three days of performance.

Fig. 2.4 Pastorela dancing. December 2009.

For the pastorela, young women wear a pink or red sïtakua (pleated skirt), but they can choose whatever color they wish for the rest of their attire. They also wear a hat decorated with bells, ribbons, and plastic flowers (mainly poinsettias and roses) and carry a walking stick, also decorated with ribbons. The first pastorela dance takes place on December 24 at the midnight mass (Misa de Gallo). The dancers, organized in parallel lines, sway from side to side with the music. On December 25 and 26, the young women visit the homes of each other's boyfriends, so each of them can take presents and bags of hard candy to the young men (fig. 2.4). In some cases, a young woman may not be dating the young man but may take him a present anyway; however, this is not as common.

On December 26, 2009, I followed the group from the barrio de arriba, as three of my research collaborators, Lourdes, Noemi, and Magali, were dancing

72 CREATING CULTURE, PERFORMING COMMUNITY

with them. The group was made up of little girls and young women. They danced through the community and visited the houses of their boyfriends. Once the group arrived at the intended house, they knocked on the door and asked for permission to enter. Some occupants did not let them in, so the groups danced in the middle of the street, throwing confetti and hard candy in the air and toward the roofs. The reason homeowners did not let the dancers in was that they intentionally broke light bulbs with their walking sticks. Misbehavior is expected during the pastorelas, as young women sometimes ignored the rules for appropriate conduct based on gender.

Older women followed the group either to accompany their younger daughters or to make sure that order was maintained. Catalina, an acquaintance of mine and a friend of my host sisters, joined me in following the group. She did not dance; she was accompanying her younger sister, who was dancing. The group was going to the house of her sister's boyfriend, and Catalina wanted to make sure they behaved and did not break anything. While we watched the group dance inside the house, Catalina made a disapproving sound and said: "I do not like how they are behaving; they are behaving like men." I looked at her quizzically and asked: "What do you mean? How should a woman behave?" She pointed with her chin at the group and said: "Not like that." I continued watching the group; the young women were dancing spiritedly, twirling fast so their skirts would go up and show their petticoats.[22] Some of them were laughing loudly and screaming with the music. After we left her sister's boyfriend's house, and she made sure that nothing was broken, Catalina said goodbye and returned to her home. I followed the group for another hour and then went home too.

Not all young women like to participate in the pastorelas. When I began my research work in Angahuan in 2005, Chucha and Pela told me about the pastorelas and said they had never participated because they didn't like how the dancers behaved.[23] When I accompanied the group from the barrio de arriba, I saw that some of the older young women were drinking tequila, acting rowdy, and dancing too spiritedly. For example, when they twirled, their sïtakua would lift and show their tatchukua. This is considered inappropriate behavior for women in Angahuan but is expected during the pastorela celebration. As I documented at other events in Angahuan, certain behaviors, such as breaking and challenging gender norms or respectable ways of behavior, are permissible. But even if those behaviors are permissible, they are still monitored (as in the case of Catalina accompanying her sister to make sure nothing was broken at her boyfriend's home) and regulated.

Some young women do not like dancing in the pastorelas, but others, like Lourdes, Noemi, and Magali, who usually avoid communal events, do like dancing in them. When I first interviewed Lourdes, Noemi, and Magali in November 2009, they told me that they have a "bad" reputation in the community because they like to break the gender rules of how young women are supposed to behave in Angahuan. They are punks and rockers, who like to travel to concerts around the state. They do not enjoy participating in many communal events, nor wear the traditional P'urhépecha female dress. For the pastorelas, however, they did wear the usual attire, but with modifications. Lourdes, for example, did not wear the traditional hat that all dancers are expected to wear. Although I was not able to interview them after they danced at the pastorelas, they had mentioned in previous conversations that they participated in a few cultural practices in the community but did so in their own way.

The kurpiti is danced by young men, and, like the pastorelas, the age group of participants varies, though they are always single (fig. 2.5). The attire for the kurpiti is slightly more complicated than for the pastorelas. The young men must procure between ten and twenty tangarikuecha (plural for tangarikua) from their female friends, girlfriends, or female relatives. The tangarikuecha are layered on top of their shoulders like capes. They wear boots and small bells tied to their ankles, a long-sleeved button-down shirt, and gloves. Their faces and heads are covered with handkerchiefs. In addition, they wear a mask decorated with colorful floor-length ribbons and bows on top of their heads.[24]

Like the pastorelas, the kurpiti dancers are divided between the barrio de arriba and the barrio de abajo. Each group must collect money to hire a wind band. The first dance of the kurpiti is on January 6 for the Epiphany procession and mass. January 7 is the big day for the kurpiti in Angahuan: this is when the dance competition takes place. Families cook a feast (mainly korunda and churipo—a beef stew) and prepare to receive guests. After the feast, almost everyone in the community goes to the plaza to watch the competition.

The rivalry is intense between the two neighborhoods. The coordinators of each group are responsible for keeping the peace between participants. Together with the kurpiticha, another group also dances, los feos, the ugly ones. The feos are also performed by young male dancers; they wear torn clothes, masks (some are Halloween masks), and wigs and tend to look dirty. Some young men also dress as women, borrowing clothes from their sisters. However, los feos only participate in the competition and not the other activities in which the kurpiticha dance. Two other characters also take part in the competition: the T'arepiti (old man) and the Maringuía (María). The old man's attire is similar to the famous attire of the Danza de los Viejitos.[25] The character wears a manta shirt and pants, a faja (woven belt), and a sash that crosses his chest;

Fig. 2.5 Cheio and cousin dressed as kurpiti. January 2009.

he covers his face with an old man wooden mask and carries a decorated cane. The Maringuía, performed by a young man, dresses in a floor-length black sïtakua, two colorful tangarikuecha, and a saco. The Maringuía also wears a pastorela hat and has floor-length ribbon-decorated braids. A beautifully carved female mask covers his face. Each barrio must have dancers for the feos, the old men, and the Maringuías, and they dance only during the competition. After the competition, the two groups of kurpiticha start dancing around the community.

On January 8, the kurpiticha from both barrios visit the homes of the girl-friends of the group's members who helped pay for the band. The brass band accompanies each group, and they are required to take presents for their girl-friends. The required gift is, at minimum, a sack of oranges, but other gifts may be given. In January 2010, Pancho, one of my host family's sons, wanted to take a sack of oranges to his girlfriend. He gave the money to his mother, and Na Juana and Ta Emiliano traveled to Uruapan to buy the oranges. Even though Pancho was not dancing that year (it was Cheio's turn), the family had contrib-uted money for the band, so they had to go to Pancho's girlfriend's house too.

If the pastorelas are a little destructive, the kurpiti are much worse. The kur-piticha not only broke all the light bulbs they could see but also threw oranges through windows. Most of the homes we visited did not let the kurpiticha in, so they mainly danced in the street. Normally, after the whole group has left, the boyfriend or suitor stays behind with some close friends to present the sack of oranges and any other gifts he brought. Gume, Inés's husband, loaned us his car so we could follow the group until it was Pancho's turn to present his gifts. After four hours, it was time to go to Pancho's girlfriend's house. We stayed on the street corner while the kurpiticha tried to enter the house; the girlfriend's family refused to let them in, so they danced outside. As soon as they were done, the main group left to go to another house. We stayed behind while Pan-cho negotiated with his girlfriend's family to open the door so he could give them the oranges. Finally, they opened the door, and Pancho left the oranges at the entrance. The young men kept dancing late into the night until they had finished dancing in or outside all of their girlfriends' homes. Because we were in the car accompanying and helping Pancho, we missed two groups taking oranges to Chucha. When we returned to the house that night, we found three sacks of oranges and several broken bedroom windows.

Unlike the pastorelas, most young men and boys *want* to participate in the kurpiti; many of them begin dancing at a young age. Most young men have danced as a kurpiti, and some offer the dance as a manda (a promise to a de-ity).[26] In January 2010, a group of young married men wanted to participate in the festivities, but because they were married, they were not allowed to dance as kurpiticha. Tomás (mentioned earlier in this chapter) told me that this group decided to run their own event: they dressed as feos, hired a band, and danced around the community.[27] They received a great deal of criticism, but as Tomás told me, they did not care and enjoyed dancing through the community. I do not know if something like this ever happened again.

Young men are expected to dance as kurpiti, but a young woman is not required to participate in the pastorelas. In fact, in more traditional or

Fig. 2.6 Carrying uarhotecha. April 2009.

conservative families, dancing in the pastorelas is discouraged. Maybe that is why Lourdes, Noemi, and Magali liked to dance in the pastorelas—because it was not done by "respectful" young women, and it was a way to continue transgressing "correct" female behavior in the community. However, the pastorelas are becoming more popular and accepted, and more families are allowing their young women and girls to participate.

Another public courtship ritual tied to the communal calendar of events is the uarhota (fig. 2.6). This is a gift from a boyfriend to his girlfriend, signaling his commitment to her. The uarhota is a log covered with palm leaves and decorated with fruit (watermelons, coconuts, pineapples, mamey sapote, bananas, and other seasonal fruits), soda and juice cans, candies, boxes of cookies, small clay pots, balloons, plastic flowers, palm leaf decorations, and any other item the boyfriend might want to include. The young man must ask his girlfriend for permission to give her a uarhota. In most cases, receiving a uarhota is an honor and a sign of a future intention to marry.[28] Fernando, a research collaborator, explained that in about 80 percent of cases in which a uarhota is given, the relationship is serious, but each case varies. Even if their intentions are not serious, some young men give their girlfriends the uarhota so they can participate in the different ritual activities and traditional practices in the community. As my host sisters explained to me, if the young woman has already eloped with her boyfriend, then he *must* present the uarhota during the first Palm Sunday after the elopement.

In 2009, Fernando described the process of going to look for the uarhota. According to him, the Viscal, one of the minor cargueros from the Iurhixu, organizes an activity called Pimu Akuri. Around two hundred young men go to the Pimu Akuri every year. Several weeks before Palm Sunday, the Viscal announces over the communal loudspeakers that interested young men should start preparing for the Pimu Akuri. The Viscal is in charge of preparing and taking food (although each young man is responsible for taking his own meal) and organizing the transportation and music. A week before Palm Sunday, the group travels to the Tierra Caliente region to look for the two different types of palms and a log. They gather in the town's cemetery, leave at noon on Friday, and return to town the next day. Upon their arrival with the palms and wood, they leave all the materials by a cross behind the cemetery (one of the religious points in the community). On Sunday, accompanied by music, they take all the materials to the Iurhixu to present them to the Virgin and have them blessed by the priest. Afterward, the Viscal and the wind band accompany the young men back to their homes. The week after, early on the eve of Palm Sunday, the uncles, fathers, and other male relatives gather in the homes of the young men to decorate and prepare the uarhota. That night, uncles and parents, but mainly female relatives, take the decorated uarhota to the intended young woman. I asked Fernando why the boyfriends did not deliver the uarhota themselves. He laughed and said that he did not know.

Late on the Saturday afternoon before Palm Sunday in April 2009, Chucha, Pela, and I walked to the plaza for two reasons: Chucha and Pela had a meeting at the church, and they wanted to see and show me the women carrying uarhotecha (plural of uarhota). There was a great deal of movement throughout the community, but, as it was already dark, I could not see the uarhota's details. After we returned home that evening, three of Chucha and Pela's cousins asked us to help carry the uarhota for the Palm Sunday procession the next day. We agreed.

At that time, three masses were celebrated on Palm Sunday, and each mass was preceded by a procession of young women and girls who had received a uarhota.[29] Each procession left from different points in the community. The first procession and mass are usually the best attended, as most of the young women want to show off their uarhota. One of the cousins, Fabiana, wanted to go to the first mass at eight in the morning. It was still dark and cold when we woke up at about six to get ready. We walked to Fabiana's home to pick her up and help carry her uarhota. Fabiana's uarhota was almost eight feet long and incredibly heavy, even though it only had one watermelon, one coconut, and one pineapple (among other smaller fruits, soda cans, clay pots, etc.). It required at least three people to carry it, so we all (Chucha, Pela, Fabiana, and me) took turns. The first procession left from the cross behind the cemetery. We arrived early at the meeting point for the procession. As eight o'clock approached, more and more groups of young women arrived carrying their uarhota. Most of the uarhota were carried by groups of three or more young women and young girls. While we waited for the procession to begin, all the young women leaned their uarhota against the walls or fences of the homes in the area.

The sun slowly came out from behind the mountains, and the morning chill began to dissipate. Shortly after eight, through the light mist that still covered the town, we saw Padre Armando, the young missionaries who were in town for Holy Week, and more young women carrying their uarhotecha, walking from the church to the place where the procession would begin. The young missionaries were carrying the image of Santo Santiago, religious banners, and candles. The group arrived at the procession's starting point. Padre Armando began the necessary ritual prayers, and the procession began. All the young women followed the procession carrying their uarhotecha. The procession was a vivid and colorful wave with over fifty uarhotecha. As we arrived at the church's atrium, most of the young women stayed outside and leaned their uarhotecha on the church's wall, although some entered the church with their uarhotecha. Before beginning the mass, the priest blessed all of the uarhotecha, including those outside the church. As the mass began, more young women, and even little girls, arrived with their uarhotecha. At the end of the mass, we returned home carrying Fabiana's uarhota and then had lunch and rested for a little while, as we needed to get ready to help Paulina (Pablo's sister) and Salma (another cousin) carry their uarhotecha to the noon mass. The second procession started in the Calvario, a small hill on the north side of town.

Salma arrived before noon to ask for help with her uarhota. Thankfully, Salma's uarhota was not that big and could easily be carried by two people. Paulina's uarhota, on the other hand, was so heavy that even the four of us could hardly carry it! Paulina's had two watermelons, two coconuts, and one pineapple, in addition to soda cans, cookies, bananas, and other types of fruit. As we walked to the church, our shoulders hurt so much from carrying it that we decided not to do the whole procession and wait on a street we knew the procession would pass. We waited until the priest and the missionaries reached us, and then we joined the procession on its way to the church. Again, we stayed outside the church while the mass took place, after which we returned home, carrying the uarhotecha. After we returned Paulina and Salma's uarhotecha to their respective homes, Chucha, Pela, and I went home, where I collapsed for the rest of the day. For the next few days, our shoulders were sore and bruised from carrying three uarhotecha.

In this first group of public courtship rituals—the Cargueros de la Resurrección, the pastorelas, the kurpiti, and the uarhota—young women and men put themselves on display in the community in activities that are for and by them. Some of the rituals, such as the Cargueros de la Resurrección, provide a space where young women and men let the community know that they are "people of respect," religious, and active members of the community. The pastorelas, the kurpiti, and the uarhota are mainly for people who are in some form of relationship or are interested in having a relationship (in the case of the pastorelas and the kurpiti). Participating in all these different activities, while not a requirement, is important for the cultural and social development of young people in Angahuan. Even if young people do not like to participate in wider sociocultural events in the community, many of them will take part in the pastorelas or the kurpiti at least once in their lifetime and in their own way. These cultural practices are one of the ways in which young people are raised and taught how to perform their membership in their P'urhépecha community and culture.

Other types of public courtship practices are those that are part of larger events, such as the aguadoras during Holy Week or the participation of young women and men during the celebration of the Assumption of the Virgin. The aguadoras are young women and men who carry clay pots filled with aguas frescas, fruit-flavored water made with rice, oatmeal, hibiscus flower, strawberry, watermelon, and lime, which they serve to church attendees. After the Via Crucis mass and the reenactment of the Last Supper on Holy Thursday, the aguadoras hand out the aguas frescas to the attendees. The principal aguadoras are the eight young men and women who hold the Cargo de la Resurrección. And while the cargueros de la Resurrección must have enough water for everyone present, any young person may bring their own clay pot filled with water to share with friends, family, or anyone they find. To pour the water, the aguadoras have smaller clay pots that they fill, share, and reuse. During the event, children of all ages run around trying to take the clay pots away from the aguadoras, while male youth dressed as Roman soldiers chase the children to "punish" them for their mischief. At the same time, young men and women share their

80   CREATING CULTURE, PERFORMING COMMUNITY

fruit-flavored water and flirt while doing so. Some young men may "spice" the water with tequila and dare young women to drink from their clay pots.[30]

As described at the beginning of the chapter, the younger relatives of the cargueros play a crucial role in the celebrations of the Assumption of the Virgin. In the early afternoon of August 16, the young men return to the cargueros' house to take the bulls to the jaripeo. For their part, the young women have flags and banners and carry presents for the jaripeo riders during the procession. After arriving at Angahuan's jaripeo arena, each carguero and their entourage dance in the middle of the rodeo, showing the prizes they have brought for the riders. Male relatives of each carguero must carry a torito. A torito is a medium-sized wooden frame in the shape of a bull laden with fireworks. The torito is lit when everybody is inside of the rodeo, and the torito must chase people and dance while the music plays. After dancing in the rodeo, all the cargueros move to the middle school, which is next to the rodeo, to dance for an hour before returning to the cargueros' house to continue the festivities; meanwhile, the jaripeo continues. This procession and dance are mainly performed by the younger relatives of the cargueros. The older generation—the mothers, aunts, and godmothers—are in charge of taking the food (mainly the nakatamales that were prepared in the morning) to the jaripeo and distributing it to the people present. The dance is a great opportunity for courtship, as the dance and procession provide the necessary space for interaction between men and women.

Dances organized in the community provide another space for courtship: the dances in honor of San Isidro (May 15) and Santa Cecilia (November 22) and, of course, during the celebrations of Santo Santiago (July 23–27), the patron saint of the community. The celebrations of Santo Santiago are a perfect time for flirting. Weeks and even months before the fiesta, young women and men save money to buy new clothes and shoes to wear during the festivities. Every night from July 23 to 27, activities are held in the main plaza. From pirekua concerts to dances, the plaza is full of life, and all the young men and women from the community participate. The plaza and nearby streets are bustling with a market, food stalls, and attractions like a Ferris wheel (and, in 2024, a virtual reality game). Every time I have been in Angahuan for Santo Santiago, I have seen groups of young men and women walk through the crowd flirting with each other. Young men invite young women to accompany them on the rides or offer to buy them tacos, pizza, or whatever they want. The middle of the plaza, where the dance occurs, is normally packed with people not only from Angahuan but also from neighboring communities. It is common knowledge in the community that during the celebrations of Santo Santiago, many young couples will elope, so everybody is prepared. This second form of public courtship allows young people to meet and interact, under the communal gaze and following certain rules or expectations.[31]

As just noted, Angahuan has a rich and diverse public courtship tradition. However, the rituals and practices just mentioned are not the only ones. The other types of courtship practice are less obvious and more private, as these rituals may take place "outside" the gaze of the whole community, even though they might occur in public spaces. For example, when I lived there in 2009– 2010, sellers came to Angahuan every Monday to set up a traveling market in the plaza. There, people could buy fruits, kitchenware, clothes, and cloth to make the traditional female dress. Bootleg music and movies were also available. By noon, and especially after the middle school and high school were dismissed, the plaza was full of women with their small children shopping, as well as young men and women walking around and flirting with the opposite sex. Young women wore their best rollo to walk around the plaza and nearby streets. Some young couples walked around, but mainly I saw small groups of young women and men. When a particular group encountered each other, they exchanged words. In some cases, the young woman covered her head and mouth with her kuanindikua to hide her laughter. I always loved going to the plaza on Mondays, as it was full of life, laughter, and cool items (such as fresh seasonal fruit) to buy.

At the time of my research, the most common method of private courtship was when the interested young man would visit the young woman at her home at night and invite her to go outside to talk. I observed that most homes had a bench or a log outside for people to sit on. During winter, people lit bonfires outside of their homes to pass the time sitting around the fire and to stay warm. Some nights, Chucha, Pela, and I would walk through the streets near their house and see many young couples talking outside of their homes. The couples never sat side by side, as public affection was and is frowned on, especially among unmarried couples. More people walked around the plaza and nearby streets on weekend nights than during the day. Groups of young men and women, all bathed and dressed nicely after a long workday, bought tacos, pizza, kamata, or tequila, and walked around to see who else was walking around. The few young men with cars drove around blasting music ranging from rock and reggaeton to banda and corridos.

Migration has had a noticeable effect on courtship in Angahuan. Many migrant young men court young women in Angahuan via telephone and WhatsApp. People who either have traveled to the United States or are returning to the community bring gifts, which help long-distance relationships. In some cases, a young man may return to Angahuan to marry his girlfriend after having a long-distance relationship. Other young men who do not have a girlfriend in Angahuan may return to find a bride, and, in most cases, get married in the first year after their return. The communal radio also contributes to the courtship practices in Angahuan, as couples send messages through the radio or request music for their loved ones.

After conducting research in Angahuan for so long, it has been amazing to see some of my research collaborators who were courting, recently married, or had small children in 2009–2010 now teaching their children how to take part in these cultural performances once they are old enough to participate. For example, Sergio and Emilia, two of my main research collaborators—who are communal leaders and have participated in many religious and political cargos—documented their oldest son's experience as a 2022 Carguero de la Resurrección and shared it on social media.[32] It was lovely to see how culture is transmitted from one generation to another, and how each generation transforms those cultural practices to reflect their own interests and cultural trends.

Next Step after Courtship

From what I observed and documented in Angahuan, public and private courtship strategies are intertwined in the community. What happens in one form of courtship will affect the other. For example, a couple may get together through private courtship practices but will make their relationship public by participating in public courtship practices (such as taking an uarhota or a sack of oranges as a kurpiti). In other cases, a relationship may begin from a public courtship (during Holy Week and the aguadoras, for example) and then continue through private courtship practices. In this regard, young people in Angahuan have many different forms of courtship available to them, and these practices are constantly fluctuating, adapting to the needs and styles of the current generation. Other courtship practices likely exist in the community, but these are the ones I witnessed during my time in Angahuan. Moreover, each generation develops, or customizes, Angahuan's courtship practices to fit their needs, interests, or trends.

Despite the specific courtship practices that abound in Angahuan, relationships themselves vary greatly. I heard of couples who had been together for many years but did not ultimately get married, while others decided to elope after only a month of courtship. Some young men and women might marry their current boyfriend or girlfriend when they decide they are ready for that step, but if he or she does not want to marry, they may look for someone else who does want to get married. For example, I know of a young man who had just returned from the United States and wanted to marry, but the young woman he had been courting refused him. Two weeks later, he eloped with someone else. While paths to marriage vary, when a couple decides that they want to marry, they all come to the same crossroads: either elope or ask for the young woman's hand in marriage. This decision is crucial because the organization and performance of the wedding will depend on this action, as will the possible future relationship between the couple's families. And that is where our story takes us next.

Notes

1. The celebrations of the Assumption of the Virgin last three days, from August 14 to 16. Each day features multiple events, processions, and masses. More importantly, during those three days, each carguero must prepare enormous quantities of food (mainly special dishes that are only made for those celebrations) that are shared with everyone present and given as special gifts to the Council of Elders.

2. Tomi did not go on the fourteenth, so I did not attend the first day of rituals.

3. The tradition of the kanakua has a long-standing history. It is practiced differently in most P'urhépecha communities, including those where kanakua refers to a dance performed by young women who carry bread crowns on their heads (Alcaraz 1925; Dominguez 1925a, 1925b; Storm 1945; Toor 1925). But however this tradition is practiced, most P'urhépecha communities use the kanakuecha to honor and celebrate. In chapter 5, I discuss how kanakua are used at weddings.

4. Chucha and Pela told me that the young men are not technically hunting or capturing the bulls, as the bulls are usually left in predetermined places on the mountain. According to them, the group of "hunters" spend the night around bonfires, drinking and eating.

5. Nakatamales are like tamales but with only a fine layer of dough, and they are filled with a beef atapakua (a type of P'urhépecha thick stew, similar to Oaxacan mole).

6. David has since married, so we were not teased about this anymore.

7. As I will explain, attaining full adulthood in Angahuan is a long process. After marriage, the young couple must contribute money to the community. But it is not until the couple has participated in the cargo system and assumed certain responsibilities (such as compadrazgo) that they are considered full adults. Most of my research collaborators in 2009–2010 were at that in-between stage of no longer being a tumbí (young man) or iurhitskiri (young woman) but not yet having become an achati (sir) or uarhiti (madam).

8. Other categories that are used, sometimes interchangeably, are adolescent, teenager, and young adult. However, each of these categories has its own historical development and uses. See Savage 2008.

9. I borrow the term customizing from Shane Greene (2009, 17), who proposes the concept of customizing Indigeneity as a tool to help explain the "*specific acts* and to a *structural process* of constrained creativity" (italics in original).

10. To explain these processes, scholars have coined the terms indigenous modernities or indigenous cosmopolitanisms. See Forte 2010; Goodale 2006; Pitarch and Orobitg 2012.

11. In general terms, a social network can be defined as "the chain of people with whom a person, more or less regularly interacts" (Jeremy Boissevain in Govers 2006, 13). Social networks are systems based on social hierarchies, that is, who has what and how others can attain/share that social capital (2006, 13). In this sense, social networks allow people to "gain resources they do not own themselves, and so broaden their resource base" (2006, 13). In Angahuan, resources extend beyond material goods, as they include labor or company during celebrations or times of crisis. The number of social networks to which one belongs or in which one participates will determine how many people will help an individual during times of duress or celebration. In addition, one's social position within a social network will determine how that person participates in events.

12. However, he is now married with children and has assumed cargos, thus reducing the ambiguity of his position within the community.

13. As mentioned in the first chapter, Angahuan privileges a male-female binary gender model, hence terminology is only assigned for male or female individuals. I have not encountered P'urhépecha communities with terminology for nonbinary genders.

14. Each P'urhépecha community may have its own variants of life stages terminology, but these are the most common terms. See Medina Pérez 2006 and Bello Maldonado 2008.

15. As explained in chapter 1, to participate in the religious cargo system, married couples must be heterosexual couples. Some scholars have documented same-sex relationships in other communities, specifically Ralph Beals ([1945] 1992) in Cherán in the 1940s, but as far as I know, there are currently no openly same-sex couples in Angahuan. Other P'urhépecha communities, however, do have openly same-sex couples, some who have celebrated their tembuchakua.

16. Levantamientos are celebrated between January 6 and March 19. Almost everybody in the community builds a nativity set during Christmas. The nativity sets have multiple images of baby Jesus. For each image in the Nativity, the host family invites a child or youth to levantar (raise) and dress one of the images. The family of the child who will dress the image must take large quantities of food to

share with all the people present. Usually, five to seven different families prepare food, including tostadas, kamata, pozole, cake, gelatin, and fruits, and the food must be given to everyone present. Young adults and adults only attend if they are taking food to the inviting house or if it is at their house. Children, on the other hand, might attend the houses of neighbors and friends. During this time, the youngest children arrived almost every night at my host family's house with the food they had received in different levantamientos.

17. For a full explanation of the concept of te toca, see chapter 3.

18. WhatsApp has become the main mode of communication in the community, to the point that the few houses with landlines have canceled them for cell phones. WhatsApp has made communication with migrant relatives easier and more accessible.

19. Other P'urhépecha communities in the Sierra, mainly San Juan Nuevo and Caltzontzin, also perform the dance of the kurpiti. The styles from San Juan Nuevo and Caltzontzin are the most popular and recognized styles, and when they are performed each year in the Music and Dance Competition of the P'urhépecha culture in Zacán (celebrated in October), the crowd goes wild. For more information on the tradition of kurpiticha from San Juan Nuevo, see Próspero Maldonado 2000.

20. At the beginning of my research in 2005–2006, Chucha and Pela told me that the pastorelas were somewhat new, that young women began to perform this ritual so they had something analogous to the kurpiticha. However, a few years later (in 2009), they said that the pastorelas were not new and that they were performed even when their mother was young. But the pastorelas had not been performed for some time; young women started up the ritual again in the mid-2000s. More research is needed to understand the "rebirth" of the pastorelas in the mid-2000s.

21. I have heard of men and women who dance with those from another neighborhood only because all of his or her friends live in that barrio.

22. As I was repeatedly informed, the sïtakua is not supposed to move much when a woman walks but just have a very subtle sway. As I walk like a Caribbean woman, I was constantly chastised because my sïtakua moved too much.

23. Pela, however, participated in the pastorelas in December 2011. She enjoyed the experience and planned to participate again, but she eloped before she could do so.

24. For additional information regarding the kurpiti attire in Angahuan and on the dance, please see Martínez-Rivera 2023.

25. The Danza de los Viejitos is a traditional dance from the Lake of Pátzcuaro area. See Hellier-Tinoco 2011.

26. Those who offer the dance as a manda may only dance on January 6, when they dance in the church.

86 CREATING CULTURE, PERFORMING COMMUNITY

27. At that time, Tomás was still single, so he could have danced with the kurpiti, but he decided to dance with his married friends.

28. I am not implying that the gift of a uarhota is analogous to an engagement ring but only that the giving and receiving of a uarhota denotes a serious commitment between the giver and the receiver of the gift.

29. As a result of the COVID-19 pandemic, there have been some changes to how many masses or processions are performed in a day, so I am unaware if the three processions and masses are still being officiated.

30. In addition to the aguadoras, other water-related rituals in Angahuan include the cleaning of the water spring (the Uekato), when the young female relatives of the cargueros of the Virgins (both Virgin of Guadalupe and of the Assumption of the Virgin) must go to the river to wash the clothes of the images. Young male relatives of the cargueros must also help the young women with their task.

31. Some of the rules in 2009–2010, or at least the main rule, was that courting couples could not hold hands or kiss. I heard of cases in which a young couple was forced to marry to restore the young woman's honor after they were seen holding hands or kissing. However, in 2018, I was told by my host sisters that this is no longer the case, as it's become more common to see young unmarried couples kissing and sharing public displays of affection.

32. Sergio and Emilia are also heavily invested in promoting traditional games and sports, as well as other youth-related cultural practices, but those stories warrant their own space.

Fig. 3.1 Bathing the bride. June 2009.

3

Te Toca

Eloping versus Asking for Marriage

I attended my first wedding in Angahuan in 2009, a week after Holy Week. It was Pablo and Lisa's wedding, described in the introduction. The afternoon before the wedding, my host sisters Chucha and Pela explained that since we were the groom's relatives, we had to bring soap and loofahs to bathe the bride at her home that evening. They said the ritual was basically to bañar a la novia (bathe the bride), but it was going to be more like a water fight between the relatives of the bride and the groom. Chucha and Pela wore their beautiful P'urhépecha attire, while I wore jeans, boots, and a warm jacket. We walked to the community's store near the main plaza to buy our soaps and loofahs. Chucha and Pela had brought two small bateas (decorated wooden trays) that they filled with our purchases.[1] Lisa lived near the plaza, so we waited there for Pablo's relatives. But we did not have to wait long. The group was fairly small, mostly made up of the groom-to-be's young female relatives (sisters and female cousins). We all walked to Lisa's home, and Chucha and Pela warned me to watch out because as soon as the water fight began, everyone would become fair game for a soaking, including me—even if I was holding a camera in my hands.

Lisa's family invited us in and directed us to Lisa's room, on the right side of the courtyard. Lisa was waiting for us, sitting on her bed dressed in her P'urhépecha attire. A line quickly formed as each person offered her their soap-filled batea. She thanked each person as she took their soaps and loofahs and placed them on her bed, returning the empty batea to its owner. I did not have a batea, so I, somewhat embarrassed, presented my gifts in a plastic bag. Lisa, surprised and chuckling softly, received my plastic bag and thanked me too. Once we finished presenting the soaps and loofahs, everybody left the room and then the house. Outside, a water tank sat full and ready for the battle to start. A large number of plastic buckets sat beside the water tank to be used during the water fight. Lisa's young female relatives were also there, to participate and "protect and defend" her. While we waited for the bathing to start, Lisa's older relatives offered us milk kamata—which was greatly appreciated given how cold it was. Paulina and Laura, two of Pablo's sisters, were in charge of instigating the fight. They gently dragged Lisa to the middle of the patio, drenching her with water and pouring liquid soap on her head. As water splashed over the patio and street, the laughter and screams of the participants could be heard throughout the block. Chucha and Pela did not want to participate in the fight because the night was cold and the water was freezing, so they stayed half a block away and waited for me to finish taking pictures. After one of Lisa's brothers decided to throw water at the guests who were only watching—luckily, I had managed to protect my camera, only getting my back wet—we decided to take that as our cue to go home.

Despite multiple previous research trips to Angahuan, that night was the first time I experienced the practice of nos toca in relation to a wedding. The reason this was the first time that I participated in a wedding was that it was our turn to do so, and people in Angahuan only attend or help at events where te toca (they have a responsibility to do so). As discussed in chapters 1 and 2, P'urhépecha culture is stratified and organized based on social position and gender. Depending on a person's gender and social position, one will have different tasks and roles during community and family rituals and celebrations, so one only goes to events where te toca. Before going to bathe the bride, I had participated in other events, such as visiting a relative who had just given birth and nos tocaba ir (we had to go) bringing presents to the baby and mother. Covering the spectrum of life events, from special milestone celebrations to routine fieldwork, sharing in a happy event or supporting each other during times of misfortune, this sense of responsibility, rooted in a reciprocity system, is a significant ingredient in the recipe that enables the continuity of P'urhépecha culture in Angahuan. In addition to this sense of responsibility, the practice of te toca brings to mind a game of taking turns, fairness, opportunity, and rotation. The practice of te toca is crucial to Angahuan daily life, and there are cultural repercussions if the order of exchange is broken. This concept and practice, therefore, directly reflects P'urhépecha worldviews and values and helps us understand how and why people make decisions about how to create and perform their cultural practices.

In this chapter, I build on the concept of te toca by exploring the differences between eloping and asking for the hand of the bride in marriage. The young couple's decision will impact how their wedding will be organized (discussed

Fig. 3.2 Taking a basket with presents. July 2008.

in chap. 4). Moreover, in both cases (elopement vs. engagement), the extended networks of the bride and groom are "activated," as is their responsibility to participate (les toca ir o les toca participar) in the different rituals associated with elopement or engagement. I begin this chapter with a discussion of te toca and how it relates to P'urhépecha worldviews and practices. Then I look at the differences between asking for a woman's hand and eloping and the ritual practices associated with each event. The chapter concludes with an analysis of how a young woman's social status might change depending on the way the couple choose to get married. Throughout the chapter, I highlight how the practice of te toca comes into play during the different ritual practices associated with

92   CREATING CULTURE, PERFORMING COMMUNITY

elopement or engagement, as the practice and idea of te toca form a foundation on which future discussions of how people in Angahuan create their cultural practices and perform their ideas of belonging to and in the community.

Theorizing with Te Toca

P'urhépecha language is very specific, especially regarding ritual practices. There are different words or phrases to describe specific rituals or cultural moments and events. The term te toca is used in Spanish-speaking P'urhépecha communities, but it is not used often in Angahuan.[2] I propose that the term te toca serve as an overarching concept to refer to the sense of responsibility, the practice of reciprocity, and the active participation in communal sociocultural and political life. In many ways, te toca is reciprocity's performative act.

Reciprocity plays a crucial role in the formation, maintenance, and negotiation of the practice of te toca. Since I started my fieldwork in Angahuan, I noticed the importance of reciprocity in the formation, transformation, negotiation, and maintenance of social relations. I observed the daily acts of someone taking a basket of food, bread, sugar, or fruit to someone else (fig. 3.2). During my time with my host family, baskets would arrive at least once every few weeks, either as a thank-you for help given at an event or as an invitation to a celebration (e.g., a wedding or baptism). And, of course, we would regularly take baskets of food to other households.[3]

Reciprocity in Angahuan is dyadic: A gives to B, and B reciprocates by giving to A. These gifts may take many forms and range from lending money or giving material gifts to help in the preparation of food, cleaning, setting up or conducting an event, or just keeping the homeowners company during a celebration or special event. In Angahuan, exchanges are symmetrical, open, and reciprocal and typically are made among peers. No one keeps an account of the exchanges, which implies "a relation of permanent mutual commitment" (Mayer 2002, 220). In addition, total prestation (the obligation to both give and receive gifts) accompanies each basket that is presented as a gift (Mauss [1954] 1967). In this sense, the practice of reciprocity can change depending on the participants' needs while still providing enough continuity and structure to help balance and organize the relationships of the people involved.

If someone fails to reciprocate as part of a social network, the consequences are varied. Gossip will inevitably follow the inaction, but the biggest impact I noticed was that, if someone broke the reciprocity, they severed a strand of their social network, a strand that might have helped them in a future misfortune or offered companionship during a celebration. I heard of celebrations, weddings,

TE TOCA

or parties that were sparsely attended because the host's social network was limited or they were not in good standing with the community. Angahuan's community members work hard to develop their social networks so that during celebrations or times of need (either due to hardship or the need for help with planting or harvesting), they have enough people helping them. My host parents, for example, work hard and provide a strong, stable support system for their godchildren, relatives, and neighbors; consequently, the members of their many social networks are always ready to help them and reciprocate favors. In addition, strong social networks are key in the performance of cultural practices in the community, whether community wide (celebrations related to the cargo system, for example) or familiar (mainly life events, like weddings or baptisms).

The practice of reciprocity, as it relates to te toca, is strongly tied to how people give or receive. In his analysis of the story *La Japingua*,[4] Agustín Jacinto Zavala ([1983] 1997) unpacks the concept of "to give" and "to receive" (dar y recibir) as a ritual activity in a P'urhépecha community. In Jacinto Zavala's framework, receiving is a dangerous act because the recipient may ultimately lose more than he gains. Jacinto Zavala ([1983] 1997, 277) argues that "dar y recibir son actividades sociales que no pueden realizarse a la ligera. Ni irreflexivamente hay que dar, ni descuidadamente se debe recibir" ("to give and to receive are social activities that cannot be done thoughtlessly. One should neither give rashly nor receive carelessly"). The object is active: "el dar es comunicación de cuerpo a cuerpo, mediante una cosa que pasa de mano a mano" ("to give is to communicate bodily through an object that goes from hand to hand") (Jacinto Zavala [1983] 1997, 279). In this framework, dar y recibir in a community are ritual acts because it is understood that the person giving is giving a part of themselves. This ritual, furthermore, is created, endorsed, and changed by tradition ([1983] 1997, 279). Jacinto Zavala ([1983] 1997, 287) concludes that this dar y recibir has a structure, and if it is broken or performed in another context, the act of dar y recibir would be the same as selling one's soul to the devil. This structure can be broken in various ways, like when a person does not participate in the communal dar y recibir, or if they give or receive at an inappropriate time or setting.

According to the concept of dar y recibir, one both dies and is resurrected; the giver symbolically surrenders their life, and the receiver has the power to dispose of it. When one gives and receives, one dies as an individual and is resurrected as a member of the community. This dar y recibir unites the giver and the receiver in a reciprocal relationship. If this exchange takes place within the appropriate structure and follows the prescribed ritualistic practices, the death-resurrection cycle is completed. But if the act of dar y recibir occurs outside tradition, then resurrection is not attained. Jacinto Zavala ([1983] 1997, 287) concludes that one who masters the art of dar y recibir becomes a k'uiripu (a person). Reciprocity, to properly give and receive gifts, is a crucial component of te toca.

While there might appear to be a relatively clear system that governs interpersonal relations, among many other sociocultural and political aspects in the community, this "system" is in constant flux. The relationship between reciprocity and confianza is dynamic and bidirectional; one builds and depends on the other. Both reciprocity and confianza play crucial parts in the negotiation, maintenance, and performance of social networks. Based on the ebbs and flows of confianza as well as day-to-day dynamics, the relationships of the people of Angahuan are continually in a simultaneous process of transformation and continuity. However, it is the very fluidity of this structure that has enabled the people of Angahuan to survive in times of stress and uncertainty.

The idea of te toca also influences behavior in terms of gender, social position in a social network, and different life stages. As discussed in chapter 2, depending on life stage (charaku versus a tumbí, for example), one must follow different rules of behavior and have different communal expectations. People participate in rituals and events if and when te toca: when it is one's turn or place and according to the expectations surrounding one's age and role in the community (see, e.g., Tomás's story from chap. 2). Depending on one's place in a social network, one has different responsibilities during events (consider the opening vignette in chap. 2 where the cargueros' young female relatives had to present the kanakua to the young men returning with the bulls). As I detail in chapter 5, te toca is instrumental in P'urhépecha core worldviews and values. By properly performing the act of te toca, as both reciprocity and a set of behavior rules, individuals in Angahuan can embody and perform the principal values of what it means to be P'urhépecha.

Ueakuarhini or Uarhipini:
To Elope or to Ask for a Hand in Marriage

Continuing with our Angahuan wedding story from the end of chapter 2, when a couple agrees to get married, they must decide whether to elope or whether the young man's family will ask for the woman's hand in marriage. Each option has different consequences, and how families act is based on that decision.

According to *Relación de Michoacán* ([1541] 2000) written by Fray Jerónimo de Alcalá, since pre-Columbian times, P'urhépecha people have performed

TE TOCA 95

marriage in at least two distinct ways: by elopement or by the young man's family asking for the woman's hand in marriage (Alcalá [1541] 2000; Beals [1945] 1992; Martínez-Rivera 2021). According to some scholars and even some of my research collaborators, the correct way is to have a uarhipini, a ritual to ask for the young woman's hand in marriage. However, elopement is much more common, and, even in the 1940s, people could not remember a time when eloping was not the common practice (Beals [1945] 1992, 418). In some ways, elopement challenges familial authority. And yet it is so widely practiced that it is implicitly accepted as normal rather than scandalous. In this sense, elopement is both the model and antimodel. For example, of my seven host sisters, only one was asked for in marriage; the others, including the two married brothers, eloped. Whether the young couple decides on elopement or engagement will influence how the tembuchakua is organized. To illustrate the differences between eloping and asking for the hand in marriage, I share some of my research collaborators' stories.

Uarhipini: Amalia's Engagement Story

In the summer of 2011, I visited Amalia at her job as Padre Armando's assistant in the parish where she oversaw the scheduling and organizing of the church's main events and served as a language interpreter between Padre Armando and parish members. I often visited her while she worked, and we spent many afternoons chatting and discussing religious cultural practices in Angahuan. That day was the first time I had seen her since I left in February 2010, so we had a lot to catch up on. After the initial greeting, she informed me that the week before my arrival in Angahuan, her boyfriend, Joaquín, had gone to her house with his family to ask for her hand in marriage. Amalia and Joaquín had talked about getting married, and he had told her that he wanted to ask for her hand during the dinner being held in honor of her saint's day.[5] An aunt was visiting from the United States, and Joaquín wanted to take advantage of her presence to ask for Amalia's hand. However, Amalia did not believe him. The next night, as promised, Joaquín arrived accompanied by his parents and aunts. Amalia was in shock. When Amalia's mother saw Joaquín's intentions, the family quickly called some of Amalia's uncles and aunts to the house to help them with the ritual. Joaquín's family had brought two baskets of presents, mainly fruit and bread. Amalia's younger sister received the baskets, and Amalia scolded her because by receiving the baskets, the family was entering into a reciprocal relationship with Joaquín's family.

Amalia told me she was shocked and embarrassed by the whole process. She had to go outside to greet his family, and then Joaquín's relatives returned the

96   CREATING CULTURE, PERFORMING COMMUNITY

greeting and gave her their blessings. She and Joaquín waited in the kitchen while their parents and relatives talked on the patio. Throughout the evening, her family repeatedly asked her about her decision and what she wanted to do. They wanted to respect her decision and especially wanted to make sure that Joaquín's family was not coaxing her to do something she did not want to do. Joaquín's family also wanted to make sure that Amalia loved Joaquín; Joaquín's mother talked to her and questioned her about her motives.

Because it was Amalia's saint's day, her family had prepared a special dinner. Padre Armando and Sandra (the priest's housekeeper), who were also Amalia's friends, had come to celebrate her saint's day. I spoke to Padre Armando afterward. He told me that as soon as he arrived, they invited him in and made him part of the council, but he did not know what was happening. He told me that Amalia looked like she was in shock. Throughout the evening, Amalia's father called from the United States. He was informed of the situation and took part in the conversation over the phone.[6] An uncle asked Amalia what she thought about the proposal. Amalia said that she did not want to say no but that she wanted to talk to her father first. By that point, her mother had already accepted tequila and was drinking, which, to some degree, signals an approval or an implicit yes to the proposal.

Amalia was studying to become a teacher, and her family was concerned that Joaquín's family, and even Joaquín, would not let her pursue a teaching career after working so hard to acquire her education. Amalia was also aware of this danger. During our conversation, she told me that she was seriously considering all her options, including postponing the wedding as late as possible to finish her degree. That night during the uarhipini, both parties agreed that they would meet again in two weeks so Amalia could give her answer. But later, and especially because the celebration of Santo Santiago was fast approaching, Amalia's family expressed a desire to postpone the decision until after the celebrations.

Several weeks after our initial conversation, Amalia told me that she still had not given the official yes. She did want to marry Joaquín, but she wanted to do things the right way. Joaquín was pressuring her to accept his proposal so they could have more freedom to spend time together. During our second conversation, she clarified that she was certain she wanted to marry him, but she wanted to understand the challenges she might face after the wedding.

Another research collaborator, Agustín, also asked for his wife's hand in marriage. Agustín, a leader in Michoacán's Indigenous teacher movement and part of a renowned and respected family in Angahuan, asked Lupe for her hand. They had formalized the relationship beforehand, as they were sure they wanted to get married. Both families agreed with the relationship, and Lupe was allowed to visit Agustín's home before he asked for her hand in marriage. However, their case is atypical, as most young people are not allowed to visit the home of their girlfriend or boyfriend before an engagement. Agustín took Lupe to his mother's house to introduce her and tell his family that they (the family and him) were going to ask for Lupe's hand in marriage. Two weeks later, Agustín's mother and close relatives went to Lupe's house to ask for her hand. They took many gifts, including food and tequila.

Asking for the bride's hand in marriage and celebrating the uarhipini is the most respectable way to formalize a relationship, but it is also the most expensive and challenging. The courtship process leading to the misa kuani is different: the groom's family must arrive with gifts, the close family gathers, and everybody is informed. A popular practice, according to my research collaborators, required that from the day the young woman was asked for in marriage, the groom's family brought her a basket with fruit, bread, and food every Sunday until the misa kuani was celebrated. The contents of the baskets changed depending on the season and the community's ritual calendar. For example, during Lent, the gifts would be fish, shellfish, and other ingredients or dishes traditional for the season. During Holy Week, the groom's family would take the ingredients for the Holy Friday feast. The future groom would give a uarhota during Palm Sunday and a basket of soaps, loofahs, milk, and chocolate on Saint John's Eve (June 23). During, and immediately after, the 2008–2009 economic recession, however, this practice was not very popular.

According to my research collaborators, another challenging aspect of asking for the bride's hand is the gossip. Amalia confessed to me that she did not want Joaquín to ask for her hand in marriage. She had told him that she would have preferred to ueakuarhini, that is, to elope with him. Amalia's older sisters had all been asked in marriage, so Joaquín felt that her family deserved respect, and he did not want to "steal" her. But, as Amalia told me, the main reason she wanted to elope was because of the gossip. Amalia and several of her peers told me that when the uarhipini occurs instead of ueakuarhini, relatives, friends, and others will often spread gossip about the future groom and bride and their families to break the engagement. Amalia informed me that less than a week after Joaquín had asked for her hand, gossip was already rampant. There were rumors that one of Amalia's ex-boyfriends was supposedly returning to Angahuan from the US to stop the marriage. There was also gossip that she was meeting other men and that Joaquín was seeing other women. One of my research collaborators told me how the families of ex-boyfriends or ex-girlfriends pressure them to leave their intended bride or groom. Agustín, for example, was bribed by the family of a wealthy ex-girlfriend to persuade him to leave Lupe

98 CREATING CULTURE, PERFORMING COMMUNITY

and marry their daughter instead. The rumors became so intense that Agustín and Lupe chose to live together rather than wait for the misa kuani, at which point the gossip stopped.[7]

I was told that people also gossip when there is a ueakuarhini, but it is not as bad as what takes place after the uarhipini ritual. In the case of Agustín and Lupe, as well as other couples who performed the uarhipini, the gossip continued until the couple moved in together or celebrated their misa kuani. Even if the couple celebrated their civil union, for the people in Angahuan, the marriage does not "count" until the misa kuani has taken place. It is only then that the gossip stops. The high costs of the uarhipini and harmful gossip are two reasons why some young couples decide to elope instead.

Ueakuarhini: Chucha's Elopement Story

An elopement can take place two ways: through violence, when a young woman is stolen (uatsïmbastpiani), or voluntarily, when the young woman leaves willingly (ueakuarhini).[8] Based on my research and conversations with research collaborators, most young couples elope. Some women even secretly move some of their belongings to their boyfriend's house weeks before the elopement (which was the case of Paulina and Mateo). Couples elope for many reasons. Some know that their marriage will not be accepted (either because they are related, because they are too young, because of economic differences between the families, or because of reputation issues) and want to force the union.

The principal event of the ueakuarhini, after the actual elopement, is the process of asking for forgiveness, the potpinsani (ir a perdir el perdón), which lasts two days. I observed that elopements normally occur at night, so on that night, the young man and woman are chastised, and the potpinsani starts and ends on the next day. In July 2010, Chucha eloped with José, now her husband (I interviewed Chucha in the summer of 2011). During the main dance of the celebration of Santo Santiago on July 25, José asked Chucha to elope with him. Chucha told me that they had talked about eloping but only teasingly. José really wanted to elope with Chucha, but she had her misgivings, as she wanted to wait for the appropriate moment. During the dance, José proposed to Chucha and asked her to elope with him. Overcoming her feelings of indecision, Chucha decided to go with him. José's parents' house is beside the plaza, so they did not have to walk far. One of Chucha's aunts lives in front of José's home and saw Chucha enter the house. Chucha told me that once she was seen, there was no turning back. She had many thoughts running through her mind: "¡No! ¿qué hice?, ya no hay para atrás, ni modo . . . es que se siente así muy raro, con miedo, porque dices ¿qué pasará?, ¿qué dirá la gente?, ¿cómo será su familia?,

TE TOCA

99

y ¿cómo serán sus hermanos? o ¿cómo me verán a mi?, ¿sí será lo que estarán esperando?" ("What have I done? I cannot go back, oh well . . . it feels really weird, scared, because you ask yourself, what will happen? What will people think? How will his family be? What about his siblings? Or, how will they see me? Will I be what they were hoping for?").

After the couple entered the house, José woke his parents to let them know he had eloped with Chucha. José's mother asked Chucha if she had been brought by force or if she had come of her own accord. After José's mother made sure that Chucha had not been forced (uatsïmbastpiani), she greeted her: "Bienvenida seas a la casa, gracias por no tenernos miedo . . . gracias por no tenerle miedo a mi hijo" ("Welcome to our home, thank you for not being afraid of us . . . thank you for not being afraid of our son"). But Chucha was afraid as she waited for her parents to come looking for her. Chucha was also afraid because her parents would scold her sisters, who were supposed to have been with Chucha during the dance. After twenty minutes or so, Na Juana, Ta Emiliano, and Chucha's older sisters arrived at José's house. Chucha told me that her sisters and mother cried together as they made sure that Chucha was firm in her decision and that she was safe. They returned to their home that same night accompanied by José's parents, who had to go to Chucha's home for the first part of the potpinsani. José's parents took some tequila to Na Juana and Ta Emiliano's home and talked with them until early in the morning, asking for forgiveness. As they were leaving, José's parents informed Na Juana and Ta Emiliano that they would return later that morning to continue the potpinsani.

That morning, Chucha helped with the chores in José's house, and Pela brought her some clean clothes. Relatives gathered at José's home and prepared food to take to Chucha's home. When José's maternal grandmother arrived, she knelt in front of Chucha and asked for her hand. Chucha was embarrassed but did as she was told. The grandmother said, "Gracias por aceptarnos a nosotros, y que te hayas animado a venir con él y que espero que él cambie ahora así contigo" ("thank you for accepting us, and that you decided to come with him. I hope that he will now change with you"). When José's paternal grandmother arrived, she did the same thing. Chucha told me that she was touched by the welcome she received. She recognized that her experience was not common, as many young women are chastised or even shunned by the young man's family.[9]

When the food was ready, José's family went to Chucha's home to take the food to Chucha's family. Chucha and José stayed at José's house, but after dinner, Chucha and José were summoned to Chucha's home. According to Chucha, José's family had told José that if Chucha's relatives insulted him, he should not say anything because he was at fault. When Chucha and José arrived at the Gómez Santacruz house, their first responsibility was to kneel in front of Ta Emiliano, offer their hands, and ask for his forgiveness. Ta Emiliano took their hands and said, "Pues ni modo, así tendría que ser" ("Oh well, I suppose this is the way it was supposed to be"). Chucha and José had to kneel in front of all of the family members, offer their hands, and ask for forgiveness.

As part of the potpinsani agreement, Na Juana did not want Chucha and José to live together before the wedding. José's family agreed; his mother believed they should wait to live together until after they were married. But that day, Chucha returned to José's house. The next day, her future mother-in-law, one of José's sisters, and José returned Chucha to her parents' home to live there until the misa kuani. That day, they took a basket of fruit, bread, and other gifts to give to Na Juana and Ta Emiliano.

I was told that the likelihood of violence in a marriage is an important factor that young women and their families consider when deciding how to respond to a marriage proposal or elopement.[10] According to my research collaborators, mothers-in-law have a bad reputation in Angahuan, and, in many cases, the mother-in-law (and even the sisters-in-law) can be more violent than the husband.[11] I heard that young women who are asked for in marriage tend to be treated better than those who eloped. But again, in many cases, even young women who have been asked for in marriage are later mistreated by their husbands' families. According to some of my research collaborators, one reason for this is that during the courtship, the husband's family spent money on her, so now she must repay her "debt." Even though eloping is more common than engagement, a young woman's reputation is "tarnished" by an elopement, and the reaction of the future mother-in-law toward this is unpredictable. In Chucha's case, José's family readily accepted her, and to this day, they continue to treat her with kindness and love. But sometimes, the young man's family is against the elopement, and, if the young woman is not returned to her home the next day, the mother-in-law and sometimes the sisters-in-law will mistreat the woman to the point of running her out of the house. Some families will take their daughter home if they hear that she is being mistreated. Social networks and the support of the young woman's family are key to helping her if she is being mistreated.

Performing Te Toca during a Uarhipini or Potpinsani

Tomás, Agustín's younger brother, witnessed both variations: when a young woman is stolen and when a woman is asked for her hand. He remembered a night when one of his older brothers returned home with his girlfriend. His mother, a widow and member of the Council of Elders, questioned them and said that although it was disrespectful, there was no turning back. She also asked if they knew what they were doing; they could still change their minds. After she made sure that her son and his girlfriend truly wanted the elopement, she left to find her son's baptism godparents and close relatives. The young woman's parents arrived at Tomás's house looking for her. Her parents also chastised them. Both families continued talking until almost two o'clock in the morning and agreed to meet the next day. Tomás did not see the rest of the event, as he was not allowed to participate, no le tocaba.

During my yearlong stay in Angahuan, I heard of many elopements and often saw Na Juana and Ta Emiliano leaving for or returning from relatives' homes after the potpinsani. But I never witnessed them in person, because no me tocaba; it was not my turn or my place to participate in those events.[12] Chucha and José also did not participate in the entire process of the potpinsani, just in the parts where les tocaba. Both during the potpinsani and when asking for a young woman's hand in marriage (uarhipini), the families' social networks play an incredibly important role during the negotiations. When a young woman's hand is asked for (as in Amalia's case), her extended family must gather quickly in her home to negotiate with the young man's family. Uncles, aunts, grandparents, and baptism godparents are summoned to be part of the council. The young man's council will also include uncles, aunts, grandparents, and baptism godparents. Depending on the degree of confianza, the first communion and confirmation godparents may also be summoned. Similarly, when a young woman elopes, her parents must gather their social network and wait for the young man's family to arrive. For the potpinsani, the young man's family, in addition to asking the woman's parents' forgiveness for their son's action, must also ask forgiveness of the young woman's parents' wedding godparents and their children. The potpinsani and the uarhipini are two rituals where social networks and the practices of reciprocity matter a great deal and where the practice of te toca is performed, as only relatives that les toca can and must participate.

After the Uarhipini or Potpinsani

After a young woman elopes or is engaged, her social status and role change. This change is more evident with a young woman who has eloped, as people consider her to be already "married"; the engaged woman is not considered married until the celebration of her misa kuani. As my host sisters explained, it is expected that as soon as the young woman elopes, she must behave as a married woman and assume the responsibilities that accompany her new status. This means that the couple must move away from the public eye and stop any activities they are participating in (working in the communal radio station or volunteering in church organizations). Young men who have "stolen" their girlfriends are also considered "married," but their status and role in the community do not really change until they have celebrated their misa kuani.

In April 2009, Gabriela eloped with her boyfriend Jonathan. Gabriela was the organizer of the Liturgy Group at the church, a very visible position.[13] After Gabriela ran away with Jonathan, some of the young women in the Liturgy Group argued that she should no longer be the organizer or even participate in the group, but Gabriela wanted to continue her role. Things became so tense that they scheduled a meeting with Padre Armando to discuss the situation. Padre Armando told them it was acceptable for a married woman to participate in the church's various organizations as long as she was properly married. Therefore, there was no reason for Gabriela to stop participating in the meetings and acting as the group's leader, especially because she was going to be married by the church soon. The tensions continued to grow, however, and Gabriela ultimately quit her leadership position and the group.

Gabriela's experience highlights the community's expectations regarding women's roles before and after they have a potpinsani or uarhipini. For example, young unmarried women can participate in social-religious community events in ways that married women cannot. Some of my female research collaborators and acquaintances, like Gabriela, also quit communal or church groups after eloping or getting engaged, and several, whom I used to see regularly, hardly left their homes after their engagement or elopement. Women's style of dress also changes. Young women tend to wear the most expensive and colorful P'urhépecha dresses, and married women do not, either because they can no longer afford them or because, according to some people in the community, it would not be appropriate.

From my observations, social change among young men is not so drastic, although some of my male collaborators mentioned that they had fewer responsibilities before getting married and could travel (for concerts, cultural events, etc.), party every weekend, and be desmadrosos (act without responsibilities). After their uarhipini or potpinsani, some changed their lifestyle, searched for stable work (if they did not have it before), and started to save money (for the tembuchakua and setting up a home after the wedding). But most of my male collaborators continued with some of their activities, such as working in the communal radio stations or going to music concerts.[14]

The time between the uarhipini or potpinsani and the tembuchakua is a liminal stage, as the young couple is no longer a proper tumbí or iurhítskiri, but they are not yet an achati or uarhiti. As I observed, this is a time when they must learn how to behave as a married couple and acknowledge the changes in their social status and behaviors. In some cases, they may not be allowed to participate in events that are for tumbí or iurhítskiri only (such as the kurpiti or the pastorelas). In addition, they will start learning how to practice te toca as a soon-to-be-married couple, as they can now begin participating in some events that are designated for married couples only.

A key feature of both the potpinsani and the uarhipini is the negotiation of the expectations between both families regarding the future relationship and the wedding rituals. This is especially important if the young woman has a profession or if her family has money or land. As illustrated in the case of Amalia, her family, especially her father, was reluctant to accept the offer unless Joaquín's family agreed to let her finish her degree and find a job. Another example is Cayetana, the oldest daughter of my host family. When she eloped with her now-husband, Beto, during the potpinsani, her parents insisted that his family had to respect that she had a profession and would not pressure her to quit her job. In addition to negotiating the terms of the marriage, during the potpinsani or uarhipini, families might also begin negotiations for the preparation of the tembuchakua, the couple's wedding, which is discussed in chapter 4.

En Route to Organizing a Tembuchakua

Based on what I observed and documented, te toca is central to how people are educated and raised in Angahuan. Te toca is a crucial component of how people are taught to live and act as members of their community. And while additional research is needed to further analyze the ramifications and relevance of this idea of te toca and how it interacts with other facets of P'urhépecha culture in Angahuan and other P'urhépecha communities, in this chapter, I introduced the idea of te toca and how it influences the processes of asking for the bride's hand in marriage, asking for forgiveness, and elopement. As I illustrate in chapter 4, P'urhépecha culture has a series of values that are central to its worldviews. But the concept and practice of te toca, which is to some degree embedded in those values, provides a nuanced and rich lens through which to understand those same P'urhépecha worldviews and values. In chapter 4, we will explore how the tembuchakua is organized and created, te toca's important part in the decision and negotiation process, how culture is created, and how ideas of community are performed in Angahuan.

104 CREATING CULTURE, PERFORMING COMMUNITY

Notes

1. The store, which is incredibly well stocked, carries almost everything that people in the community need: personal hygiene products, alcoholic beverages, religious paraphernalia, groceries, cleaning products, and even special items, such as spaghetti and other products that are otherwise only available in the city.

2. My host family, when explaining in Spanish why we were doing things or had to go somewhere, normally said to me, "porque nos toca" (because we have to / it's our turn).

3. For example, as Lisa, Pablo, their families, and I had entered into a reciprocity relationship since I participated and provided gifts during Lisa and Pablo's wedding, they reciprocated with a fruit and bread basket on my birthday.

4. The story of the Japingua is the tale of a lazy man who makes a deal with the devil to have riches. In payment, the man must give his soul to the devil at his death. At the beginning, all goes well for the man, but later, he suffers a horrible and painful death, and his soul is taken by the devil. I am sure there are many variations of this story throughout the continent, but this story, in particular, allows Jacinto Zavala to study in depth the system of dar y recibir in a P'urhépecha setting.

5. In México, it was traditional to name newborns after Catholic saints (a child was named after the saint who is celebrated on the day of their birth according to the Catholic calendar). While at present most families do not follow this practice strictly, many people in Angahuan celebrate their saint's day, or "día de su santo," instead of their birthday. However, this practice is changing with younger generations.

6. Amalia's father works in the United States, and at that time (2011), he had not returned to the community in almost ten years.

7. If the young woman is asked for in marriage, the couple are expected to live in their respective parent's home until the misa kuani, even if they were married by the court. However, as the case of Agustín and Lupe illustrates, there are exceptions, and some couples do live together before their misa kuani.

8. The Spanish term for this is robo de la novia ("stealing of the bride"), and it applies to both cases: when the bride is taken by force or when the bride leaves of her own accord. In P'urhépecha, they recognize the difference.

9. I was told of a case in which the young man's mother forcibly returned the young woman to her home.

10. While there are no reliable statistics on physical or psychological family and domestic violence, both are quite common in Angahuan. However, according to my observations and those of my research collaborators, family and domestic violence in the community are similar to national averages.

11. Even during the Virreinato period, chroniclers of Michoacán—Fray Pablo de la Purísima Concepción Beaumont (17??—1779), for example—wrote

about the mistreatment suffered by many P'urhépecha women at the hands of their families-in-law (in León [1889] 1982, 77).

12. In a future publication, I plan to theorize how the concept and practice of no/te toca also impacted and guided my fieldwork.

13. Men can participate in the Liturgy Group, and one of my (male) research collaborators was a member of the group in the mid-2000s. However, young women have traditionally dominated the group, and, at that time (2009), the members were all young, single women.

14. I must confess that I am much more aware of the social changes to young women in Angahuan compared to young men, as I spent most of my time in female spheres.

Fig. 4a.1 Decorating for a wedding. October 2009.

4

Creating Culture

Organizing a Tembuchakua

During my yearlong research stay in Angahuan (2009–2010), I was formally asked to be a godmother twice.[1] In late September, after a long day of fieldwork, I was in the kitchen with Na Juana and Leti, working on my embroidery. Leti, under Na Juana's supervision, was making rice kamata—one of my favorite kamata! The afternoon rain had ended, and the day was transitioning into a sunny but chilly and humid afternoon. The sun was slowly setting behind my two favorite mountains, showering Angahuan with different shades of red and crimson. Just before 7:00 p.m., Na Juana's sister-in-law, Na Antonia, arrived with one of her daughters. They sat down with us, commented on my embroidery, and then began talking about the upcoming wedding of Joel, Na Antonia's son. Na Juana and I knew the main reason for their visit: they wanted to ask me to be a godmother at Joel's wedding. Several days before, Na Antonia had mentioned to the family that they wanted to ask me to participate as a godmother in the wedding. Because I am considered part of the Gómez Santacruz family, it is proper to ask Na Juana and Ta Emiliano before approaching me. Even though both Na Antonia and her daughter speak a little Spanish and I understood a little P'urhépecha, they were waiting for Chucha so she could translate. Once she arrived, they officially asked me to be a godmother. They still did not know how I could help; they needed to talk to Daniela's family (the bride-to-be) first. But they were considering me for helping to decorate the church (mainly buying the flowers) or for the cake. They needed to check with the church because the weekend of the wedding was also the celebration of Saint Teresa, and one of the church groups would likely be in charge of the decorations. If that were the case, I would then be the godmother of the cake. I agreed and thanked them for the honor. After drinking kamata, Na Juana left with Na Antonia and her

108   CREATING CULTURE, PERFORMING COMMUNITY

daughter to visit Daniela. They wanted to talk to Daniela's mother and female relatives about organizing the final details for the wedding. They needed to divide the tasks—who would be responsible for choosing the wedding godparents as well as other minor godparents—and agree on which rituals would be performed during the misa kuani. Chucha and I retreated to the girls' room to watch television and wait for Na Juana to return with news. In the end, it was decided that I would be the cake godmother.

The second time I was formally asked to be a godmother was for Gabriela and Jonathan's wedding. Several days after Na Antonia's visit (late September), Gabriela and Jonathan came to the house. They arrived as we were starting to eat supper. Taking advantage of the fresh seasonal corn from the family's tareta, Na Juana had made uchepos (a type of tamal made with the first corn of the season; because the corn is fresh, the uchepos tend to be sweet and fluffy), which we were having with milk. We were gathered in the kitchen, sitting around the parangua, talking, eating, and getting warm. Gabriela had already talked to the family about their intention to ask me to be a godmother for their wedding, so I was aware of the purpose of their visit. Since they were technically my guests, I greeted them at the door and invited them to come in and sit down with us near the fire. I helped Cayetana serve them uchepos. We talked about work, family, and other everyday issues. As we finished our uchepos, I noticed that Gabriela and Jonathan were whispering to each other. Even with my limited P'urhépecha, I could understand that they were trying to decide how to bring up the subject. I was beginning to get nervous. We all knew what was going on, but I was unsure about the protocol, so I decided to help them out. I said, "Bueno, ¿en qué puedo ayudarles, que ya han venido cuatro veces a buscarme?" ("Well, you have come four times looking for me, so how can I help?"). Everybody started laughing. Gabriela, between giggles, said, "Well, we came looking for you to ask for a big favor."

"Well, if I can help, it will be my pleasure," I answered.

"We would like for you to be a godmother in our wedding."

Before Gabriela even had a chance to finish, I responded: "Yes, of course, it would be my pleasure! Thank you so much for the honor."

After a very brief silence, I asked, "Godmother of what?"

A new wave of laughter ensued, and Na Juana said jokingly, "Of the cake!"

Gabriela looked at her with surprise and said, "Yes, of the cake."

"Well," I said, "the good thing is that I will have experience." By this point, we were dying of laughter, and Gabriela and Jonathan, while also laughing, did not fully understand why we were laughing so much about the idea of me being godmother of the cake. Na Juana explained to them that I was also going to be godmother of the cake for another wedding that same month (both weddings were in October). Gabriela and Jonathan stayed a little longer, finished their uchepos, and left. Even after they left, we were still laughing. Na Juana teased me because I had said yes even before they had asked me for the favor. I had not followed the protocol for how to accept (or reject) favors (see chap. 3's discussion of dar y recibir). Both of these events are examples of the padrinu arhip'eni niani (to go ask for a godparent) and are part of the wedding organization process.

In the first part of this book, I introduced Angahuan and some of the historical, economic, and political contextual details that influence social and cultural organization based on gender, age, and social position (chaps. 1 and 2). I have also shared some of the main courtship rituals and youth vernacular cultural practices (chap. 2). In chapter 3, I described how the preparations and organization of a tembuchakua in Angahuan begin with either the young woman's elopement or a young man and his family asking for her hand in marriage. Families begin planning their children's upcoming nuptials during the potpinsani (when the young man's family asks for forgiveness after eloping with the young woman) or the uarhipini (when the man has asked for the young woman's hand in marriage). This decision and negotiation process is crucial because it determines how the tembuchakua will be performed.

In this chapter, I present the first strand of my interwoven arguments / axes / points of encounter, which is the creation of culture. Building on the work by Eva María Garrido Izaguirre on P'urhépecha aesthetics, I explore the cultural elements that influence people's decision-making processes that lead to the creation of culture. Then I briefly describe the sivil kuambuni, the celebration of which determines how the misa kuani will be organized. In the third section of the chapter, and with special attention to the process of recruiting wedding godparents and general godparents, I focus on the organization of the wedding, mainly the decision-making processes, as an example of creating culture. These decision-making processes are important because negotiations between the families will determine how the wedding will be performed. Additionally, I focus on how young people participate in the negotiating and organizing processes, playing a crucial role in the transformation of the wedding. Focusing on how Angahuans negotiate and make decisions about organizing and performing a wedding can help us unpack how they are actively (re)creating their cultural practices. This highlights how culture is neither static nor set in stone but alive and in a constant creative process. Hence the process of organizing the wedding is crucial to understanding the transformation of P'urhépecha cultures: transformative decisions made during the organization stage are later

Creating Culture and P'urhépecha Cultural Creativity

During my time in Angahuan, each of the weddings I participated in was a little different. Some had more ritual events than others, or the rituals were performed differently (more on this in chaps. 5 and 6). In this sense, the tembuchakua is not fixed or static but in flux, directly dependent on the participants and organizers of the event. However, even though the tembuchakua is fluid, a particular cultural logic ruled by expectations and ideas of cultural creativity influences the organization and performance of a wedding in Angahuan.

I do not intend to revisit the discussion on culture (what it is, how to define it, how it works, etc.) since the culture concept is one of the most studied in anthropology, folklore, and similar fields. Also, I am not interested in rearticulating the conversations regarding authenticity, acculturation, or any other concept that has served to diminish or colonize Indigenous cultural creativity and diversity. However, I do want to highlight some works that have influenced my thinking and have helped me understand some of the dynamics that I observed in Angahuan. In particular, I was and still am deeply inspired by scholars who focus on Indigenous creativity and how people make decisions regarding their own cultural production.

In his 2009 book, *Customizing Indigeneity: Paths to a Visionary Politics in Peru*, Shane Greene (2009, 16; italics in original) proposes the concept of "customization to refer both to *specific acts* and to a *structural process* of constrained creativity." Greene articulates the process of customizing Indigeneity in three analytical dimensions: the logics of custom, the phases of articulation, and the act of customizing. The logics of custom refer to the "ideological references that make the practices appear meaningful" and that "actions correspond to socially produced values" (2009, 17). The logics of custom, therefore, refer to the worldview and cultural logic that are particular to each group. During the phase of articulation, a group of people must first grow accustomed to "something that at first appears foreign but becomes a bit more familiar over time" (2009, 17). The last phase, the act of customizing, refers to the creative act of adapting and owning that which is foreign based on the cultural logic of the group. An important consideration in this customization process is that "any project of customization is . . . constrained by the politics of customization in which it is enmeshed" (2009, 18). Greene stresses that customization is "both continuous and open to change" and that these changes follow an internal logic

CREATING CULTURE   111

and a process of negotiation among the different social actors (2009, 19). He mainly focuses on the relationship between customization and the politics of Indigeneity, paying close attention to the relationship of the state and Indigenous leaders, Aguaruna Indigenous leaders with Indigenous leaders from other communities, and what it is to "customize oneself as Aguaruna" (2009, 26).

Building on Greene's conceptualization of customizing, I propose that the act of creating culture, in addition to being a process of customizing foreign cultural practices, also entails the customization of local practices. In this regard, I see people in Angahuan engaged in multiple processes of customizing foreign and local cultural practices simultaneously. Expectations play a crucial role in the customizing processes, as some people organize their wedding (or other ritual events) based on the expectations of family members or neighbors.

In previous works (Martínez-Rivera, 2014, 2018), I focused on the Indigenous rock music movement in México and presented different models to discuss, unpack, or approach Indigenous popular culture as an example of Indigenous cultural creativity. I do not wish to revisit those conversations, but I do want to highlight some of the ideas that have influenced those works as well as this one. For example, Phillip J. Deloria's *Indians in Unexpected Places* (2004) and James Clifford's "Indigenous Articulations" (2001) challenge negative and limited representations of Native Americans and Indigenous individuals and their cultural productions. Through his proposal of Indigenous articulations, Clifford highlights the complex identity politics and realities of Native Pacific Islanders and the diversity that exists within the term Indigenous. He argues that "articulation as I understand it evokes a deeper sense of the 'political'— productive processes of consensus, exclusion, alliance, and antagonism that are inherent in the transformative life of all societies" (2001, 473). It is in these dynamics of articulation that the people of Angahuan engage to create their vernacular cultural practices.[2]

Specific to the P'urhépecha area, scholars have paid close attention to many P'urhépecha vernacular cultural practices, such as rituals and festivals, music, food, dance, art (or artesanías), vernacular architecture, and others, and how they relate to P'urhépecha worldviews and values. Instead of focusing on the vast literature on P'urhépecha cultural practices, I highlight Eva María Garrido Izaguirre's (2020) recent publication *Donde el diablo mete la cola: antropología del arte y estética indígena*. In this richly detailed book, Garrido Izaguirre focuses on Ocumicho (a P'urhépecha community in the Cañada de los Once Pueblos) and their well-known devil clay figurines. Based on more than twenty years of research in Ocumicho, Garrido Izaguirre provides an in-depth view of the experiences and lives of female artesanas, the government structure that influenced the creation of the devil clay figurines, and the complex communal dynamics that resulted in the creation of such figurines. More importantly, Garrido Izaguirre outlines different cultural practices or ideas that influence P'urhépecha aesthetics and the creation of cultural objects. In her analysis, Garrido Izaguirre highlights the relationship between creativity and culture and how ideas of aesthetics are tied to ideas of ethics, as the ideas of aesthetics and ethics influence how things (either material culture or cultural events) are created. While Garrido Izaguirre focuses primarily on material culture, she does not ignore the relationship between material culture and cultural practices and how they influence one another. To better understand aesthetic ideas among Ocumicho's inhabitants, she also documented communal celebrations and life cycle events. Therefore, to unpack ideas of aesthetics, she had to pay attention to "la lógica de la cotidianeidad" (roughly translated as the logic of everyday practices) (2020, 453). This logic helped her understand what is considered good versus bad, expectations, what should and can be done, what is considered ethical, and other elements that influence P'urhépecha aesthetic values. As previously mentioned, these ideas influence how culture (i.e., material culture or cultural practices) is created. Some of the main elements that influence P'urhépecha aesthetics according to Garrido Izaguirre (or that people consider when creating a piece of art) are the importance of "el costumbre" in the decision of what to do or how to do something,[3] ideas of good versus bad, the importance of symmetry, and the "armonía global del conjunto" (the total harmony of a piece) (2020, 506). Garrido Izaguirre concludes that "el sistema estético Purépecha y ocumichiense gira en torno a la noción de persona perceptible y de orden grupal, es decir, el cuerpo, gesto y comportamiento social conforman un núcleo del que derivan la mayoría de los valores estéticos-éticos purépechas" ("P'urhépecha and Ocumicho's aesthetic systems move around individual and group notions, i.e. the body, gestures, and social behaviors form the nucleus where the majority of P'urhépecha aesthetic-ethic values reside") (2020, 533).

Garrido Izaguirre's framework for discussing P'urhépecha aesthetics has been vital to my understanding of the logic that influences the creation of culture in Angahuan. As discussed in the following sections, the negotiation of the tembuchakua is influenced by the aesthetic-ethics dynamics that Garrido Izaguirre saw in Ocumicho. More importantly, during the negotiation and organization of the wedding in Angahuan, families must contend with their ideas of good, what should happen, and expectations among other community members. These elements in turn influence how culture is created (and performed) in Angahuan.

Fig. 4a.2 Taking ocotes on the eve of a sivil kuambuni. June 2009.

Organizing the Tembuchakua: Celebrating the Sivil Kuambuni

When planning a tembuchakua, one of the first decisions involves whether the sivil kuambuni and the misa kuani will be celebrated on the same day or on different days.[4] The sivil kuambuni can be celebrated days or even months before the misa kuani. However (as I discuss in chap. 6), beginning in 2009, some families decided to celebrate the sivil kuambuni and the misa kuani on the same day to cut costs and avoid organizing two different wedding celebrations. This decision has allowed for new changes to the wedding, as families negotiate which rituals they will perform. Even though some families combined their celebrations of the sivil kuambuni and misa kuani, during my time in Angahuan in 2009, it was more common to celebrate both weddings separately. Most families planned for the sivil kuambuni first and then organized the misa kuani. To ensure coherence and clarity, I first describe how the sivil kuambuni is celebrated, and in the next section, I focus on how the misa kuani is negotiated and organized.

The civil ceremony is a relatively new wedding practice in the P'urhépecha area.[5] While the Civil Registry is over 150 years old, the practice of being married by the church and the courts is relatively recent (specifically dating to after the Mexican Revolution of 1910). Researchers from the first half of the twentieth century documented that civil marriage was a somewhat recent practice in P'urhépecha communities, especially after the church started asking for the civil marriage certificate before the religious ceremony (Barragán and González Bonilla 1940). According to George Foster ([1967] 1988, 70), "Most villagers believe that people are not really married by the civil act. They look upon it rather as Americans view a marriage license: as an expression of intent." Based on reports and my research, Foster's perception is still valid, and in Angahuan, a couple is not considered "officially" married until they celebrate their misa kuani (see chap. 3). This could explain why the sivil kuambuni rituals are not as elaborate as those of the misa kuani.

The sivil kuambuni is generally less formal and features fewer rituals and events than the misa kuani, providing more space for negotiation between the families. The newlyweds' peers perform most of the rituals celebrated during the sivil kuambuni, primarily the bathing of the bride and taking wood to the bride's home. According to my research collaborators, these two rituals were originally celebrated only in the misa kuani, but today, they might occur in both types of weddings. Some families decide that both rituals should be performed in both weddings, while others decide that if the bathing and gifting of wood were performed in the sivil kuambuni, they do not need to be repeated in the misa kuani. Other families might decide to celebrate the sivil kuambuni as simply as possible and postpone most of the rituals for the misa kuani. It all depends on the preferences and circumstances of the families involved.

Angahuan has its own Civil Registry office, but a judge must travel from Uruapan to officiate at wedding ceremonies. Before my first sivil kuambuni, Chucha and Pela explained that the first event was the bathing of the bride. After the bride has been bathed, she is dressed to be taken to the Civil Registry, where the groom and his family are waiting. After the legal documents have been signed and the couple has been married by the state, the wedding party walks to the groom's house, where they are fed birria (a beef-based dish).[6] Afterward, the bride and her relatives return to her house, and the celebrations continue at both houses. In the early evening, the groom and his older relatives go to the bride's home where they wait for nightfall. As soon as it gets dark, the groom's young relatives gather in his house with trucks full of ocotes (pine torches) and wood to give as gifts to the bride's family (fig. 4a.2). After assembling at the groom's house, the young men leave in a procession with the wood and ocotes while carrying torches. As soon as the young men arrive at the bride's house, the bride's young female relatives welcome them and offer

CREATING CULTURE 115

them alcoholic drinks. Ritual drinking ensues, with much merrymaking that continues late into the night. In sum, and as described by Chucha and Pela, a civil wedding, in addition to the ceremony officiated by the judge, has three components: the bathing of the bride, the gifting of wood, and ritual drinking.

In early June of 2009, Fabiana and Salvador celebrated their sivil kuambuni. Since we were distant relatives of Fabiana and lived near her house—nos tocaba—we had to participate; specifically, we had to "defend" Fabiana when Salvador's relatives came to bathe her. Because of the timing of the couple's civil wedding ceremony, they reversed the order of events. They got married before bathing Fabiana, and after the civil ceremony, the wedding party went to Salvador's home for lunch. Next, Salvador's relatives brought Fabiana to her parents' home for the bathing. After that, the celebration continued in the expected order: the celebration was divided between both houses, and, by nightfall, the groom's relatives went to the bride's home for the gifting of wood and ritual drinking.

On the day of Fabiana and Salvador's sivil kuambuni, I went to the main plaza at noon to do some errands. On my way to the store, I ran into Salvador, who was already outside the courthouse waiting for Fabiana. We greeted each other, and I teased him because he seemed nervous. His parents' house, which is several houses down from the Civil Registry, was already decorated and ready for the festivities. On my way back from my errands, I saw that Fabiana had already arrived at the Civil Registry, and the wedding ceremony was underway. As I walked to my host family's house, I ran into a huge convoy of the Policia Federal Preventiva (the Federal Police; PFP) driving through Angahuan in a menacing manner.[7] Some people were outside their homes watching them pass by, while others were hiding their children. Just to be safe, I ran home. When I got there, everybody was sitting outside the house watching the PFP convoy drive by.

Tomi, Caye, and Lisa (the wife of a recently married cousin, whose wedding I described at the beginning of this book), along with other relatives, had come to the house to wait for Fabiana's return and to participate in the bathing / water fight (fig. 3.1 is of Fabiana's bathing). We did not have to wait long for Fabiana or Salvador with his relatives and the water truck. My host sisters took center stage in defending Fabiana. However, the groom's relatives always catch the bride and cover her in soap, so it was inevitable that Fabiana would be soaking wet and covered in soap very quickly. Salvador was not supposed to be there, as this is a female-only affair, so he also got "bathed." Salvador's older brother Fernando was also there, and a group of young women ran after him with buckets filled with water until they got him wet as well. Laugher and

116   CREATING CULTURE, PERFORMING COMMUNITY

screams (especially when the cold water hit someone who was still dry) could be heard throughout the neighborhood. Like all the other times I participated and documented the bathing of the bride, at some point, I had to run unless I wanted to get soaked too. Because I was carrying my equipment, I was granted some leniency. In the end, however, I had to run to the house to leave my camera bag there and return to the water battle to accept my fate. My host sisters mentioned that the battle had not been balanced because Fabiana's relatives were not well prepared; they had too little water and ran out quickly and thus were at the mercy of Salvador's relatives and their water tank. At the end of the event, we were all wet and shivering from the cold but incredibly happy.

After Fabiana's "bathing" and water fight, our duties were completed since we were not close relatives of Fabiana or Salvador, hence no nos tocaba attend the wedding or to help or participate beyond the bathing ritual. We stayed at the house for the rest of the afternoon. That night, we went outside to wait for Salvador's relatives to arrive. The night was pitch-black and cold because it had rained in the afternoon. We could hear the music and merrymaking coming from Fabiana's home, and other families were also outside waiting for the young men with ocotes. Then we saw the torches from afar and heard the music coming from their trucks. The puddles from the rain reflected the fire from the torches, covering the young men in an eerie light. But they were singing with the music, laughing, and joking in loud voices that could be heard at a distance, dispelling any sense of dread caused by the torches. As soon as they arrived at Fabiana's house, they unloaded their cargo and entered. The drinking and celebration continued late into the night.

The bathing of the bride ritual for the sivil kuambuni is different from the one in the misa kuani in some ways (at the start of chap. 3, I described Lisa's bathing before her misa kuani). The main difference is that the bathing for a sivil kuambuni is done during the day; for the misa kuani, it is celebrated at night. Since this ritual occurs at night for the misa kuani, the bride's relatives offer kamata afterward to all who are present, especially those who have gotten wet, as the kamata will help warm them. The bathing of the bride normally happens only once, meaning the bride is not bathed for both the misa kuani and the sivil kuambuni. In some cases, if the bride is bathed during the celebrations of Saint John the Baptist (June 23–24), she might not be bathed again for her misa kuani. But even if the bathing does not happen, the gifting of soap and loofahs *must* occur. In one misa kuani (Daniela and Joel's wedding in October 2009), we did not bathe Daniela because she had already been bathed for Saint John's Day and the sivil kuambuni. However, on the day before her misa kuani, we did take her soaps and loofahs, and her family offered kamata, as was expected.

CREATING CULTURE 117

As I detail in chapter 6, young people have been actively transforming the wedding ritual in the last twenty years. However, I regard the inclusion of the sivil kuambuni as one of the first main transformations of the tembuchakua in the last sixty years. The civil wedding, as a practice imposed by the Mexican state, was customized to the cultural logic of the community.[8] All of the rituals performed in the sivil kuambuni are also practiced in the misa kuani, and some of them, mainly the gifting of firewood, have pre-Hispanic roots (Martínez-Rivera 2021). While the earliest documentation of the bathing ritual is recent (Ojeda Dávila 2006), the importance of water during courtship rituals is well established (Barragán and González Bonilla 1940; Beals [1945] 1992; Foster [1967] 1988; León [1889] 1982; Lumholtz 1904; Mendieta y Núñez 1940). I posit that when people in Angahuan were forced to celebrate civil weddings, they incorporated some of the rituals already performed in the community into this foreign practice. In the process, they turned the civil wedding into the sivil kuambuni. This shows how the misa kuani serves as a cultural template that allows for the customization of foreign practices and the active creation of vernacular cultural practices.

Creating the Misa Kuani: Decision-Making and Asking for Godparents

Based on conversations with research collaborators and my host family, preparations for the misa kuani are a delicate and complicated matter and may require diplomatic skills. The celebrations are generally not planned for months in advance; in some cases, the entire event can be organized within a month. It depends on many factors: if the groom's and bride's families can find godparents quickly, if the bride is pregnant, or if the season when weddings are celebrated is nearing its end (see the intro., where I discuss Angahuan's wedding season). The first decision regarding the celebration of the misa kuani involves setting the wedding date and selecting and asking the wedding godparents.[9] Choosing godparents is a delicate matter in Angahuan. In most cases, there is no prior relationship between the godparents and the godchildren. After the wedding, however, the godparents will be a constant presence in their godchildren's lives.[10]

One Saturday in November, I walked to the home of Margarita (a friend and research collaborator). We discussed her sister Gabriela's wedding (which occurred in late October and is described in chap. 6), Gabriela's due date (in mid-February), and where she and her husband-to-be, Jonathan, were going to live. I also asked Margarita about the process of selecting the wedding godparents.

In some cases, couples offer themselves as godparents, but, according to Margarita, it is mostly a family decision. The bride's and groom's immediate families must agree about the candidates for wedding godparents. The families must evaluate them to see if they have a good or bad reputation. In some cases, the intended godparents are not available on the day of the wedding. Gabriela and Jonathan had a specific couple they wanted as godparents, but they were not available until January. By that time, Gabriela's pregnancy would have been too far along for her to participate in her own wedding. So they had to look for another couple to fill the role.

According to Margarita, the groom's parents sometimes choose the wedding godparents and inform the bride's parents. If both of the newlyweds' parents do not agree with the choice of godparents, the entire wedding can be fraught with tension.[11] Because people already know that the selection of godparents might be problematic, some couples asked to serve as wedding godparents do not agree to do so unless they are sure that all parties involved agree. After the couple and their families have chosen whom they want as wedding godparents, the next step is to ask the prospective godparents.

The protocol for asking prospective godparents is formalized. The bride's and groom's parents, together with close relatives, must visit the candidates to ask them to be godparents. This type of visit is called padrinu arhip'eni niani (to go ask for a godparent). One night in April 2009, we had an unexpected visit. As we were finishing our supper, two couples arrived at the house. They came with bottles of tequila. After greeting everybody, they offered us tequila. Na Juana and Ta Emiliano accepted the drinks; nobody else was allowed to accept, as no nos tocaba. Chucha and Pela cleared away the dirty plates and set up chairs for the visitors. Then they gave me a sign that we should retire to our bedroom—it was not our turn or place to be present. We left as another couple arrived at the house. Pela explained that it looked like the visitors had come to ask Na Juana and Ta Emiliano to be godparents for a wedding. She was not entirely sure, but, in her experience, when a couple arrives with a bottle of tequila, they are there to ask for a compadrazgo (described in chap. 1). The next morning, we found three empty bottles of tequila and Ta Emiliano with a hangover. They had talked until three in the morning. Pela was correct: the visitors had come to ask Na Juana and Ta Emiliano to be godparents in a wedding. Na Juana and Ta Emiliano did not answer because they needed to discuss the matter further. The wedding was scheduled for June, and June would be a difficult month for the family financially, as the three boys were graduating from school and the family needed to pay for three celebrations. The visitors said they would come back in a few days for an answer.

CREATING CULTURE 119

Several weeks passed before the bride and groom-to-be's relatives returned for the answer. They were willing to move the wedding to September if Na Juana and Ta Emiliano accepted the request to be the godparents. Na Juana and Ta Emiliano had no choice but to accept. The family members agreed to return at a future date to discuss the wedding details. When I left the following February, they had not yet returned. According to Chucha, the bride-to-be was pregnant; they had to wait until she had the baby, and the baby was big enough to participate in the wedding. The wedding took place in January 2014.

Based on my experience and what my research collaborators shared with me, when a couple arrives at the house of the intended godparents for the padrinu arhip'eni niani, they begin the visit with small talk. Everyone present knows their intentions, but they wait to broach the subject. After the topic has finally been raised and the visitors have explicitly asked for the godparenthood, the intended godparents are expected to say that they will think about it and that the visitors should return on a later date (as in the case of Na Juana and Ta Emiliano or when Amalia's hand was asked in marriage—see chap. 3). It is bad form to agree immediately to any type of proposal, which is why everybody laughed when I broke protocol after Gabriela and Jonathan asked me to be a godmother at their wedding. As explained in chapter 3, reciprocity in P'urhépecha culture is a serious practice; people must be careful not to break the structure of dar y recibir. This act must be performed properly. Expanding a social network based on the practice of reciprocity must be seriously considered. This is one of the reasons that choosing the godparents and asking for the compadrazgo are so crucial: the performance of the wedding and the newlyweds' future life both are at stake. However, the protocol is changing as more young couples are taking charge of the decisions regarding their wedding and the people they want as godparents. I expand on this development later in this chapter.

After the date has been set and the wedding godparents have been confirmed, the groom's and bride's families must decide how they want to perform the tembuchakua. Na Juana, for example, believes that the groom's parents are responsible for most decisions regarding the tembuchakua. One reason is that most of the rituals and wedding expenses are paid for by the groom's family. For her daughters' weddings, Na Juana left all decisions regarding the godparents and the organization of the tembuchakua to the future-in-laws. My host sisters said that their mother helped them avoid problems with the grooms' families during the organizing of the tembuchakua in an effort to ensure that the beginning of their married lives would be as easy and tension-free as possible.

Social status and economic affluence also play a part in the decision-making process. If the bride's family is well-off, they may make the decisions.

120   CREATING CULTURE, PERFORMING COMMUNITY

For example, in July 2011, a month in which weddings are not traditionally celebrated in Angahuan, a distant male relative of my host family got married. The bride's family was more affluent than the groom's family, so they could afford to celebrate a wedding several weeks before the celebration of Santo Santiago. The groom's family had to go into debt to fulfill their part and celebrate the wedding that the bride's family was expecting. I heard about other cases where the bride's family took over the major decisions because she was their only daughter or their youngest daughter and they wanted to celebrate with a lavish wedding. This may happen regardless of socioeconomic status.

Another element that greatly influences how the misa kuani will be performed is the music. To celebrate all of the rituals performed during the misa kuani, the groom's family must hire a wind band or orchestra. The bride's family might decide to hire a band too, but this is up to them. In recent years, and for the more costly weddings, families have hired bands with stages, sound systems, and light shows. Some of these bands play a variety of music, such as banda, cumbia, or grupera, rather than only pirekua. Sometimes, the groom's family hires a wind band for the rituals, and the bride's family might hire a band with a stage and sound system for the final dance. If the families cannot hire a wind band or orchestra, the format of the misa kuani will change significantly (see chap. 5). If the groom's family hires a wind band, then the parties involved in the wedding (the bride's family and wedding godparents) know that certain rituals will occur and they must prepare accordingly.

The families must also agree on the attire of the bride and groom for the misa kuani. As chapter 6 describes, the format of the wedding will change depending on the bride's attire in the misa kuani (i.e., if she goes to the mass in the traditional P'urhépecha dress or in a white gown). In Angahuan, it is expected that the groom's family provides the clothing for the bride, and vice versa. In some cases, the groom's family might not be able to afford a white gown in addition to a P'urhépecha dress. In this case, if the bride wants to get married in a white gown, the families might agree that each party will be responsible for his or her own wardrobe. In other cases, the bride's family might force the groom's family to provide the white gown or any other attire the bride wants. Chucha, for example, wanted to get married in a white gown but did not want to impose on her future in-laws. However, her mother-in-law wanted to buy her a white gown, so she took Chucha to Uruapan to buy the dress. Chucha was not expecting a P'urhépecha dress as well, so her mother and sisters saved money to buy the cloth for a new P'urhépecha dress for Chucha's wedding day. But when José's family arrived to bathe Chucha on the day before their wedding, they brought both the white gown and a beautiful and expensive P'urhépecha dress.

CREATING CULTURE

Another factor open to negotiation is whether the groom's family will give wood and bread to the bride's family. The wood is used for cooking, and the bread is used for the invitation baskets. A week or two before the misa kuani, the groom's young male relatives take wood and his young female relatives take bread to the bride's house. The day the bread and wood are taken to the bride's house, her young relatives must be there to welcome the groom's relatives with alcohol and food. On their way to the bride's house, the groom's male relatives sweep the ground while carrying the wood on their way to the house. This ritual action is a clear continuation of a preconquest practice in which the groom gathered wood and swept the path to his bride's house after the wedding (Alcalá [1541] 2000; Martínez-Rivera 2021).

In Angahuan, invitations to a wedding (and most events) are made personally and, depending on one's status and relation to the family, each invitee will receive a basket with bread and fruit. But even the giving and receiving of bread can be a delicate and complicated affair. In the week before the wedding, the bride's mother takes bread to the homes of relatives to invite them to her daughter's impending nuptials. The relatives who receive the bread must then take presents to the groom's house the night before the wedding.[12] However, if the groom's family gives too little bread and the bride's family does not have enough bread to invite people, some of the bride's relatives may feel slighted. In other cases, if too much bread is given, and the bride's family does not have enough guests, the groom's family might feel offended because they will not receive gifts in proportion to the bread they gave. In some cases, when a great deal of bread has been given away but too few relatives reciprocate with gifts, tension arises between the families. Na Juana, after suffering both extremes of having too much or too little bread, decided that the groom's family should not give them bread so that they might avoid potential friction with family members.

Pirjo Kristiina Virtanen (2012) observed that young Manchineri, an Indigenous group in Brazil, are becoming more active and participatory in their education as members of their community. I saw this same dynamic in Angahuan. More young people in Angahuan are participating and making decisions about how their weddings will be performed. In some families, the mothers and aunts do all the wedding planning. In others, the future newlyweds are encouraged to participate or say that they want to participate. Chucha was fortunate: her mother-in-law was very helpful and generous with the preparations for her wedding. She constantly asked Chucha and her family for their opinions and solicited their input for all preparations. José's mother urged José and Chucha to choose their wedding godparents because they were going to be a big part of their lives. While José and Chucha had the final decision, they still wanted to consult with their parents. When the time came to tell their parents their choice for wedding godparents, Chucha and José resorted to "drastic" measures, according to Chucha. They analyzed couples, street by street in the community, beginning with Chucha's neighbors. Then they mentioned names and discarded them. One of their choices was a couple who had many wedding godchildren, and for that reason, they discarded them, as they would not be able to be active participants in Chucha's and José's lives. They ultimately chose a couple who lived near Chucha's parents.

Chucha and José also had to choose all their other godparents (for the cake, music, rings, bouquet, Bible, etc.). They divided the work, and each chose a group of godparents. They also selected alternative options for each godparent, as they were not sure if everyone would agree. Chucha and José took charge of asking people to be their godparents and performing the padrinu arhip'eni niani. As Chucha told me her wedding story, she confessed that she felt somewhat guilty because people told them that what they were doing was not correct: their parents should be asking people to be godparents; it was not their turn/responsibility to ask for godparents. But José felt that it was their task to choose their own godparents. In the end, they asked close friends to be the godparents for most of the church-related responsibilities, thereby avoiding the tension and criticism they first received. This situation is similar to that of Gabriela and Jonathan, who also asked friends to be their godparents. As I describe in chapter 6, this is understandable because their wedding deviated from some of the expectations of how a misa kuani should be performed.

These are some of the main issues negotiated by the groom's and bride's mothers and other older female relatives over many meetings. As mentioned, these negotiations are crucial for the successful performance of the wedding and to help the new couple form strong and lasting relationships with a new family social network. More importantly, vernacular cultural practices are shaped during these conversations. In other words, through these negotiations, culture is created and is later performed during the actual wedding ritual.[13] As we have seen, this negotiation is a delicate and complex matter, where issues of social reputation, gender, economic affluence, and other sociocultural elements are considered. The practice of te toca is also embedded in these negotiations, as are cultural expectations of how the tembuchakua is supposed to be performed. Moreover, young people are becoming more active participants in the negotiation and organization of their weddings, which further contributes to the creation of their cultural practices and the cultural transformations of and in the tembuchakua.

Creating the Tembuchakua as an Example of Creating Culture

Organizing and planning a tembuchakua (both the sivil kuambuni and the misa kuani) involves a series of diplomatic meetings between the groom's and bride's families and the wedding godparents. During these meetings, which are normally attended by the mothers and older female relatives, tasks are divided and the main rituals of the wedding are organized. The successful performance of the wedding depends on the effective negotiation and diplomacy of the parties involved. These negotiations are the building blocks for the creation of culture in Angahuan.

Using Garrido Izaguirre's model for understanding P'urhépecha aesthetics, we can elucidate some of the main considerations that influence the creation of vernacular cultural practices in Angahuan. Of the multiple elements that Garrido Izaguirre mentions, and based on what I documented, there are three primary elements: the importance of symmetry, the total harmony of the piece, and the relationship between individual choice and the communal order and expectations.

For Angahuans and P'urhépecha people in general, symmetry is incredibly important. As Garrido Izaguirre (502–503) documents, dances, altar and image decoration, and the embroidery of traditional dress follow particular symmetric patterns; in this way, people create harmonic and balanced pieces. I have observed these same dynamics in Angahuan: the community is traditionally divided into two barrios, dancers move in parallel lines, and other examples. In terms of the wedding, during the negotiation process, people consider ideas of symmetry in terms of how they organize the division of labor, how gifts (such as wood or bread) are presented and used, and how to ensure there is a balance/symmetry between what the groom and bride contribute to the wedding (e.g., bread translates into household gifts).

The second element documented by Garrido Izaguirre, and something I have also seen in Angahuan, is the idea of armonía global del conjunto (total harmony of the piece). While Garrido Izaguirre primarily focuses on pottery and material culture, in the case of the tembuchakua, this element or consideration influences the negotiation process, as people are constantly aware of the final product—the wedding. Based on what I have documented—and not only regarding the planning of a wedding—people make decisions based on how the final product (be it a dance, ritual, altar, etc.) must be or look at the end. Therefore, during the negotiation stage, people carefully contemplate the different elements necessary for the performance of a wedding.

One of the final elements highlighted by Garrido Izaguirre, and one she considers to be the most significant, is the relationship between individual choice

Fig. 4a.3 Soaps and kamata. October 2009.

and communal expectations, especially because the majority of P'urhépecha aesthetics-ethics values derive from this relationship. And, as I have documented, this is apparent in Angahuan as well. I observed many times how people negotiated between their individual preferences and communal expectations. As I discuss in chapter 5, people perform what it means to be a member of their community during the tembuchakua, thus reinforcing this relationship between the individual and the group. The ideas and practices of te toca also play an important part in the relationship between individual and group, as it guides expectations regarding communal/group ideas. Similarly to Greene's ideas regarding customization or Clifford's views on Indigenous articulations, individuals and communities transform and create their own culture and vernacular cultural practices following the cultural logic of the community.

Preparations for the Misa Kuani: Days before the Misa Kuani

Before detailing the events of the main day of the misa kuani (see the upcoming interlude and chap. 5), I want to describe what occurs weeks and days before and on the first official day of the misa kuani.

CREATING CULTURE

Before Daniela and Joel's wedding, Chucha explained everything that had to be prepared (in the upcoming interlude, I describe in detail Daniela and Joel's misa kuani). Joel is Na Juana's nephew, so we had to help with all stages of the preparations for and during the wedding. On the Sunday before the wedding, Joel's young relatives took bread and wood to Daniela's house. On Monday and Tuesday, family members went to their tareta to gather corn leaves. The corn leaves are used for the korunda, and as thousands of korunda would be made, family members offered their cornfields so they could cut as many leaves as possible. On Wednesday, Na Juana and Ta Emiliano accompanied Ta Sergio and Na Antonia (Joel's parents; Ta Sergio is Na Juana's older brother) to the mercado de abastos in Zamora, a city on the other side of the Sierra, to buy the ingredients for the three-day celebration. The mercado de abastos is a large food market and distribution center for local farmers, and the prices are cheaper there. On Thursday, a cow was killed and it's meat prepared; some of the meat would be used for cooking and some for the ritual gifts. Friday, the first day of the misa kuani, was a long day. The house was put in order and decorated, and food was prepared for the evening rituals. The main day of events was Saturday.

When I arrived at Ta Sergio's house the afternoon before the wedding (Friday), some of the cousins and relatives were decorating the outside of the house (fig. 4a.1). Chucha, Pela, and Tomi were directing the decoration efforts. Most of the decorations were blue balloons, garlands made with white cardboard doves, and white drinking straws. Noel, one of Joel's brothers, was blocking the road in front of their home by putting large stones on the street so that cars would not drive through until after the wedding. A large tarp had been placed over the entire street. As I entered the house, I saw that the older women were in the kitchen helping to prepare the meal for the night's guests. The churipo was ready, so the women were cutting the meat into smaller pieces for serving. The korunda were also ready and in baskets. All the food was in one room; both the prepared dishes and the ingredients for all the cooking that would be done over the next few days. In the room were baskets with korunda, bread, sodas, and sacks of vegetables. In another room, dangling from the roof, were the legs of the cow that had been butchered for the wedding. The legs would be offered as gifts to the bride and godparents on Saturday.

As soon as Chucha, Pela, and Tomi finished putting up the decorations, I went with Chucha to buy soaps for Daniela. It was almost 5:00 p.m., and the town's loudspeakers were already announcing that we were already about to take the soaps to Daniela's house. Chucha and I ran to the store. When we returned to Ta Sergio's house, young female relatives were beginning to gather at the entrance. All the young women had a batea with loofahs and soaps. We also carried a large basket filled with soaps and loofahs, another gift from Joel. Since Daniela had already been bathed twice (for the sivil kuambuni and Saint John's Day), we were not going to do it again, but we still had to give her the soaps. Together, we went to the couple's future wedding godparents' home to look for their young female relatives. After visiting the wedding godparents, we walked to Daniela's house. We ran into Daniela and her mother who were on their way to the church to talk to the priest and make sure that everything was organized for the next day. When we arrived at Daniela's house, they gave us kamata while we waited for her to return. For the groom's close relatives (i.e., us), the kamata was served not in plastic cups but in clay dishes in the shape of tree leaves (fig. 4a.3).[14] After waiting for half an hour, Daniela's relatives decided to start the ritual and chose one of Daniela's cousins to receive the soap. They directed us into a room where Daniela's cousin received our bateas, poured the contents on the bed, returned our bateas, and thanked us for the presents.

After gifting our soaps, we thanked Daniela's family, accompanied the wedding godparents' relatives to the godparents' home, and returned to Ta Sergio's house. By then, it was past 7:00 p.m. and already dark and cold. Our responsibilities as the groom's young relatives were almost finished. Chucha, Pela, Joel's sisters, and other female relatives went with Noel and his pickup truck to get the baskets of bread for the next day's breakfast. They came back with approximately ten extremely heavy baskets full of loaves of bread. After nightfall, the older relatives of Ta Sergio and Na Juana's generation began arriving with presents for the bride and groom. The gifts were mostly kitchen utensils and household items, such as pots, pans, plates and cups, wool blankets, pillows, clothing for the groom, and comales. In return, the relatives received a plastic bowl filled with churipo and a bag of korunda as thank-you for their presents. After Chucha and Pela returned from picking up the bread and we had finished helping, we returned home. It was almost 11:00 p.m.

We had left just in time because a huge group of relatives was approaching the house through the plaza. The group included more than fifty people, all couples and belonging to the same generation as Ta Sergio and Na Juana (fig. 4a.4). Each couple carried baskets or boxes with their gifts inside. This type of visit is called tsïpini niani (to take a gift on the eve of a wedding). They were the bride's relatives who had received the bread/invitation. Na Juana and Ta Emiliano stayed to help and partake in the ritual gift exchange.

In the new modality of celebrating the misa kuani and the sivil kuambuni on the same day (see chap. 6), some families must decide which rituals are most important to perform and which can be set aside. In some cases, like Chucha and José's wedding (which was celebrated as a joint misa kuani-sivil

Fig. 4a.4 Taking gifts on the eve of a misa kuani. October 2009.

kuambuni), everything was squeezed into three days. On the eve of the wedding, José's cousins brought the soap and ocotes. Chucha's family hired a water tank for the "bathing," and José's relatives also had a water tank. As part of the events, José's sisters brought the wedding gown and a P'urhépecha dress. As they had brought the wedding attire, Chucha had to call one of her aunts so the aunt could receive the gift. Chucha explained that it would look bad if she accepted the dresses herself.[15] The aunt had to warmly thank the groom's family for the gift. José's sisters then asked permission from Chucha's aunt to bathe Chucha. Even Chucha's brothers and male cousins participated. It was a big group, especially on Chucha's side, and with two water tanks, there was plenty of water. Chucha reported that they had a good water fight.

While the young relatives enjoyed their water fight, a group of women diligently prepared ichuskuta and other food for José's relatives who would arrive that night with the ocotes. Chucha's older relatives (the ones who received the bread as an invitation to the wedding) also gathered and organized to take the gifts to José's home. That night, after Chucha's relatives had left, José and his relatives arrived with the ocotes. They drank, danced to banda and P'urhépecha music, and then went home. They did not stay long because the next day was going to be a long one.

Ready for the Misa Kuani

We have now arrived at the eve of the main day of a misa kuani. Gradually, the different strands of this wedding story have come together to explain how culture is created and community is performed in Angahuan. This chapter specifically focuses on how culture is created in Angahuan. The process of organizing and negotiating the tembuchakua, deciding how to celebrate the sivil kuambuni and the misa kuani, choosing wedding godparents (and other, minor godparents), and deciding what rituals will be celebrated are some of the key elements that influence the creation and performance of the tembuchakua. As an example of a vernacular cultural practice, closely examining how the tembuchakua is organized can help us understand some of the building blocks of creating culture in a P'urhépecha context, such as the importance of symmetry, the total harmony of the piece, and the relationship between individual choice and the communal order and expectations. Moreover, the idea of te toca also influences how culture is created and, later, performed.

The rituals performed the day before the wedding—the bathing of the bride and the exchange of gifts—are a prelude to the various rituals that will be performed on the actual day of the misa kuani. The rituals held on the day before the wedding start the formation of a new social network, which is negotiated and performed during the misa kuani. The bathing of the bride, for example, directly relates to other rituals performed during the misa kuani, specifically the kanarperakua and la víbora de la mar (discussed in chaps. 5 and 6), which demonstrate that the bride and groom are not alone but have a strong support network and a family willing to fight for them. In the upcoming interlude, I describe Daniela and Joel's wedding, and in chapter 5, I analyze their wedding to understand the different ritual forms and the principal P'urhépecha worldviews and values represented in their wedding celebrations. This helps to unpack how ideas of community are performed in Angahuan.

But first, a note on the interlude. This section follows in the path of other scholarly works that ask us to embrace the slow approach (Perez 2023). For example, in his award-winning book *We Will Dance Our Truth: Yaqui History in Yoeme Performances* (2009), David Delgado Shorter includes interchapters called "Ethnographic Dialogues," in which he explores different ways of presenting and engaging with ethnographic stories and storytelling formats. David J. Siegal's recently published book, *The Interlude in Academe: Reclaiming Time and Space for Intellectual Life* (2023) explores how interludes—as "disruptions to our usual rhythms, rituals, and routines"—can offer opportunities to "experiment with alternative modes and models of intellectual life" (2023). More

CREATING CULTURE

importantly, during Angahuan weddings, people typically take breaks between rituals to eat, rest, and prepare for the next set of rituals. Therefore, I invite you to pause and, hopefully, enjoy a brief detailed description of the main events of a wedding before we continue on our journey to unpack how culture is created and how community is performed in Angahuan.

Notes

1. In a Catholic wedding, in addition to the wedding godparents, one also has godparents for the Bible, the arras (thirteen gold-painted small coins that are used during the wedding ritual to symbolize prosperity), the rings, and the lasso (either a decorated white "rope" or a large rosary that is used to "tie" the bride and groom together during the ceremony). The church service requires this group of godparents, as they are part of the wedding ceremony. Mexican mestizo weddings also have godparents for the cake, music, drinks, decorations, and more. These forms of godparenthood, while not as formal as ritual godparenthood (baptism, first communion, confirmation, and marriage), serve to unite a community; expand social networks; and, most importantly, enable families to pay for special events, such as weddings.

2. Jeff Berglund, Jan Johnson, and Kimberli Lee (2016) and John Troutman (2009) also build on Clifford's idea of Indigenous articulation and have been crucial in influencing my work.

3. See n. 30 in the introduction for an explanation of El Costumbre.

4. The civil wedding, as established by federal law, is celebrated before the religious wedding.

5. During the colonial period, the Catholic Church was the official entity in charge of compiling census information as well as officiating unions, annulments, and funerals. After México gained its independence, the church held its power in the newly formed state. However, the Constitution of 1855 decreed a separation of church and state. While the lands of the Church were expropriated in 1859, the final separation of church and state was established in the Constitution of 1917, which revoked the judicial entity (personalidad juridical) of the Church. From that point on, the Church was no longer in charge of maintaining birth, marriage, and death records. These powers and responsibilities were granted to the Registro Civil (Civil Registry). Mexicans who want to marry and are religious must celebrate two wedding ceremonies: a religious one and a civil one.

6. While in Angahuan, I noticed—and my host family corroborated—that people prepare specific dishes for particular events or celebrations. Each dish is considered appropriate and correct for a certain event. For the misa kuani, for example, people expect churipo and korunda, and for the sivil kuambuni, people

expect birria. However, I did attend a misa kuani where birria was served—during the dinner, my host sisters commented on the oddness of the choice of dish.

7. The convoy was checking out Angahuan, and several days later, over a thousand members of the PFP surrounded the community. For more information on this event, see Martínez-Rivera 2021.

8. An etymological analysis of the terms sivil kuambuni, misa kuani, and tembuchakua might further illuminate the process of customizing, but at this stage, I have neither the data nor the resources to do this.

9. The civil wedding does not use wedding godparents but witnesses. In some cases, the witnesses are the wedding godparents, but in others, the couple asks another couple, or relatives, for the civil wedding. However, the wedding godparents "who count" are the ones for the misa kuani.

10. After the wedding, the bride and groom are expected to stay at the bride's house for a short period. Then they are taken to their wedding godparents' house. After another short time, they are taken to the groom's house, where they are supposed to live until they have a house of their own. During this period, they must completely obey their parents and godparents, and neither the bride nor groom may work. They must be available to help their parents or godparents with whatever they may need. The bride, for example, must help with kitchen and house chores, while the groom must complete whatever tasks his father-in-law or godfather assigns to him. This period of transition is crucial for the development of the relationship between the couple and their godparents.

11. I was told of a case in which the bride's mother did not agree with the choice of godparents and so refused to participate in the kamataru niani, one of the most important rituals of the wedding (see chap. 5). Her family tried to convince her, even attempting to drag her to the godparents' home, but she locked herself in her bedroom and refused to leave. The situation was even more complicated because the bride's father was in the US, so neither of the bride's parents attended this important event. According to my research collaborators, the relationship between the compadres is strained, to say the least.

12. Most of the presents are household items, pots and pans, kitchenware, and wool blankets.

13. To some degree, this process is what Richard Schechner (1985) refers to as a bounded performance and, as such, we can study and analyze the different components of the performance, such as training, workshops, rehearsals, warm-ups, the actual performance, and the aftermath.

14. The dish in which kamata is served is not necessarily traditional: it can have many shapes; the important thing is that they used special clay dishes for the occasion.

15. This practice, an elder accepting a gift during a special occasion, is common in Angahuan.

Fig. 4b.1 Waiting for Joel and Daniela's wedding mass to end. October 2009.

Interlude

Joel and Daniela's P'urhépecha Wedding (October 2009)

We woke up early on the morning of Joel and Daniela's wedding. I do not know at what time Na Juana and Ta Emiliano arrived home from the previous night's ritual events (described at the end of chap. 4), but at five in the morning, Noel (Joel's brother) came looking for them to make sure they were able to help Na Antonia (Joel's mother) with the day's initial preparations. By 6:30 a.m., Chucha, Pela, and I were almost ready to go to Ta Sergio's house to help with last-minute preparations and attend the wedding mass, scheduled for 7:00 a.m. We needed to arrive at the church before the mass ended so we could be ready to throw confetti and, in my case, take pictures of the newlyweds. When we left our house, the sun had not yet appeared over the mountains, and a light, cold mist covered the town. Nonetheless, Angahuan was already stirring. Women fully covered by their tangarhikuecha and men in jackets and hats walked briskly through the streets to try to stay warm. The sounds of hens, roosters, pigs, and cows waking up emerged from the patios, and the loudspeakers broke the morning quiet with various announcements, including information about Joel and Daniela's wedding.

Ta Sergio's house is beside the church, which simplified that morning's errands and rituals. The house had been decorated the day before, and it was now ready for the rituals that would be celebrated during the day, the misa kuani's main day of ritual events. After arriving at Ta Sergio's home and helping with last-minute food preparations, Chucha, Pela, and I ran to the church. I waited outside with a group of young female relatives with our baskets and bags full of confetti (fig. 4b.1). When I saw that the mass was about to conclude, I entered the church and made my way to the altar. The church in Angahuan is always beautifully decorated because different religious groups oversee decorating and

Fig. 4b.2 Procession toward Joel's home. October 2009.

general maintenance. Flower bouquets covered the altar and dotted the length of the church, and garlands made with pine needles and white and yellow plastic ribbons hung from the ceiling. In front of the altar, a pew was covered with a white blanket decorated with flowers and two white cardboard doves. In the pew, Joel and Daniela were standing next to each other, flanked by their wedding godparents.

Daniela is the only daughter in her family so her parents wanted her to have a big wedding. Therefore, Daniela se casó de blanco (more on this in chap. 6). She wore a white wedding gown with a long train, and Joel wore a black suit and tie. The godmother wore the traditional P'urhépecha female dress, and the godfather was dressed in jeans, a button-down shirt, and a jacket. After a brief photo shoot inside the church, the wedding party moved outside where the wind band was waiting for the newlyweds to exit the church so they could start playing. The young female relatives were ready with confetti, and other family members greeted the newlyweds as soon as they walked outside. The young women threw confetti, and other young female relatives passed out wedding mementos to the attendees. The older relatives approached Joel and Daniela, who stood in the doorway of the church to receive hugs, congratulations, and blessings (fig. 5.1). Relatives also took that opportunity to have their picture taken with the couple. Joel and Daniela, as well as most of the guests, were quickly and completely covered in confetti.

After all the relatives had congratulated the newlyweds, the procession began. Joel and Daniela, flanked by their wedding godparents, headed the procession (fig. 4b.2). Dressed in a black suit, one of Daniela's young cousins carried Daniela's wedding dress train. Joel's cousins and sisters followed the newlyweds, throwing more confetti. Next came the rest of the relatives: women on one side and men on the other. The procession ended with the wind band, which had been playing nonstop. Our destination was Ta Sergio's house, which was right next to the church, so we circled the plaza before arriving at Joel's house. Once we got there, the principal guests (the wedding godparents with their relatives and the newlyweds' older relatives) sat down at the tables, along gender lines, while the younger female cousins ran inside the house to help serve breakfast: hot chocolate with bread. A group of older female relatives were in the kitchen organizing, preparing food, and making sure everything ran smoothly. As soon as everybody had a piece of bread and a cup of hot chocolate, the first series of rituals relating to the white/mestizo wedding began (described in chap. 6).

Once the events of Joel and Daniela's white/mestizo wedding had ended, the preparations began for the procession and the start of the P'urhépecha wedding. It was already noon, and the skies were bright and clear. The sun was warming up Angahuan before the afternoon rain clouds arrived and covered the community in damp cold. In a P'urhépecha wedding, following breakfast at the groom's house, the bride and her relatives and the godparents and their relatives are taken to their respective homes, where they will have their own celebrations. The groom's older relatives, together with the band, accompany the bride and the godparents. When the bride's and godparents' guests leave after the white wedding celebration, the young women who stayed at the groom's house quickly begin to clean, organize, and help older female relatives prepare the food for dinner. In the kitchen, women were already hard at work making korunda, while others prepared the ingredients for the churipo (figs. 4b.3 and 4b.4). After cleaning and putting everything in place, the young female relatives got ready to take ribbons to Daniela so we could make her braids. But we had to wait for the band and our turn to go to Daniela's home.

After taking the bride and godparents to their respective homes, the groom's older relatives arrived. However, they immediately left again to take the ingredients for the churipo and korunda to Daniela's and the godparents' respective

Fig. 4b.3 Preparing churipo and korunda. October 2009.

Fig. 4b.4 Preparing churipo and korunda. October 2009.

Fig. 4b.5 Taking ingredients as gifts during a wedding. April 2009.

homes. They carried a cow's leg, baskets full of corn, corn leaves, salt, onions, chiles guajillos, a water jug, and a bundle of firewood (fig. 4b.5). Before leaving for Daniela's house, they danced to one song on the patio. The procession of older relatives carrying food danced all the way to Daniela's home followed by the wind band. When they arrived, the groom's relatives danced on the house's patio and then presented the gifts to Daniela's relatives. After this, the groom's and bride's relatives danced together, while the bride's relatives held the gifts they had received. After concluding this gift-giving ritual, the groom's relatives returned to Joel's home to gather more food to take to the wedding godparents' home.

While the older generation was taking gifts to the bride, the communal loudspeakers announced that Joel's young female relatives were getting ready to take the ribbons to Daniela's house and that those who were participating should come to the house as soon as possible. One by one, young women arrived at Joel's house. As soon as the older generation returned from the bride's home, we headed to the godparents' home with them, followed by the band (fig. 4b.6). At the godparents' home, the older generation danced and presented gifts to the godparents' relatives. After Joel's older relatives completed their gift-giving ritual, they left, and it was our turn to dance. The

Fig. 4b.6 Taking ribbons to Daniela's home. October 2009.

Fig. 4b.7 Preparing Daniela's floor-length, ribbon-covered braids. October 2009.

wind band played a short abajeño, and all the groom's relatives danced while holding our ribbons. After we danced and all the godparents' young female relatives had arrived, we left in a procession for Daniela's home. She was ready for us. She had changed into her traditional P'urhépecha dress, and her hair was braided into two French braids. One of Daniela's relatives put a straw mat on the floor in one corner of the patio for Daniela to kneel on. We then presented our gifts to her: colorful ribbons, each a meter long, until she was surrounded by a sea of vibrant material. After all the ribbons had been presented, everyone paired off to make small bows with the ribbons. Daniela was measured for her braids, and a small group of older cousins made two floor-length braids with black yarn. As soon as the bows were ready and the floor-length braids had been woven into Daniela's hair, two women began tying hundreds of bows into Daniela's long braids. Between the colors and the types of ribbons, the braids looked beautiful, and a huge and heavy colorful cascade fell down Daniela's back (fig. 4b.7). Since Daniela's grandmothers were there, dancing and enjoying the celebration, we took the opportunity to put bows in their hair as well.

After we finished preparing Daniela for the next set of rituals, we left to take the relatives of the godparents to their respective celebrations and then returned to Joel's house to see if we could help with anything. Na Juana told us to get ready for the dance. Chucha, Pela, and I ran home to bathe, change, and get ready. We could hear the loudspeakers calling for Joel's relatives to come to his house; it was a little after five in the afternoon. We ran back to Ta Sergio's home, but Joel's young relatives had already left for the godparents' home. We were not alone, however. Many people had just arrived, including my other host sisters, Caye, Inés, and Tomi. We all walked to a corner where we would meet the main group when they returned from the godparents' home. While we waited, a group from another wedding came our way and danced on our corner. We waited for over twenty minutes until our party showed up. Once they got there, we joined them and began dancing and participating in the uarhantsani (figs. 5.2 and 5.3).

Our group was the largest I had seen at a wedding: at one point, we had close to seventy dancers. The ages of the people dancing varied from Caye and I (the oldest of the group in our late twenties) to some even younger than Leti (ten years old). Several of the older dancers were carrying satchels with tequila bottles and soda to mix and give to other dancers. In other weddings I had attended, I had not seen married people participate in this event, but Caye, Inés, and Tomi told me that anybody who wants to dance may do so. The only requirement is that the dancer belongs to this particular generation / social group. Everybody was dressed in their best clothing or wearing something new (Chucha was wearing new shoes, and I was wearing a new traditional dress). Some of the dancers, both male and female and of different ages, were carrying dolls tied with a tangarikua on their backs.

After joining the main group of dancers, we proceeded to dance through the streets, stopping and dancing at specific corners. The dancing path, interestingly, follows the same route as other religious, civic, and military processions in the community. However, we did take some detours, as we needed to dance at the godparents' and bride's homes. People came out of their houses to watch us dance, and some passersby would join us for a little bit and then go on their way. After completing the main dancing route, we escorted the godparents' relatives to their respective celebrations to get ready for the final set of rituals. We danced for over four hours around Angahuan, finishing close to 10:00 p.m.

While we were dancing, the older generation and the newlyweds participated in one of the day's most important rituals, the kamataru niani, at the godparents' house. After we finished Daniela's braids, the godparents and their relatives left to look for the groom and his family, and then they walked to the bride's home. The bride and her relatives left with the godparents and the groom's relatives for the godparents' home where everybody was offered kamata. Afterward, the godparents, the newlyweds, and their parents moved to a private area where a Diosïri uandarhi (a person who talks about God) directed the most important ritual of the day. This is when the godparents, the newlyweds, and their parents are reminded of their responsibilities and the compadrazgo is formalized. After the kamata, everyone returns to the groom's house where they are once again fed churipo and korunda. Next, the groups return to their respective homes to wait for the youngsters to finish dancing through the streets so the last set of rituals can be performed.

After dancing and returning the godparents' relatives to their homes, the papu (the papu refers to a person, a chair, and a song) is brought out from the godparents' home (figs. 5.4 and 5.7). When we arrived at the groom's home, the papu was already there and Na Juana was dancing with it. After several dances, everyone left in a procession to the bride's home. I went with Inés and her husband in their car to help transport the kanakua and bread necklaces for the final ritual of the evening. As we followed the procession of the papu, we saw many people standing in their doorways, enjoying the procession.

Fig. 4b.8 Pela dancing with Daniela during the kanarperakua. October 2009.

Once we had arrived at Daniela's home, the next ritual, the kanarperakua, was quickly organized. The kanarperakua is a gift-giving ritual accompanied by a display of force demonstrated by the groom's and bride's families. The kanarperakua is performed by the same generation as the newlyweds. Before I went to my first wedding, Chucha and Pela described it to me as a luchita (wrestle), a struggle between the family members of the bride and groom. There was a long line of gift givers, so Joel and Daniela danced at the same time. Daniela danced while holding pots, pans, or a comal, and Joel had a shirt or scarf wrapped around his neck. Joel's relatives tried to trip Daniela, but her family was there to help her, either by taking what she was holding or by trying to stop the "attack." At one point, Daniela danced with Noel, her new brother-in-law, and Joel danced with one of Daniela's relatives. Noel gave Daniela a huge pot, but as she put it down so she could dance, he quickly went in for the attack, taking Daniela in his arms and carrying her. Daniela was laughing and covering her very embarrassed, red face. At the same time, one of Daniela's relatives took hold of Joel and started to wrestle with him. Relatives of both families joined the struggle and either defended or attacked Joel. People were shouting and laughing at the "fight" (fig. 5.8). Na Juana, who was the elder monitoring the event, told the band to stop playing so the "fighters" would stop dancing. As the music stopped, Noel let go of Daniela, and the scuffle with Joel abruptly ended. Everybody was unhurt, laughing, and enjoying the event. The kanarperakua continued for a long while. After all of my host sisters had finished presenting their gifts, we left (fig. 4b.8). It had been a long day—it was almost midnight— and we were exhausted from all the work, dancing, and celebrations. And there was still one more day of celebrations left.

Fig. 5.1 Daniel and Joel covered in confetti. October 2009.

5

Performing Community

Following the Confetti Trail

During my many visits to Angahuan, I noticed the widespread use of multicolored confetti in the community. It is generally used to celebrate life cycle or community events, and people buy bags of confetti by the kilo. At times, the roads in Angahuan are covered in confetti, and one could follow the confetti trails to the homes where a celebration was taking place. My host family always has a spare bag of confetti, just in case it is needed. People grab a handful of confetti and toss it over the heads of others so the confetti rains down on them. While attending celebrations such as weddings, I always ended up with confetti covering my hair and clothes, and it could take days to get all of it out of my hair and scalp.

Confetti is also used to celebrate other-than-human beings, as I witnessed one May 15 during the celebration of San Isidro, the patron saint of farmers and the rainy season. That day, Na Juana brought home a bag of confetti, which she handed to her children so they could throw it on their tareta behind the house. The youngest grabbed the bag and ran to the back of the house, laughing and shrieking with joy. When I asked what was going on, Pela told me that as it was San Isidro, it was the tareta's Saint's Day and we had to properly celebrate the occasion with confetti. Confetti not only marks a celebration and its participants but also helps people, especially children, learn how to behave, celebrate, and perform their belonging in the community.

Thus far, we have walked through the streets of Angahuan and explored the community's sociocultural organization, youth cultural practices, courtship rituals, and the impacts of elopement versus getting engaged. In chapter 4, I discussed the negotiating and planning stages of the tembuchakua. Specifically, I described the process of asking for godparents and how the future newlyweds' families carefully negotiate all of the wedding ritual details. By analyzing these negotiating practices, I unpacked the first of my interwoven arguments, exploring how the process of creating culture is rooted in P'urhépecha worldviews and ideas of aesthetics. My inclusion of the interlude was inspired by how people take small breaks during celebrations, so we paused to enjoy a detailed description of Joel and Daniela's P'urhépecha wedding. Chapters 5 and 6 of the book focus on the main day of the misa kuani and present my last two interwoven arguments: how cultural practices are performed to reflect specific ideas of what it means to be a member of a community and how people in Angahuan transform their cultural practices to fit their preferences, needs, and expectations.

As already mentioned, the present-day misa kuani in Angahuan is composed of multiple ritual events celebrated over three days and following, with some room for variation, the same sequence of events. To better understand the different rituals celebrated during the misa kuani, and using Daniela and Joel's wedding as an example, in this chapter, I propose a three-part framework that explains the different ritual forms performed during the three days of celebrations: *rituals in movement, rituals of controlled violence,* and *relationship-formalization rituals.* Each ritual form has its own purpose and style and is composed of multiple ritual instances. To understand how each ritual form contributes to the performance of community, I discuss four P'urhépecha values: kashumbikua or kaxumbekua, jakajkukua, anchikuarhua, and p'urhekujkua. These four values are practiced and performed in the different ritual forms during the tembuchakua. Therefore, in this chapter, I argue that P'urhépecha rituals are interwoven with four of their principal values, and I showcase how people perform their belonging in the community by their active participation in these different rituals.

Performing Community and P'urhépecha Values

Similar to my goal in chapter 4, I do not aim to provide an exhaustive analysis of the vast literature on "community" or "performance"; however, I do wish to highlight how people in Angahuan perform their belonging to their community and culture. More importantly, I showcase how these ideas of community are rooted in P'urhépecha worldviews and practices and are reflected and performed during rituals.

Many years ago, at a meeting of the group Kw'aniskuyarhani, P'urhépecha scholar Tata Pedro Márquez Joaquín (QEPD), said that belonging to this scholarly and community-based group was about being present and actively participating in the discussions, not about *saying* that you belong. When I heard

Tata Pedro say this, some of the dynamics I had seen in Angahuan began to make sense to me. Based on experience and from conversations with elders, to be and become P'urhépecha is about action, what one does, how one behaves. One *is* because one *does*, because one is present. Based on this, most P'urhépecha principal values and worldview tenets relate to behavior and reciprocal relationships.

In a previous article (2020), I briefly presented some of the main values or ideals as discussed with me by Tata Pedro Victoriano Cruz, a community leader in San Lorenzo (a neighboring P'urhépecha community). Tata Pedro Victoriano explained that P'urhépecha worldviews have four principal values or ideals. Those four ideals are kashumbikua or kaxumbekua, which refers to being honorable or behaving honorably, being a person worthy of respect; jakajkukua, which means the belief in P'urhépecha worldviews and following the rules of nature and the community; anchikuarhua is service to family, community, and nature; and p'urhekujkua refers to the warrior spirit to defend the community and P'urhépecha culture. As Tata Pedro Victoriano informed me, by practicing and performing these values, individuals signal their belonging to their P'urhépecha community. These four values and ideals are practiced and performed in many ways, from daily life behaviors to special events. P'urhépecha scholars use these values and ideals to theorize and create knowledge built from, with, and by P'urhépecha worldviews.

The Seminario de la Cultura P'urhépecha (SECUPU), composed only of P'urhépecha scholars, has been meeting for over ten years to theorize P'urhépecha cultural practices through P'urhépecha worldviews and language.[1] The group aims to "[generar] metodologías de construcción del conocimiento con base en la lengua y cultura P'urhépecha" ("generate methodologies for the construction of knowledge based on P'urhépecha culture and language") (Cortés Máximo 2019, 10). One of the first SECUPU sessions discussed the concept of juramukua: which translates to "mandato y obediencia" (to order and obey).[2] The group analyzed how a person with juramukua must maintain order among humans, nature, and other-than-human beings. Building on their discussion of juramukua, in 2019, SECUPU members published the edited volume *Marhuatspeni: El servir sagrado entre los P'urhépecha* (Cortés Máximo 2019), which discussed the concept of marhuatspeni, which translates to "mandar obedeciendo a fin de servir a la gente" ("order while obeying to serve the people"). Each contributor to the volume used the concept of marhuatspeni to analyze different case studies, such as communal political systems, traditional medicine, the cargo system, and music. In this regard, the concept of marhuatspeni highlights the importance of sacred service performed in reciprocity among P'urhépecha people, nature, and other-than-human beings. In addition to the concept and practice of marhuatspeni, the other four values, kaxumbekua, jakajkukua, anchikuarhua, and p'urhekujkua, are practiced in many ways. Because ideas of community are rooted in these values, people who learn and practice them can become a k'uiripu and a respected member of P'urhépecha communities.

As I observed, weddings in Angahuan help negotiate, transform, and contest social networks as well as transform everyday life. Rituals involve participants performing their main cultural tenets in a dramatic fashion; thus, they provide a compelling bounded performance for analyzing the idea of performing community and how culture is created. Scholars often emphasize a ritual's positive effects, such as bridging social divisions, regenerating the social charter, and reinvigorating the individual (Cohen 1993; Durkheim [1915] 1965; Schieffelin 1985; Turner 1982). Rituals can also control, persuade, and highlight power relations (Brandes 1988). In addition, rituals "affect the transition of everyday life to an alternative context within which everyday life is transformed" (Govers 2006, 20). According to Roy A. Rappaport (1992, 254), "ritual *embodies* social contract . . . it is the fundamental social act upon which human society is founded" (italics in original). Victor Turner ([1969] 1977, 97) asserts that ritual creates *communitas*, "an essential and generic human bond." According to Rappaport (1992, 249), ritual is "understood to be a form or structure, that is, a number of features or characteristics in a more or less fixed relationship to one another." Ritual, then, is composed of different elements that come together during a particular performance. Therefore, ritual must be performed; it must be acted out. Following Rappaport's and Turner's descriptions of ritual, I am interested in the embodiment of the wedding, in how people perform and embody P'urhépecha values and main cultural beliefs during a wedding to showcase their belonging to their community.

Joel and Daniela's wedding allowed me to take part in and observe wedding preparations from the inside, but, more importantly, I was also able to participate as one of Joel's young relatives. This provided me with the unique experience of performing some of the main P'urhépecha values as well as the practice of te toca. Using their wedding as a template, in the next section, I illustrate and analyze my proposed framework of three ritual forms (rituals in movement, rituals of controlled violence, and relationship-formalization rituals) and unpack how each ritual form helps people in Angahuan perform what it means to belong to their community. To provide a fuller picture, I combine my observations and experiences of Joel and Daniela's wedding with those of other weddings I attended or documented.

Unpacking the Misa Kuani: A Framework for Understanding P'urhépecha Rituals and the Performance of Community

Pablo and Lisa's wedding was the first time I participated in a tembuchakua in Angahuan, and I was overwhelmed by the number and diversity of rituals. I took small breaks throughout the day to try to write down as much as I could. By my third wedding, however, I was more familiar with the events and what I could expect. Moreover, as I had already participated in and documented other life cycle events and communal celebrations, I started to see patterns and similarities.

One of the key features during a tembuchakua is the constant movement of the participants through the community from one house to another. The three main houses—the groom's house, the bride's house, and the wedding godparents' house—are the key locations. Rituals in movement, therefore, are those that involve the participants going from one location to the next in a predetermined or orchestrated pattern. Rituals of controlled violence refer to those that, through the performance of controlled violence, aid in the formation and negotiation of new social networks and families. The third type of ritual forms are those that formalize relationships and are the most private and exclusive events. These rituals can be understood as "a special form of symbolic communication that can create strong emotions of togetherness and belonging" (Govers 2006, 20). As we will see shortly, each of these ritual forms has its own function and structure and provides a framework that allows people to successfully perform their membership in and belonging to Angahuan. Through these three ritual forms, therefore, community members learn, practice, and perform four of their main P'urhépecha values.

Rituals in Movement

Scholars have highlighted the importance of movement and walking among different Indigenous communities, as part of a religious ritual or to mark off their territory. In her article "La Fuerza de los Caminos Sonoros: Caminata y Música en Qoyllurit'i," Zoila Mendoza (2010) illustrates the relationship among movement, sound, and the visual during the Lord of Qoyllurit'i pilgrimage in the Peruvian Andes. According to Mendoza (2010), the union of movement, sound, and visual makes the pilgrimage a unique experience, as it provides participants with a way of learning and accessing their ancestral knowledge. In the case of Wixárika people in México, movement, mainly walking, as part of their pilgrimage to the deserts of Wirikuta, helps them to access their ancestral knowledge and demarcate their territory (Liffman 2005, 2011; Myerhoff 1974).

Fig. 5.2 Uarhantsani during Daniela and Joel's wedding. October 2009.

While movement between homes remains an important part of most P'urhépecha rituals, curiously, in P'urhépecha scholarship, movement as an intrinsic element of rituals has not been analyzed.[3] Therefore, I propose that rituals in movement include all rituals performed while moving through the community and that allow participants to access, create, perform, and experience their cultural knowledge.[4] This chapter describes how each ritual in movement has its own expectations or rules, but they share some key features.

The first characteristic of rituals in movement is the importance of music. Music is a key component of the wedding, and it will help define how the wedding is celebrated and which rituals are performed. My research collaborators explained that because the groom's family oversees most of the rituals in movement celebrated throughout the day, they are the ones who hire the wind band. The bride's and godparents' families can choose to hire an additional wind band, an orchestra, or a sound system to enliven their festivities, but it is not required or necessary. If the groom's family cannot afford a wind band or a traditional orchestra, the wedding takes place without music. However,

Fig. 5.3 Uarhantsani during Daniela and Joel's wedding. October 2009.

when the wedding is celebrated without music, most rituals in movement are not performed.

Another characteristic of most rituals in movement is that they are divided by social status / age group or gender. For example, with few exceptions, most parents do not participate alongside their children in rituals in movement, and vice versa. Another element is that, by moving through the community, the participants are visually mapping their new social network and reaffirming an old one. Finally, participants insert themselves into the larger community by following the path of communal processions. In this sense, rituals in movement inscribe the participants' social position in space and mark them as belonging to the community.

In her work on the Patum, a traditional festival in Berga, Spain, Dorothy Noyes (2003, 4, 127–139) discusses the idea of incorporation. She describes how through different "techniques of incorporation" outsiders, such as herself, can

152 CREATING CULTURE, PERFORMING COMMUNITY

be incorporated into the Patum and the community. The Patum, according to Noyes, is the space where the people of Berga build, practice, and maintain their communitas. Participation in the Patum marks them as members of the community. While participation in rituals in movement in P'urhépecha communities does not make a turisï part of the community, it does incorporate community members into different social networks, reiterating, expanding, and enhancing their belonging within their community.

As I explain shortly, through rituals in movement, people in Angahuan practice and perform the values of kaxumbekua (to behave honorably), jakajkukua (to follow the rules of nature and the community), and anchikuarhua (to be of service to family, community, and nature). The different rituals in movement, as performed in the tembuchakua, help people to learn and practice these values, and in the successful performance of a wedding, individuals perform what it means to be part of their community.

The first procession takes place after the mass: the entire wedding party walks to the groom's home (fig. 4b.2). After the first meal of the celebrations (be it breakfast or lunch), the generation of the groom's parents organizes a second procession to accompany the bride and her wedding party, and the godparents and their wedding party, to their respective homes. Ritual drinking may start at this time.[5] The bride and groom are separated for most of the day and will not be together again until the kamata is served at the godparents' house. Each household group is responsible for the part of the celebration that takes place at their home. During the third procession, the groom's relatives dance through the streets while carrying food as gifts (meat, corn, etc.) to the respective homes of the bride and godparents (fig. 4b.5). The fourth instance of ritual in movement is when the young female relatives of the groom and godparents take the ribbons to the bride and prepare her for the kamataru niani (figs. 4b.6 and 4b.7). The wind band accompanies each procession, and as soon as the group arrives at their destination (be it the godparents' home or the bride's home), they must dance to a song.

After the bride is ready with her ribbon-filled, floor-length braids, the young relatives of the groom and godparents prepare to dance through the streets of Angahuan. This event is called uarhantsani, which means to dance through the streets during a wedding. The uarhantsani is a great example of symmetry among P'urhépecha cultural practices. The dance is organized in two columns of dancers facing each other (fig. 5.2). One column starts moving to surround the other. After they return to their original places, the other column does the same thing. At the beginning of the evening, the lines are kept separate and tidy. But as the evening progresses, people start running, teasing, and

Fig. 5.4 The papu. October 2009.

breaking the lines for fun. The dance might last up to four hours. By the end, some of the older dancers may be drunk or tipsy. For the three to four hours that the dance might last, the wind band follows the group and plays almost continuously (and this is after playing for most of the day already!). The bride's young relatives only dance if the bride's family has hired a band; if not, they do not participate.[6] If the bride's family cannot hire a band for the whole day (the cost of which might be over $10,000 MXN, roughly $1,000 USD in 2009), they might hire the band for the dance only.

154   CREATING CULTURE, PERFORMING COMMUNITY

After the dance comes one of the last rituals in movement: the papu (fig. 5.4). The term papu can refer to a song (an abajeño), a person, or a chair—or all three at once. The papu-chair is decorated with gifts—mainly kitchenware (brooms, pots and pans, comales, grinding stones) that are tied to the chair in an artistic manner. The chair is also decorated with ribbons and balloons, which sometimes cover the gifts. The chair is quite heavy, so one of the sons of the new wedding godparents' wedding godparents is responsible for carrying the papu.[7] The man covers his head with a scarf or sweatshirt and paints his face with soot. When the papu has been fully assembled, the papu-person dances to the papu song, and, by playing pranks on the onlookers, he becomes a trickster. The papu-chair-person opens the procession and dances from the godparents' house to the groom's house and, finally, to the bride's home. Sometimes the dance is more like running through the streets than following any particular steps; as far as I could tell, there are no specific steps for the papu dance. As soon as they arrive at the bride's home, the whole party dances to the papu song one last time. The man carrying the papu is relieved of his burden, and the papu-chair is carefully stored away.

Of the different rituals in movement, the uarhantsani and the papu are the most symbolically rich and complex. Some of my research collaborators explained to me that the uarhantsani might be a fertility ritual because the groom's young relatives, mainly his sisters but also brothers and close relatives, dance with dolls tied to their backs (fig. 5.3). I asked my collaborators about the significance of the dolls. While they were not entirely sure what they meant, they believed that the dolls tied to their backs brought the newlyweds good luck.

One of my collaborators, Agustín, explained that in the misa kuani's traditional format, the uarhantsani was supposed to end with the gifting of bread dolls in the shape of children to the bride and a rope or embroidered napkin to the groom. The bride's and groom's siblings, mainly the sisters, were supposed to give a piece of clothing and make the bride or groom carry the childlike figure made with bread. According to Agustín, this was a way of telling the newlyweds, "Aquí esta el deseo de que tengas a tus hijos" ("Here is the wish/hope that you may have children"). The figure of the child was then tied with a kuanindikua to the bride's back. The groom's gift of rope or napkin also has symbolic meanings. As Angahuan is mainly a forested community, the rope represents the act of the man going to the forest to get wood, and the embroidered napkins reference him taking his ichuskuta to eat while working in the forest. The uarhantsani ends with the bride and groom dancing with their gifts. In all the weddings I attended, this final dance was not performed. As I was informed, it does still occur at some weddings, but it is rare.

According to my research collaborators, some of the characteristics of the uarhantsani have changed a lot. In the past, the bride's relatives did not dance, but now, if there is a band, they can dance (e.g., for Chucha's wedding, my host sisters hired a wind band so they could dance). While everybody is allowed to dance, only the groom's relatives are responsible to wish fertility to the newlyweds. Agustín told me that during the wedding of a female cousin, he tried to carry a doll for the dance but was told he could not do so, as that was the role of the groom's relatives. In addition, the dolls the groom's relatives carry on their backs used to be made of bread and dressed as little children (León [1889] 1982; Lumholtz 1904), but now the dolls are market-bought plastic dolls (fig. 5.3).

Drinking is also part of the ritual. The groom's close relatives must carry enough alcohol to give to everybody who wants to drink and dance. As children also participate, some of the older dancers tend to stay sober to help keep control and make sure everything goes well. These dancers are also the ones who direct where the group must dance next. The uarhantsani is an opportunity for young people to flirt with each other (see chap. 2 for courtship rituals that are part of bigger events) as well as a space where tensions may arise. During the dance, young people who do not get along may "bump" against each other or throw tequila "by mistake" at somebody—as I witnessed in several of the uarhantsani I attended. While I have not heard of uarhantsani that ended in a fight, during the dance, tensions may increase setting the stage for future confrontations.

The ritual dancing through the streets is rich in symbolism and shows how many different P'urhépecha values are (re)enacted, formed, and negotiated. It also supports the creation and strengthening of new social networks and inscribes the participants into the communal cultural fabric. The first layer of this ritual is the union of three families—the groom's, the bride's, and the wedding godparents'—into one. While only the relatives of the groom and the godparents participate in the uarhantsani, by dancing at the bride's house, they are performing the inclusion of the families. For me, this event was important because in all the weddings I attended as a relative of the groom and therefore a participant in the uarhantsani, I was able to establish new friendships with the groom's or the godparents' relatives with whom I was not familiar. This was not limited by my status as a turisï, but I noticed that while my host sisters knew some of the godparents' relatives, as was the case at Joel's and Daniela's wedding, they created new bonds of friendship or an acknowledgment of that relationship with the godparents' relatives by dancing. Thus, the first symbolic layer not only signals the formation of a new social network but also helps friends and relatives to form new relationships with the newlyweds' and godparents'

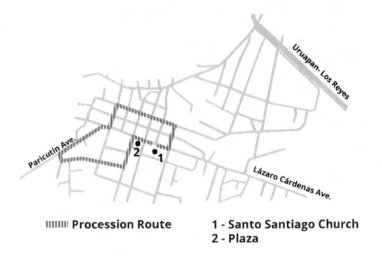

Fig. 5.5 Map of communal processions. Map prepared by Yuiza Martínez-Rivera.

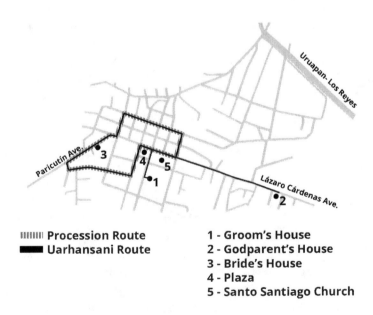

Fig. 5.6 Map of Daniela and Joel's uarhantsani. Map prepared by Yuiza Martínez-Rivera.

families. The new social network reinforces the old ones, and it is through the performance of the uarhantsani that the social networks have meaning.

Like all the movement-related rituals during a misa kuani, the dance through the streets has three focal points: the groom's home, the bride's home, and the godparents' home. However, while the groom's and godparents' young relatives must dance at these three locations, they must also follow the traditional paths of community-wide religious and military processions that culminate in the plaza (fig. 5.5). Therefore, the second symbolic layer of the dance inserts the new social network into the larger social-communal fabric (fig. 5.6). The plaza is where many rituals and celebrations take place and also serves as the starting and ending point for the kurpiticha, the pastorelas, processions for saints (San Isidro, Santo Santiago), and the military parade commemorating the anniversary of Mexican Independence on September 16. This is why arriving at the plaza and dancing there is a key feature of the uarhantsani. By dancing on the streets and following the traditional communal paths for processions, the participants of this ritual are performing not only their membership in their families but also their membership in the community, thereby integrating the newly formed family into Angahuan's social fabric.

The papu is an interesting part of the wedding (fig. 5.7). As mentioned, the papu can be a decorated and gift-covered chair, a song, or a person—it can be these three things separately or together. The papu is the last ritual in movement to be performed during the wedding, and it is fitting that it is a gift-giving ritual as well. The papu ritual, similar to the exchange of gifts in the afternoon, serves as a way to create new social networks and reaffirm old ones based on the practice of reciprocity and te toca. The papu also helps extend the social relationships of the newlyweds to wider networks (such as the wedding godparents of the new wedding godparents) and provides a way to share the costs of organizing and performing a wedding beyond the main participants (groom, bride, and wedding godparents).

Rituals in movement, therefore, have different functions. By dividing the different rituals among social groups, people are reminded or taught how to behave in ritual contexts based on their social position and ideas of te toca. For example, by participating in the rituals that te toca, people learn the value of kaxumbekua (to behave honorably) and jakajkukua (to follow the rules of nature and the community). P'urhépecha values of solidarity and reciprocity, such as anchikuarhua (service), are performed in a dramatic fashion, which also help the negotiation and creation of new social networks as well as reinforcing the old ones. By moving through the community, participants are inscribing not only themselves but also the newlyweds into the communal fabric by

Fig. 5.7 Newlyweds with their papu. January 2010.

following some of their main values. In this sense, and similar to the pilgrimage experience of the community members of Pomacanchi (Mendoza 2010), the people of Angahuan (re)create their community through the visual, auditory, and kinesthetic experience of movement.

Rituals of Controlled Violence

Some of the final ritual acts that occur during the wedding are those of controlled violence. I use the term rituals of controlled violence to refer to those

Fig. 5.8 Daniela and Joel's kanarperakua. October 2009.

rituals that, through the performance of controlled violence, aid in the formation and negotiation of new social networks. According to David I. Kertzer (1988, 131), "Rituals can provide an important safety valve for political tensions." Rituals, in this sense, help to restore order and, in some cases, maintain the status quo. Stanley Brandes (1988, 2), for example, explored how fiestas in the P'urhépecha community of Tzintzuntzan, while seemingly chaotic and formless, "promote order and social control." The main ritual of controlled violence during the wedding is the kanarperakua, an event in which the groom's and bride's young relatives "wrestle" while presenting gifts to the bride and groom. A person attending their first misa kuani might find the kanarperakua to be a chaotic, out-of-control event. But the kanarperakua is tightly controlled and monitored by older relatives who make sure chaos does not erupt. If we argue that during the kanarperakua the participants are in a liminal stage, and that the kanarperakua provides a space where rules and regulations are suspended, but as Victor Turner (1967, 106) argues, even in this stage, "liberty has fairly narrow limits."

John H. McDowell (2002, 19) describes violence as "a communicative exchange between two parties, sometimes unilateral, sometimes mutual, in which destruction of property and infliction of physical harm (sometimes unto death) is the essential mode of signification." Moreover, "violent behavior... establishes a common frame of interaction while pointing to perceptions of structural discontinuities" (2002, 20). Regarding the kanarperakua, the exchange is between two or more people and is intended more to embarrass than cause physical harm. My research collaborators explained that the kanarperakua may become violent, which is why older relatives monitor the event. But more than the actual act of controlled violence, one of the principal aspects of this type of ritual in P'urhépecha culture is that people practice how to properly behave and successfully engage in gift giving and exchanges. In addition to contributing to the creation and negotiation of the newlyweds' new social network, ritualized controlled violence highlights the practice of reciprocity and allows participants to learn and practice two of their main values: jakajkukua (to follow the rules of nature and the community) and p'urhekujkua (to defend their community and P'urhépecha culture with a warrior spirit).

The kanarperakua occurs after the papu arrives at the bride's house. The term kanarperakua refers to the act of presenting gifts to the bride and groom. Gift giving in Angahuan follows a particular set of rules: at some events, one cannot present gifts to one's relatives but only to his or her spouse. For example, the wedding kanarperakua is an exchange of gifts from the bride's relatives to the groom and vice versa. The celebration of the kanarperakua is important because gifts made by the young relatives of the newlyweds are *only* presented during then. If there is no kanarperakua, the newlyweds' young relatives do not present their gifts. I attended a wedding where the kanarperakua was not performed, and my host sisters returned home with their gifts for the bride (we were relatives of the groom, hence nos tocaba give gifts to the bride).

While I observed the kanarperakua at other events—in August 2011, when Carmen and Juan (two of Na Juana and Ta Emiliano's wedding godchildren) were cargueros for the celebrations of the Assumption of the Virgin—the principal difference is that the wedding kanarperakua is accompanied by a moment of ritualized controlled violence, called either luchpani or kamandini. Luchpani translates to "wrestle" (lucha) and refers to the wrestling match between the groom's and the bride's relatives. Kamandini translates to "carrying/hugging the bride" ("cargando a la novia") (fig. 5.9). The bride's relatives must luchpani with the groom, and the groom's relatives must kamandini the bride. After the relatives of the bride and groom present their gifts and dance with either the bride or groom, the gift is taken from the bride and groom (depending on the type of gift), and the luchpani or kamandini begins.

This event is monitored by a group of older relatives who stop the ritual immediately if they see it is beginning to get out of control. As I saw at Daniela

Fig. 5.9 Daniela being carried by her new brother-in-law, and Joel (in the green shirt) wrestling with Daniela's relatives. October 2009.

and Joel's wedding, if the older relatives give the command to stop, the band immediately stops playing and the wrestlers stop their "fight." In general, the atmosphere of the kanarperakua and the events that follow is one of happiness, expectation, and goodwill. I have been at weddings where the kanarperakua and therefore the luchpani and the kamandini were not celebrated, as the older relatives felt that the young people were too drunk and that the event might get out of control. I also attended weddings at which the kanarperakua was stopped because the bride's cousins tackled the groom violently, twice—an event that I describe shortly. However, I also attended weddings where the kanarperakua was a fun event wherein the young relatives played with the bride and groom, and everybody was able to present their gifts to the newlyweds. Sometimes, however, people take advantage of the kanarperakua to settle scores with the groom and bride or to express their discontent with the union.

As I noticed at several weddings, even those where the luchpani became a little violent, most of the attendees were laughing and enjoying the celebration.

A research collaborator shared with me that her wedding kanarperakua became somewhat violent: her cousins started fighting with the groom even though the bride and her sisters had told them not to start a fight. In the end, the groom was bleeding and the bride's feet had been stomped on as she tried to defend her husband. Her sisters told her that she should not cry, as that was normal and even expected during the kanarperakua. My collaborator's sisters said that they had had fun during the kanarperakua and knew their male cousin would get violent during the luchpani. The violence was expected and regulated. Although violence is generally not tolerated in Angahuan, many people in the community understand that violence is an integral part of certain events or cultural practices, and, in that context, violence that is monitored and controlled is allowed and even expected. As I discovered during my years in Angahuan, everything has a place and a time, including violence.[8]

The key feature during the luchpani and the kamandini is that the bride and groom are not alone in the "fight" with the relatives of their new spouse. Their family members will support and defend them during the encounter. At Yennifer and Luis's wedding (Yennifer is Na Juana and Ta Emiliano's niece), I was with one of the bride's older cousins (Agustín) and her younger brother (Jesús). The papu had arrived, and everything was in place to start the kanarperakua. The ritual began as expected; people were having fun and presenting their gifts. As Agustín and Jesús prepared to dance with Luis, they discussed their plans to tackle him. Jesús went first. After dancing for a little while with his new brother-in-law, he moved in, grabbed Luis by his waist, and "body-slammed him lucha libre–style." Luis lay on the floor until his relatives picked him up. Everybody was laughing and praising Jesús for his mastery of the luchpani. Luis was apparently hurt and did not want to continue the kanarperakua. While his relatives tried to convince him to continue dancing, Yennifer danced with several of her husband's relatives. As soon as Luis agreed to continue the kanarperakua, Agustín walked forward to offer his gift and participate in the luchpani. After a minute of dancing with Luis, Agustín made his move. As Jesús had done, Agustín grabbed Luis by the waist and slammed him into the concrete floor. This time, Luis had had enough. The kanarperakua was officially canceled, and the last set of rituals (the crowning of the newlyweds) was not performed.

At the end of the kanarperakua, I asked Agustín and Jesús about what had happened and why they had tackled Luis. Agustín explained that it was important that Luis's family know that Yennifer is not alone and she has family to protect her. Agustín said that Luis got hurt because his relatives did not protect him like they were supposed to do. As I have seen at other weddings, the bride's and groom's relatives defend them during the luchpani or kamandini,

PERFORMING COMMUNITY

ensuring that the event does not turn violent and the newlyweds do not get hurt. At this wedding, the groom was not protected by his family and, consequently, got hurt.

The kanarperakua has at least two distinct functions: to help control possible future violence and to further establish the bonds of reciprocity and social networks that have been created during the many rituals celebrated over the first two days of the misa kuani. One aspect of the luchpani and the kamandini is to test the strength of both families and to signal that neither the bride nor the groom is alone: they have a network of people willing to defend them. This is especially important given the high incidence of family violence in the community and P'urhépecha area in general (Hernández Dimas 2004; Huacuz Elías 2009). A week after Yennifer and Luis's wedding, Luis got drunk, became violent, and hurt Yennifer. As they were at her parents' home, her family intervened and defended her. The violence was controlled from the beginning, and her family monitored the situation to make sure he did not become violent again (however, they divorced several years later).

Another way to understand the kanarperakua, along with the luchpani and the kamandini, is to conceptualize the luchpani and the kamandini as events that help formalize relationships based on the practice of reciprocity and the idea of te toca. As discussed previously, the central component of the kanarperakua is the exchange of gifts. If the kanarperakua is not performed, the exchange of gifts between the newlyweds and their young relatives does not take place. Therefore, we can understand the luchpani and the kamandini as two instances that reinforce the exchange of gifts and strengthen relationships being created and performed. Chapter 3 explored how social networks and the practice of reciprocity, as influenced by ideas of te toca, must be performed. During the luchpani and the kamandini, social networks are performed (signifying who is a relative of the bride and groom, whose social network is stronger, etc.). The practice of reciprocity and te toca thereby signals a person's position inside a particular social network (signifying who must give gifts to whom, who must defend whom, etc.), but it also helps negotiate and create the newlyweds' new social network. Therefore, during the kanarperakua and as an example of rituals of controlled violence, the different families involved, specifically the groom's and bride's families, are incorporated (but with a warning) into a single network through the practice of reciprocity.

Rituals of controlled violence exist in liminal spaces where regulated violence may occur. The point of the ritual is not to cause bodily harm but to disrupt the established order—although, in some cases, people are harmed. Rituals of controlled violence may also be regarded in the Bakhtinian sense as

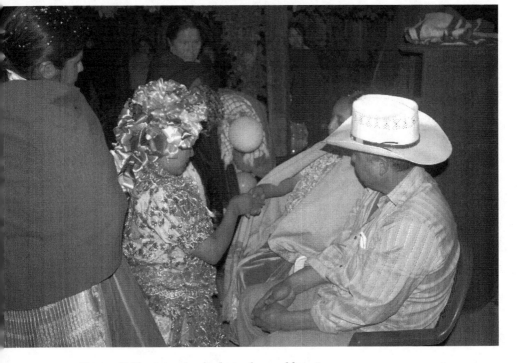

Fig. 5.10 Bride giving thanks during her wedding. January 2010.

a pressure valve that allows tensions to lessen, thereby maintaining harmony and order in the community. Rituals of controlled violence can also serve, as during a wedding, to highlight gift exchanges, help incorporate and reaffirm social networks, and show the strength and force of particular social networks. Furthermore, these rituals of controlled violence, with specific rules of engagement, are mainly performed by young people who use them to learn and practice p'urhekujkua and jakajkukua.

Relationship-Formalizing Rituals

The third type of ritual form, relationship-formalizing rituals, includes the most private and exclusive events of the misa kuani and helps consolidate the social networks being created that day. Relationship-formalizing rituals are characterized by the performance of ritual speeches and acknowledgments of the people who participated and helped during the wedding. During the misa kuani, the first two ritual forms—rituals in movement and rituals of controlled violence—help create the newlyweds' larger social network, which consists mainly of their extended families. Relationship-formalizing rituals, however, establish the newlyweds' immediate social network. During this ritual, the last one of the day, the newlyweds are formally presented as a married couple, signaling the end of the day's celebrations. Through the different relationship-formalization rituals, participants learn and practice kaxumbekua (to behave honorably, as a person of respect) and are admonished to follow jakajkukua (to believe in P'urhépecha worldviews and follow the rules of nature and the community) and anchikuarhua (to be of service to family, community, and nature).

The first relationship-formalizing ritual and the most important of the rituals celebrated during the day is the kamataru niani. The kamataru niani is celebrated at the home of the wedding godparents and is a very private event.[9] After the bride's floor-length braids are prepared (fig. 4b.7), the wedding god-parents' relatives go to the groom's house to pick up the groom and his family. From there, they walk to the bride's house to gather her and her relatives. Everyone then congregates at the godparents' house where milk-based kamata is served to everybody. While the guests take their kamata, the bride, groom, their parents, and the godparents adjourn to another room or private space. During this event, everyone involved is either seated or kneeling. For Chucha and José's wedding, for example, their godparents had prepared an altar with chairs in the middle of their inner patio. The godparents sat beside Chucha and José for the ritual. The Diosïri uandarhi (a person that speaks of God) then made Chucha and José exchange their cups of kamata to symbolize their commitment to each other.[10]

During the ritual, the Diosïri uandarhi talks to the newlyweds about their responsibilities as a married couple and gives advice to the parents and god-parents. The speeches are improvised, and the themes and topics vary from person to person.[11] Ta Manuel Sosa has several recordings of different Diosïri uandarhicha. One was made by an older man who worked in the mountains and whose speech was colored by nature metaphors and images. Ta Manuel told me that while the practice is still central to weddings in Angahuan, less people practice the craft of the Diosïri uandarhi; if the wedding godparents forget to procure a Diosïri uandarhi, they may choose somebody else who is at the celebration.[12]

Although I was unable to witness or acquire a recording of a Diosïri uan-darhi, during the summer of 2011, I spoke to Na Dionisia Rita Toral about her role as a Diosïri uandarhi.[13] Na Dionisia told me that while she knows what she wants to tell the newlyweds, she does not prepare a speech beforehand. When she is invited as a Diosïri uandarhi, she encourages newlyweds to be smart and mature about their relationship and to work so they have a successful marriage

166   CREATING CULTURE, PERFORMING COMMUNITY

that does not end in divorce.[14] Because she is a devout Catholic, she told me that her speeches are colored by her faith. She highlights the importance of God and his love and encourages newlyweds to make time to pray, go to church, and read the Bible. She also urges them to work through their problems in peaceful ways, to refrain from using violence, and to talk with each other and look for help if the problem is too complicated. She tells them to go to their godparents for help and counsel. Her married experience was a happy one, so she tells them about what she and her late husband used to do to maintain a happy marriage. She encourages the newlyweds to be considerate with one another, to be patient, "que haya amor, que haya respeto" ("let there be love, let there be respect"), and that they should love their relatives, their parents, and their elders. She also talks about gender equality, explaining that a woman is not less than a man and that the husband should respect his wife. She highlights the unity of the family, not only the nuclear family but also the extended family. She talks about how the couple's well-being also affects the extended family. During her speeches, Na Dionisia shares her wisdom and teaches new couples to follow the four P'urhépecha values discussed in this chapter.

In addition to the ritualized speech by the Diosïri uandarhi, the bride's and groom's parents formalize their compadrazgo with the wedding godparents. When the Diosïri uandarhi is finished, they signal the start of the next ritual "bueno ya pueden hacerse compadres" ("well, now you can become godparents"). According to Ta Manuel, the people in Angahuan already use a ritual formula to become compadres. This formula, with slight variations, is used for all of the different events involving compadrazgo (baptisms, confirmations, and first communions). If this formula is not uttered, the people involved do not become compadres. The formula goes something like this:

> De aquí en adelante ya vamos a ser compadres. Usted disculpe si el día de mañana me lo encuentro por la calle y si de un de repente no lo saludo.
>
> From henceforth we will be godparents. Please forgive me if tomorrow we cross paths and I do not greet you.

After this phrase is uttered, the person being addressed responds with "mamguani," which means "likewise," and they shake hands. As greeting people in the streets in Angahuan is a key feature of the community's social norms, this formula serves as an anticipated apology that aims to avoid future confrontations and help maintain social cohesion. As Ta Manuel told me, this event helps expand the godparents' social network. In some weddings, the extended family is included, mainly the close blood relatives and the newlyweds' baptism, first communion, and confirmation godparents, but this varies according to each case and the families involved.

After finalizing the kamataru niani ritual, the entire party leaves for the groom's home, where they eat more churipo and korunda. Afterward, the bride and her relatives are taken to the bride's home to wait for the papu, while the groom stays at his home with his relatives.

The blessings and coronation of the newlyweds occur in the bride's house after the papu, uarhantsani, and kanarperakua. During the blessing, an informal yet important part of the celebration, the bride and groom go to each of their relatives, offer their hand, and bow their head or kneel (fig. 5.10). The relative must then offer some words of wisdom and their blessing. The bride and groom must respond by saying Diosï Meiamu uajia (thank you) or a similar phrase. The celebration continues while the bride and groom give thanks and receive blessings, with music playing, people dancing or eating, and so on.

Cultural and social acknowledgment is important in Angahuan. In many rituals and celebrations, there must be an acknowledgment of all the people involved. In the case of the misa kuani, people expect to be acknowledged by the bride and groom and given thanks. In some cases, the bride and groom give their hand to everybody present, as they do not want to forget or offend anyone. At Yennifer's wedding, an aunt led her to the people to whom she had to give thanks and ask for a blessing.[15] Yennifer came to give me thanks, as I had been cake godmother. She offered her hand, which I took; I stared at her and asked, "What am I supposed to do?" Yennifer smiled and said, "I cannot tell you what to do or say, so just say something." I laughed and thought of what I could say. Finally, I wished her good luck and that her marriage be a blessed one. She bowed her head and gave me thanks. Her aunt then took her to the next person she had to thank. Luis followed suit. I noticed that neither Yennifer nor Luis went to their peers to receive blessings, but only to their elders, that is, their parents' generation. I believe the bride gave me thanks because I had been the cake godmother.

This offering of appreciation and receiving of blessings, while a somewhat informal ritual, is quite significant. By going from person to person and showing respect to each one, the bride and groom acknowledge their old and new family members and continue the process of creating their new social network. For example, when my host sister Inés and her husband Gume baptized one of their sons, Inés and her sisters went to all of the baptism godparents' relatives, offering them their hand and thanking them for accepting the compadrazgo. Inés's sister Tomi told me that if this is not done, the compadrazgo is not official.[16] Therefore, giving the hand, bowing the head, giving thanks, and

Fig. 5.11 Pablo and Lisa crowned at the end of their wedding. April 2009.

receiving blessings have at least two main purposes: showing respect that helps consolidate new relationships and reiterating that these new relationships are now part of a larger kin configuration.

After the bride and groom have presented their respects, given their thanks, and received their blessings, they are crowned with kanakuecha.[17] Days before the wedding, relatives of the groom must have commissioned two kanakuecha, two bread necklaces, and two pieces of bread in the shape of a hand or foot from one of the town's bakers. The bread necklaces are small bread ribbons, which are then tied to a string.[18] The groom's aunts are in charge of ordering the kanakuecha, and they also direct the bride and groom to the middle of the patio or a central space where the celebration is being held. First, the bread necklaces are hung around their necks. Next, the groom and the bride are crowned with the kanakuecha, and then they are presented with the bread shapes. Everybody claps and cheers for the newlyweds, who are then escorted to their wedding bedchamber. After that, in most cases, the celebration continues late into the night.

Although the kanakuecha is an important part of a P'urhépecha wedding, it is not always celebrated—usually because the groom's relative in charge of commissioning and preparing the kanakuecha forgot or did not want to do it. As my research collaborators explained, while the newlyweds' relatives might be offended by the absence of the kanakuecha, there are no major repercussions beyond gossip and some slight social exclusion. But with the placing of the kanakuecha, the official wedding day rituals are concluded. The next day, there are other rituals, but only for the parents of the newlyweds and the wedding godparents, and those are also examples of relationship-formalizing rituals (more on this in the conclusion).

Relationship-formalizing rituals are the most private and exclusive among the three rituals discussed here. One of its key elements are the ritualized speeches, such as the one by the Diosïri uandarhi or the one to become compadres. While speeches are not scripted, they follow a cultural-linguistic pattern that frames them as a ritual speech. Another important element of relationship-formalizing rituals is the public acknowledgment of participation and aid during a celebration, either as a participant or when accepting a compadrazgo. Body movement—mainly the bowing of the head, kneeling, or asking for someone's hand—is another important framing device of this ritual, as it signals appreciation of the blessings received and recognizes the honor the person has bestowed on the receivers. Relationship-formalizing rituals are closely tied to the practices of reciprocity; if the ritual is not performed, the act of dar y recibir is broken, and the participants do not become a full person, a k'uiripu (Jacinto Zavala [1983] 1997). As the most private and important ritual mode, relationship-formalizing rituals encompass all the values shared in this chapter (kaxumbekua, jakajkukua, anchikuarhua, and p'urhekujkua), as individuals are encouraged and taught how to properly behave based on core P'urhépecha values and worldviews.

Taking the Confetti Trail Back Home

By following various confetti trails, this chapter has explored the three main ritual forms in P'urhépecha culture—rituals in movement, rituals of controlled violence, and relationship-formalizing rituals. Each one can help us unpack and highlight the different ways in which people in Angahuan, and more generally in the P'urhépecha area, organize, perform, create, and practice their main values through ritual performances. And while these three ritual forms occur together in the misa kuani, I have seen them performed separately at other events. For example, at baptisms, rituals in movement are performed between the parents' and the baptism godparents' homes. The parents and baptism godparents also perform relationship-formalizing rituals, and, in the case of the celebrations of saints by the cargueros (e.g., the Assumption of the Virgin or the Virgin of Guadalupe), most of the rituals performed are rituals in movement. The kanarperakua is performed during celebrations tied to the cargo system, but only the gift exchange is performed, not the luchpani or kamandini. The kurpiti and the pastorelas are also rituals of controlled violence, as violence, in the form of breaking light bulbs and windows, is expected yet monitored and controlled. Weddings, therefore, provide a unique opportunity and serve as a distinctive event to observe the many different ritual forms in P'urhépecha culture. They also show how some of the principal tenets of P'urhépecha worldviews are taught, practiced, and performed. By engaging in these rituals, individuals in Angahuan perform what it means to be a member of a P'urhépecha community.

As we approach the final chapter of our journey, we will weave the last strand of my argument by looking at the cultural transformation of the tembuchakua. By defining transformation as the simultaneous process of continuity and change, I highlight how cultural transformations follow the internal cultural logic of the community and are influenced by P'urhépecha values and worldviews. By focusing on how people create, curate, and transform their cultural practices, we can understand how they rearticulate and perform their own identity. We will explore all of this while covered in confetti.

Notes

1. SECUPU is composed of Pedro Márquez Joaquín (QEPD), Alicia Lemus, Amaruc Lucas, Néstor Dimas, Abraham Custodio, Juan Carlos Cortés Máximo, Elías Silva, and Celerino Felipe Cruz (who left the group after the initial meetings).

2. The edited volume based on SECUPU's first meeting focusing on juramukua was published in late 2023. See Márquez Joaquín 2023.

3. I would like to clarify that P'urhépecha scholarship has described movement during rituals (see, e.g., Ojeda Dávila 2006), but it is not analyzed as an intrinsic part of rituals in the way that I am proposing.

4. Rituals in movement are not the only way in which P'urhépecha can access, create, and experience their cultural knowledge, but movement is an important component of their cultural practices in general.

5. During my time in Angahuan, the preferred form of drinking was a shot made of tequila and soda. I was told that when a drink has been offered, one must accept it. If a person does not want to drink, a close relative may accept the drink

PERFORMING COMMUNITY

instead or may take the drink and spit it out. It is more appropriate to spit out the drink than to refuse it.

6. In general, the bride's relatives, specifically the bride's young relatives, have hardly any ritual responsibilities during the celebrations, as most of the celebrations are the responsibility of the groom's family and godparents.

7. As an example, in June 2022, two wedding godchildren of Na Juana and Ta Emiliano, Carmen and Juan, were wedding godparents. My host siblings, then, where in charge of preparing the papu, and Pancho carried it, becoming the papu-chair-person.

8. For example, people expect that the kurpite and the pastorelas will be disruptive and in some cases violent, as described in chapter 2. Controlled violence may also be part of the celebrations of Santo Santiago or during the jaripeos.

9. This is the only part of the wedding that I have not seen and likely never will. All of my married research collaborators only witnessed this event at their own weddings. My unmarried collaborators had never seen it, or, if they had, they were too young and did not remember it. I confess that I struggled with the decision to share this ritual, given its private, although not secretive, nature. However, my collaborators gave me permission to share their stories and experiences participating in the kamataru niani.

10. The role of the Diosïri uandarhi is a clear descendant of the pre-Hispanic priest who gave the ritual speeches during the weddings of the nobility in the Tarascan Empire (see Alcalá [1541] 2000; Martínez-Rivera 2020). The Diosïri uandarhi can be a man or a woman; the only qualification is that he or she must be a wise and respected person. The godparents oversee finding a Diosïri uadarhi.

11. The Diosïri uandarhi's speech may not have a structure, but it is framed as ritualized speech. Although I do not have a recording of the event, it would be interesting to analyze the speech to understand the different framing devices.

12. While in Angahuan fewer people practice the craft of the Diosïri uandarhicha, in the neighboring community of San Lorenzo, the craft is highly respected. According to Ta Manuel, some of the most sought-after Diosïri uandarhicha live and perform in that community. There are, however, several recognized Diosïri uandarhicha in Angahuan.

13. Na Dionisia is a passionate and hardworking woman; she is a member of the Council of Elders and one of the cultural and religious pillars of the community. Her late husband, Valente Soto Bravo, was one of the first Indigenous filmmakers in México, a Jefe de Tenencia in the community, and one of the first Indigenous scholars to graduate from the Centro de Cooperación Regional para la Educación de Adultos en América Latina y el Caribe (CREFAL) in 1982. Na Dionisia and her children continue the legacy of their late husband and father.

14. We also discussed the importance of ritual speeches in P'urhépecha culture and how the younger generations of other communities no longer want

the traditional speech, but in Angahuan, the practice is still very much alive. Na Dionisia is extremely aware of the different social problems affecting the community, such as family violence and the fragmentation of families. To help the community, she has tried to convince the priest in Angahuan to create seminars to help prepare couples as Diosïri uandarhicha so they can help younger couples with their marriages. At the time of this writing, these seminars have not been established.

15. Yennifer was raised and lives in Southern California and met her then-husband, Luis, in Angahuan during a visit. While she does understand P'urhépecha, she does not speak it; therefore, her relatives assume that she does not know what to do during certain rituals. At her wedding, older female relatives were always directing her so she could do what was expected of her.

16. In this case, only the parents of the baby who is being baptized utter the traditional formula of anticipated apology.

17. For some people, the kanakua is one of the clearest examples of P'urhépecha culture continuity in the wedding. Other communities, such as Caltzontzin and Nuevo San Juan Parangaricutiro, also use kanakua during the wedding (Ojeda Dávila 2006). One of the earliest mentions of the kanakua in relation to weddings that I have found is León's ([1889] 1982), in 1889, of the celebration of the kanakua the day after the wedding as the exchange of gifts between the groom's and bride's relatives. In 1925, R. Saavedra reported in the *Magazine de Geografía Nacional* that the "Canacua" was still celebrated the day after the religious ceremony, mainly in the communities from the Sierra. But other writers report that the kanakua is celebrated more as a ritual to honor someone who is respected in the community or an important visitor than during the wedding (Alcaraz 1925; Dominguez 1925a, 1925b; Storm 1945; Toor 1925). In Angahuan, the kanakua are used during a wedding and given as gifts to the young men who procured the bull for the Assumption of the Virgin (see chap. 2). While the origin of this ritual may be contested, for some of my research collaborators, it is authentically P'urhépecha.

18. Agustín hypothesizes, although somewhat tentatively, that the necklaces could be an imitation of the wedding lassos used during the Catholic mass. He mentioned that people might have liked that idea and started making the bread lassos for the kanakua, as they could not afford the store-bought lasso.

Fig. 6.1 Daniela and Joel's white wedding. October 2009.

6

Transforming the Tembuchakua

January and early February 2010 were packed with celebrations, as Lent was fast approaching and most people in the community had completed their harvest. Every weekend in January, we had weddings, levantamientos (a special celebration in honor of baby Jesus), baptisms, and other community and family events. On the weekend of my going-away dinner at the end of January, there were at least six weddings and even more baptisms, probably setting a record for community-wide celebrations at that time. As I explained earlier in this book, people only attend celebrations based on their position in that particular social network, if les toca. While many of my host family's relatives got married in January 2010, in most cases, we were distant relatives of the bride or were not close to any of the families involved in the wedding; therefore, our responsibilities were limited, as was our participation in those weddings. For example, we took soaps to many brides-to-be on the eve of their weddings but had no other responsibilities during their tembuchakua. Among the many weddings celebrated that month, however, we were close relatives of the bride at only two and were expected to participate in those celebrations. In both cases, I offered to be the wedding photographer, and I was asked to be the cake godmother at one and ring godmother at the other. One of those weddings was Yennifer and Luis's, a misa kuani that began with the white/mestizo wedding. The second wedding, Paulina and Mateo's, was different: they celebrated the sivil kuambuni and the misa kuani on the same day. As described in chapters 4 and 5, while certain rituals are expected at a wedding (such as the exchange of gifts and the kamataru niani), the families involved decide which rituals are to be celebrated and how. If the groom's and bride's families decide to celebrate

175

176   CREATING CULTURE, PERFORMING COMMUNITY

the misa kuani and the sivil kuambuni on the same day, this will determine which rituals are performed.

On this final part of our journey, I present my last interwoven argument / axis / point of encounter: the tembuchakua provides a cultural template that allows for the transformation of P'urhépecha culture. Cultural transformations, as I observed in Angahuan, are not "dramatic changes in form or appearance" (as defined in Oxford Languages online dictionary) or instances of A becoming B. They are rather a simultaneous process of continuity and change influenced by ideas of innovation and expectations. I also bring together the other main threads discussed throughout the book, mainly the practice of te toca and how people in Angahuan create their culture and perform their ideas of belonging to their community. Therefore, this final chapter weaves together all of the different threads/stories discussed so far to showcase how people in Angahuan create, curate, perform, and transform their cultural practices.

As I mentioned in the introduction, during my time in Angahuan in 2009–2010, I was able to fully document four weddings. Those weddings, while sharing the three ritual forms described in chapter 5, were all different. Therefore, in this chapter, I use those four weddings to explore the process of cultural transformation. I begin with Daniela and Joel's white/mestizo wedding. This type of wedding includes some of the most common elements of Mexican non-Indigenous weddings: the waltz, the cake, the champagne toast, la víbora de la mar, and the bouquet and garter toss. By analyzing the white/mestizo wedding, we will see the process of customization of foreign traditions into Angahuan P'urhépecha culture. Next, I present a wedding that did not conform to expectations of what a misa kuani "should be" in Angahuan. Gabriela and Jonathan's wedding, however, is a clear example of the continuation of certain preconquest P'urhépecha wedding practices. Then, using Chucha and José's wedding, I elaborate on the community's recent tendency to celebrate the sivil kuambuni and the misa kuani on the same day. I end the chapter by discussing a recent trend of reviving older ways of celebrating the misa kuani. These four different weddings showcase the agency people in Angahuan have over their culture and further elucidate how ideas of te toca, expectations, and values influence the transformation of Angahuan's vernacular cultural practices.

Cultural Transformations in Angahuan

One of the interwoven arguments in this book suggests that cultural transformations are influenced by cultural ideas and practices tied to each community. Previous chapters have described how the wedding, as an example of vernacular cultural practices, is organized and how people in Angahuan signal their belonging to their community through the performance of the different rituals. I also highlighted how, through the performance of each ritual form, they practice some of their main values and learn what it means to be a k'uiripu. In this framework, transformation is a crucial component of these processes, as it is the transformation of cultural vernacular practices that brings them to life and makes them relevant to current and future generations. Additionally, transformations, as I witnessed in Angahuan, are composed of two separate yet simultaneous processes: continuity and change.[1]

Throughout this book, I have relied on the concept of customization as an alternative to the idea of change (see chap. 4). The concept of customization, as articulated by Greene (2009), elucidates the internal cultural logic of a particular group that is in the process of customizing something. However, Greene mainly focuses on the process of customizing foreign cultural practices. And while the people in Angahuan have customized foreign practices into the tembuchakua (such as the sivil kuambuni and the white/mestizo wedding), they also customize local cultural practices. This dual process of customizing foreign and local cultural practices allows for the continuation of P'urhépecha cultures.

The way I see continuity at play in Angahuan is not merely through a direct connection to the past of a particular cultural practice (although in some instances, that may be the case) but rather through a process of traditionalization. Engaging with the work of Charles Briggs (1996) and Jason Jackson (2008), who move away from constructivist views of the "invention of traditions," we can understand traditionalization as "the ways that all people connect with (and create/recreate) their own understanding of culture, the past, and tradition through every day, but often artful and powerful uses of language, social action, and material culture in situated moments of human encounter" (Jackson 2008, 14). Traditionalization, therefore, can be understood as a creative and constant process of interpreting and performing local cultural practices. Some of the ritual events in the tembuchakua have preconquest roots, such as the movement between the newlyweds' houses, the speeches by a Diosïri uandarhi, the food, and the types of gifts. Others have a more recent past, such as the kanakua and the sivil kuambuni. The idea of tradition provides a framework within which to create and re-create an understanding of a particular cultural practice and also serves as a "core evaluative standard to be used in interpreting both ritual practices and everyday community life." (Jackson 2008, 13). Each culture has its specific mechanisms and cultural metacommunication devices that will distinguish particular cultural practices (i.e., genres) (Bauman 1977). Those framing devices, and what is considered the correct performance of a particular cultural practice, are "situated within and rendered meaningful with reference to relevant contexts" (Bauman 1977, 27). Therefore, the idea of tradition provides a framing device and, as such, a means of evaluating the performance.

In their chapter "Innovation as a Key Feature of Indigenous Ways of Learning: Individual and Communities Generating Knowledge," Francisco J. Rosado-May et al. (2020) argue that Indigenous Knowledge Systems can help and support schooling and general education systems. The authors explore the concept of innovation and how it relates to Indigenous ways of knowledge creation and learning. They challenge narrow understandings of Indigenous cultures and ways of knowing that portray them as static and unchanging and highlight the dynamism and constant innovation of Indigenous cultures. Building on Little Bear's idea of "dynamic without motion," they state that "cultural practices are constantly in motion, with moments in which an untrained eye might not see any change" (2020, 83). Moreover, Indigenous ways of knowledge creation and learning are built around doing: actively participating in everyday practices and special communal events. Constant innovative change, the authors claim, "is fundamental to the very existence, continuance, innovation, and renewal of cultural patterned behavior itself" (84). Those innovative changes, which may not be noticeable to outsiders, are guided by Native wisdom, which "provides guidance for the future" (83). Hence, cultural transformations/innovations, as a simultaneous process of continuity and change, are both necessary and intrinsic for the continuation and flourishing of Indigenous cultures.

In the case of P'urhépecha cultures, some of the factors that influence cultural transformations are the practice of te toca (chap. 3), ideas of creativity and aesthetics (chap. 4), and the principal values that influence P'urhépecha worldview (chap. 5). I would also add the idea of expectations and how expectations influence and guide the creation of culture as well as reflect specific ideas of what it means to belong to a community. In the case of Angahuan, expectations—se espera, se supone (it's expected, it's presupposed)—greatly influence how cultural practices are organized, performed, and transformed. Expectations can be seen as a form of social control. During my research, I frequently heard comments like the following: "X event is supposed to occur in this manner"; "Y is supposed to happen like this."[2] In general, expectations influence how an event will be organized and performed. In Angahuan, people expect to see a traditional event, but they also want to see something grander and more elaborate than previous performances. In this regard, expectations can be considered a central force that encourages the simultaneous process of

Fig. 6.2 Daniela and Joel dancing the waltz. October 2009.

change and continuity in Angahuan and influences the creation of culture and the performance of community.

According to some of my research collaborators, during the economic growth of the 1990s, celebrations in Angahuan became bigger: more music, more food, more alcohol. Other cultural practices that had not happened in years, such as the pastorelas, began to be performed again (as described in chap. 2). Therefore, event expectations increased and changed. In 2010, two of my collaborators, Sergio and Emilia, became cargueros of the Virgin of Guadalupe. At the beginning of the couple's year of service, Sergio told me that a relative commented on what he expected to see in Sergio and Emilia's home during the celebrations of the Virgin. Sergio and Emilia were in a bind. They wanted to organize a simple celebration with all the necessary rituals without going into considerable debt. However, because of the relative's comment, they

180   CREATING CULTURE, PERFORMING COMMUNITY

had to adjust their plans for organizing their service as cargueros to meet the new expectations. Another example of high expectations relates to migrant workers. As was shared with me, and as I witnessed, families of migrant workers are perceived to be economically affluent. Any celebrations in their homes are expected to be plentiful and elaborate.

To showcase the process of cultural transformation, the rest of the chapter focuses on four different wedding styles: a white/mestizo wedding; a wedding that broke with expectations; a sivil kuambuni-misa kuani wedding; and a new "traditional" wedding. Each style performed the many rituals of the wedding in its own way, signaling the family's agency in the decision-making process of organizing a tembuchakua. However, even though families can choose how to organize and celebrate a tembuchakua, they must also contend with familial and communal expectations. Therefore, I show the tembuchakua's transformation and how expectations can affect how a wedding will be performed or how its performance will be judged.

Joel and Daniela's White/Mestizo Wedding and the Customization of *Turisï* Practices

Over one hundred guests arrived at Joel's house during Joel and Daniela's white/mestizo wedding, which occurred directly after mass.[3] The guests were scattered throughout three main areas. The main table was at the home's entrance, under the huge tent that covered the road. All the men sat at three long tables near the main one. Women and children sat on wood benches lined up in front of the entrance and outside under the tent. The wind band played music outside, only taking breaks to eat or drink. The kitchen was run by a contingent of more than thirty women of various ages. There were paranguecha inside and outside the kitchen where women made hot chocolate, ichuskuta, and churipo for lunch. As soon as everybody started sitting down, a group of young women began distributing breakfast, which consisted of a cup of hot chocolate and bread.

After breakfast, the next part of a P'urhépecha wedding in Angahuan involves the groom's family taking the bride, her relatives, and the godparents and their relatives to their respective homes (as described in the interlude). But as Joel and Daniela se casaron de blanco (got married in a white dress, signifying a white/mestizo wedding), we did not take the bride and her family to their homes. Instead, we waited a little while before serving lunch and performing the rituals associated with the white/mestizo wedding.

During breakfast, I noticed that two couples had arrived with presents for the newlyweds. The first couple carried a basket full of kitchenware (pots,

Fig. 6.3 Kneeling and giving thanks. October 2009.

pans, plates, cups, etc.) and a metate (a grinding stone made of volcanic rock). Another couple brought a box full of plates and cups, a basket with buckets, and smaller baskets for ichuskuta. The two couples were Joel's baptism and confirmation godparents. While the lunch of churipo with ichuskuta was being served, one of the older female relatives placed a petate, a straw mat, in the middle of the patio for some of the gifts. The groom, bride, their parents, the wedding godparents, and older close relatives knelt and bowed one by one in front of the gifts and offered their thanks (fig. 6.3). After they finished with the first set of gifts, they repeated the procedure with the second set.[4] During this ritual, the band played outside, and young female relatives served food, cleared the tables, washed dishes, made ichuskuta, and performed other chores. When the ritual was completed, the gifts were put away, the mat was removed from the floor, and the white/mestizo wedding rituals began.

182 CREATING CULTURE, PERFORMING COMMUNITY

All of the rituals were performed under the outside tent. The first event was the waltz (fig. 6.2). The wind band played an arrangement of Johann Strauss's "The Blue Danube." Joel and Daniela danced together first, and then with their parents, wedding godparents, and close older relatives. After the waltz, they played the game la víbora de la mar.[5] This game is popular at weddings in México, but in Angahuan, they put their own spin on it. In turisï weddings, the bride and groom stand on a chair and use the bride's veil to make a "bridge." Players grab each other by the hand or waist to form a "snake." As the music plays, the snake must move faster and faster until everyone is running under the bridge, through tables, around the guests, and so forth; in most cases, people fall or the snake breaks—which is, to some degree, the point of the game. Angahuan's version, however, is a bit more intense, and only the newlyweds' generation plays. Daniela and Joel climbed up on the chairs, and three relatives of each surrounded them, protecting them in the chairs. Two groups, or snakes, were formed: one with Joel's relatives and one with Daniela's. To help the snakes stay together, each person tied a kuanindikua to their waist for the person behind them to hold on to. The band began to play, and the snake made up of Daniela's family began to run between the newlyweds. The snake quickly surrounded Joel and tried to push him off the chair so they could take his shoes (that is why three relatives were surrounding and protecting him). By the end, Joel had lost his shoes. Then it was Daniela's turn. The snake made up of Joel's relatives was just as fierce as Daniela's relatives. At one point, both snakes surrounded Daniela and Joel, and both lost their shoes (fig. 6.4). Everybody was laughing and enjoying themselves. By the end of the game, Daniela and some of the relatives had scratches and bruises, but everybody had a great time. To get their shoes back, Daniela and Joel had to dance with the person who had taken them.

After la víbora, Daniela and Joel threw the bouquet and the garter, respectively. The woman who caught the bouquet danced with the man who caught the garter. Next, a group of young female relatives uncorked champagne, and all the guests toasted to Joel and Daniela's health, although there were no speeches (as there would have been at a mestizo wedding). Finally, it was time for the cake. As cake godmother, I had ordered a three-tiered cake with a larger cake on the side. The cake was brought out from its safe place, but before it was cut, some of the relatives began shouting "¡Mordida, mordida!" (Bite, bite!). Joel and Daniela refused at first, then agreed. Their heads were pushed into the cake, and they ended up covered in cake.[6] Laughing, Daniela and Joel left to clean up so I could take photographs of them cutting the cake. With the help of Chucha, Tomi, Pela, and some other cousins, we cut and served the cake, after which, the ceremonies were over and most of the guests left. The procession to take

Fig. 6.4 Playing the víbora de la mar. October 2009.

Daniela, the wedding godparents, and their respective relatives to their homes began. Next, the second type of wedding, the P'urhépecha wedding, would begin (see the interlude and chap. 5 for a detailed description of this event).

My research collaborators told me that casarse de blanco was a relatively new practice that began in the late 1990s, a time of economic expansion and population growth in Angahuan. Electricity service was widely installed in the community, and televisions became affordable. Tomás hypothesized, as did some of my other collaborators, that the white/mestizo wedding is inspired by the popular telenovelas on Mexican television, which romanticized the idea of getting married in a white gown. Tomás remembers that one of his older sisters was among the first in Angahuan to wed in a white gown.

In most P'urhépecha communities, the bride wears a white gown. She might change into the traditional dress, but this depends on the community and the

184   CREATING CULTURE, PERFORMING COMMUNITY

families involved (Ojeda Dávila 2006). In Angahuan, marrying in a white gown is an addition, not a substitution, meaning, if a bride marries in a white gown and the families celebrate rituals associated with the white/mestizo wedding, the bride will later change into a traditional P'urhépecha dress and the rituals associated with a P'urhépecha wedding will be performed.

Getting married in a white gown is now more common in Angahuan, but in 2009–2010, it was considered a sign of a higher socioeconomic status, as a misa kuani that begins with the white/mestizo wedding is more elaborate and expensive. The wedding wardrobe is purchased by the groom's and bride's families (the groom's family buys the bride's attire and vice versa), so both families must be in accord, especially the groom's family, as they carry the larger financial burden during the celebration. I heard of cases where the bride wanted a white dress, but the groom's family could not afford it, in which case either the groom and his family had to work out a deal where each party bought their own clothes or the groom's family had to borrow money to buy the gown. For example, Joel's family could not afford Daniela's gown, so the families agreed that each family would be responsible for their own attire. I have also heard of brides who do not want to marry in a white gown, as in Chucha's case. She did not want to burden her future in-laws, but they wanted her to marry in a white gown and bought the dress for her.

More and more brides in Angahuan are getting married in a white gown, but it is still a personal and familial decision. Some families with more money might decide against a white/mestizo wedding, while families with less money might choose one. Some families might be against the white/mestizo wedding because, as a research collaborator told me, they view it as a sign that the community is losing its traditional way of life. For example, of all the weddings I documented and participated in during my 2009–2010 stay, only two had a white/mestizo wedding. Since then, however, my younger host sisters have all had a white/mestizo wedding compared to the older sisters who had P'urhépecha weddings.

While the white/mestizo wedding could be seen as a move toward modernity within the traditional-modern paradigm, I argue that it is more a process of customization and innovation. During the white/mestizo wedding, the cake, toast, waltz, víbora de la mar, and bouquet and garter toss are visibly turisï. But the way in which those elements are performed remains very much in line with P'urhépecha values, aesthetics, and ritual forms.

One of the clearest examples of customization and innovation during the white wedding is how the víbora de la mar is played (fig. 6.4). As described above, the víbora de la mar in Angahuan becomes a competition between the bride's and groom's young relatives to seize the shoes of the newlyweds and knock them off the chairs. Older relatives of each of the newlyweds protect them from the others. At Daniela and Joel's wedding, la víbora was controlled, but I have seen and heard of weddings in which the game became more violent, to the point that the bride's veil (and, in one case, her dress) was torn apart. In most cases, the bride, groom, and relatives playing the game might have scratches on their faces, arms, and legs, as well as torn clothes and stomped-on feet by the end. One of the most extreme cases I heard of was when the bride fell off the chair and broke her arm. Before the wedding, the bride and groom might talk to their relatives and ask them to control themselves, urging them not to incite violence. I had been told about a groom who asked his relatives not to hurt his bride. As the game became animated, the groom grabbed his bride and left the celebration. Their relatives were in shock, but, after a little while, the wedding resumed in peace.

As performed in Angahuan, the víbora de la mar is an example of ritualized controlled violence and can be considered parallel to the luchpani and the kamandini that are performed during the kanarperakua (see chap. 5). Like the luchpani and the kamandini, la víbora de la mar might seem to be an out-of-control violent affair, but it is closely monitored and controlled by a group of older relatives who, at any sign of violence, signal the band to stop playing, thus ending the game. As soon as people stop, in most cases, they are laughing and enjoying the event. By playing la víbora de la mar similarly to how they perform the luchpani and the kamandini—and not how la víbora is tradition-ally played during turisï weddings—people in Angahuan are customizing a mestizo tradition and making it their own.

The practice of the white/mestizo wedding was created by the younger gen-eration. In addition to the possibility that people wanted to imitate what they saw in telenovelas, the white/mestizo wedding allows for more direct partici-pation of the bride's and groom's generation than the traditional P'urhépecha wedding does. As I described in chapters 2 and 3, different generations in Angahuan do not participate in the same celebrations because people only participate in those that te toca, and only in the way that they are supposed to. The ritual space changes depending on the person's function or role. For example, a mother and daughter might be in the same physical space, but ritualistically, the mother is in another space—for example, drinking and dancing—while the daughter is helping in the kitchen or serving the food that the mother will eat. During a P'urhépecha wedding, the newlyweds' genera-tion has distinct and somewhat limited roles: the young female relatives of the groom and the godparents take ribbons to the bride to prepare her for

Fig. 6.5 Gabriela and Jonathan cutting their wedding cake. October 2009.

the compadrazgo ceremony at the godparents' house, dance during the uarhantsani, and participate in the kanarperakua. In a white/mestizo wedding, the younger generation has a more active role because they get to participate in la víbora de la mar, the toast, the cake, and the bouquet and garter toss. In this sense, traditions associated with a turisï wedding (the cake, the toast, etc.) have been doubly customized. The first level of customization is the P'urhépechization of the traditions, that is, performing foreign practices in a P'urhépecha way. The second level is the appropriation of those practices by and for the newlyweds' younger relatives, which showcases the importance and agency of youth participation in the transformation of P'urhépecha vernacular cultural practices. This first wedding style, therefore, showcases the different levels of customization as part of larger processes of cultural transformations in Angahuan.

Departing from Expectations: Gabriela and Jonathan's Wedding

Of all the weddings I participated in, Gabriela and Jonathan's wedding was the most unusual, even by my turisï standards.[7] My host family and I were not close relatives of either of the newlyweds (and, therefore, Chucha and I were unsure of our role during the misa kuani), and the general organization of the misa kuani departed from expectations. Gabriela and Jonathan were fairly well-off, so people had high expectations of their misa kuani and assumed the wedding would be more elaborated. Their wedding gave me a clearer insight into how people make decisions about organizing and performing the misa kuani and their cultural practices in general.

For several reasons—mainly the availability of the godparents—Gabriela and Jonathan's wedding took place on October 31, the day before Days of the Dead celebrations began. As described in chapter 4, the couple whom Gabriela and Jonathan had wanted as their wedding godparents would not be available until January, and, as Gabriela was pregnant, they could not wait that long. The couple they ended up choosing as godparents were only available the weekend of October 31. I think the fact that the misa kuani took place on October 31 is why it felt so different from other misa kuani I had participated in. As stated in the introduction, people in Angahuan do not celebrate weddings in November to respect Days of the Dead celebrations and remember their dearly departed. Therefore, the fact that the wedding was on the eve of this celebration affected how many people participated in the wedding. Another notable difference was that this misa kuani began at midday: the mass was at noon, rather than seven in the morning. This meant that either most of the rituals would not be performed, as there would not be enough time, or the rituals would be performed incredibly quickly.

As my host family had no close relationship with any of the families involved in this misa kuani, only Chucha and I attended the wedding. Gabriela and Jonathan asked me to be their cake godmother weeks before the wedding (see chap. 4), so even though we were not relatives, I still had some responsibilities. Chucha also had some duties, as she was a friend of Gabriela's, and both participated in the Liturgy Group at the church. When we arrived at the plaza on the wedding day, we found Jonathan outside the church waiting for Gabriela. The church was beautifully decorated with a pine needle carpet, flowers on the side, and pine needle garlands hanging from the ceiling. Not long after Chucha and I arrived at the church, we saw Gabriela coming down the street. She was dressed in a new traditional dress: an expensive sïtakua, and her tangarikua featured hand-embroidered flowers, which were becoming fashionable and

188   CREATING CULTURE, PERFORMING COMMUNITY

are quite expensive. Gabriela arrived accompanied by her family and wedding godparents. After the wedding party was gathered, Padre Armando gave his initial blessing and began the procession down the main aisle of the church.

After the mass, I organized a photo session with Gabriela and Jonathan's relatives and all the wedding godparents inside the church. Then Gabriela and Jonathan walked outside the church where their relatives, both older and younger, and the band were waiting for them. As soon as they exited the church, the band began to play and their female sisters and cousins began to throw confetti and give away mementos. The older generation got in line to congratulate them and offer their blessings. After the newlyweds were covered in confetti and all of the relatives had given their blessings, we had another round of pictures with relatives and the procession to Jonathan's home began.

The main celebration took place outside Jonathan's house. Huge tents crossed the street with tables and chairs set up underneath. The cake was beautifully displayed on a table surrounded by wedding presents. A little farther away from the tables, men were assembling a stage for the band that was going to play during the evening for the final dance.

I was surprised by the fact that there were not a lot of guests. I had expected more people because of the newlyweds' financial situation. One of the reasons there were so few guests from Angahuan might have been because most people were at the cemetery cleaning the graves and getting ready for Days of the Dead celebrations. Another reason is that perhaps Jonathan's and Gabriela's families did not fully participate in the communal dar y recibir. However, there was a large group of turisï guests. Gabriela is a teacher, and many of her coworkers, who are not from the community, came to her wedding. Therefore, the composition of wedding attendees was also different.

During most of the tembuchakua, Chucha and I felt lost because we were guests, not helpers or participants, per se. At other weddings, we were given a role and therefore had to help, but that was not the case at Gabriela and Jonathan's wedding.[8] Because the wedding started later than usual, we were not served the traditional hot chocolate with bread but went straight to dinner. The menu was another unique aspect of this wedding: instead of menudo (which I have seen the hosts normally give out before the churipo), they gave us birria, which is traditionally served at the sivil kuambuni, not the misa kuani. Another main difference was that the ichuskuta were not handmade but store-bought.[9]

The wedding was technically not a white/mestizo wedding because Gabriela did not get married in a white dress, but they still had the cake, which is not part of the P'urhépecha wedding. This led me to conclude that Gabriela and Jonathan had clearly participated in the decision-making process of which rituals and activities they wanted to have at their wedding. Gabriela's family had prepared gelatin to serve with the cake, so we waited to serve the cake until they arrived with the gelatin. Gabriela and Jonathan cut the cake, and then Gabriela's relatives made Jonathan take the traditional mordida. After that, Chucha asked some of Jonathan's relatives if they could help us serve the cake and gelatin. With so much cake and very few people, we served the guests huge pieces. At the end, we still had one large layer of cake left, so we took it to Gabriela's house for her relatives to enjoy.

After the cake, Chucha and I felt it was time to go home; we had fulfilled our responsibilities. We told Gabriela and Jonathan that we were leaving and would take the rest of the cake to her house for her family. She told me to wait while she went to the kitchen and returned with a plastic container filled with birria and a basket with ichuskuta wrapped in an embroidered napkin. Gabriela told me that the basket and the napkin were for me, a gift for being the cake godmother. I thanked her, and we left for Gabriela's home.

The party there was also small; there were few guests, but they all seemed happy and were enjoying themselves. We gave the cake to Margarita, one of Gabriela's older sisters, and, in return, she gave us another container with churipo and a bag with korunda. Chucha and I went home, carrying our gifts. I went back that afternoon to continue participating in the festivities. Specifically, I went to dance in the uarhantsani.

On my way to Gabriela's, I ran into Margarita, Sandra, and Marbella (Sandra works at the church, and Marbella works at the private primary school; both are turisï, like me), who were also going to Gabriela's home to start dancing. When I arrived, there were very few people. Gabriela was at the godparents' house for the kamataru niani. The band was there, but the groom's and godparents' relatives were not. Once the groom's relatives had arrived, it was decided after a brief discussion that we would start dancing at the bride's house instead of the groom's. We danced at Gabriela's house before starting our route. It was unusual because the event did not unfold in the expected way. We danced to Jonathan's home to look for his relatives, and then we went to the godparents' home where they were still in the middle of the kamata ritual. Then the dancers followed the established pattern for communal processions. After dancing with the group for a couple of hours, I went home.

Gabriela and Jonathan's wedding allowed me to experience a wedding that was unusual on many levels. As I was not a close relative of the bride, groom, or godparents, I was able to experience the wedding as a guest. Guests are not common in Angahuan, as one normally attends celebrations in which te toca. If te toca, if it is your turn to attend a celebration, you know what to do and how

190   CREATING CULTURE, PERFORMING COMMUNITY

to act. But at this wedding, neither Chucha nor I knew what the expectations were or how we were supposed to behave. The biggest difference, however, was the format. Although Gabriela did not marry in a white gown, there was a cake. The menu at Jonathan's home was not the traditional menu served in the misa kuani. As the mass was celebrated late in the day, most of the rituals in movement that are usually performed in a misa kuani were not carried out. Jonathan's relatives did not give Gabriela ribbons; therefore, she did not wear long and colorful braids for the kamata ritual in the wedding godparents' home. The processions for the exchange of gifts (mainly the ingredients for the churipo and korunda), the papu, and the kanakua were not performed. The uarhantsani was also different because the bride's and groom's families split the cost of hiring the band. Typically, the band is hired by the groom's family, and the bride's family is not supposed to dance with the groom's and godparents' families. In this case, in addition to everybody dancing together, the bride's family took the lead. However, the kamataru niani was performed, which highlights the central importance of this event in the misa kuani.

Not all families can afford to have a full misa kuani. Some have a simple misa kuani without the wind band or orchestra. For example, Inés and Gume had no music at their wedding. Neither family was financially stable at the time, so they could not afford to hire a band. During Inés's misa kuani, a radio played music at my host's family's home, but nothing more. As she recounted her wedding to me, Inés remembered that her wedding mass was early in the morning. After the mass, the wedding party went to Gume's house for the chocolate and bread, and later she was brought back to her home. In the afternoon, Gume's cousins brought her ribbons, made her braids, and prepared her for the kamataru niani. After that, they went to Gume's home for churipo and korunda. After dinner, the wedding party walked to Inés's home where Gume and Inés stayed. That was the end of the celebrations. The exchange of gifts, the papu, the uarhantsani, and the kanakua were not performed. For all of these ceremonies, which are rituals in movement, the band must be present. But at some weddings without music, if relatives want to give gifts to the newlyweds, they may do so anyway. There was a band at Jonathan and Gabriela's wedding, but most of the rituals in movement were not performed, which made it even more unusual. In this way, Jonathan and Gabriela's wedding followed the format of the misa kuani without music.

Gabriela and Jonathan's wedding is a clear example of the flexibility of the misa kuani, as it highlights each family agency's over the events to be celebrated. To some degree, the tembuchakua in Angahuan has a particular framework that each family must follow, as they must contend with different social

Fig. 6.6 Chucha and José's civil wedding. October 2010. Photo provided by the Gómez Santacruz family.

pressures, expectations, and obligations. These pressures and expectations are what create this framework. However, each family can negotiate what to do and in what way. Gabriela wanted a cake at her wedding, and she did not have to get married in a white gown to have cake.[10]

Another important feature of Gabriela and Jonathan's wedding was the rituals they did celebrate, mainly the kamataru niani. The role of the Diosïri uandarhi in the misa kuani is one of the clearest examples of continuity in the P'urhépecha culture (see chap. 5; Alcalá [1541] 2000; Martínez-Rivera 2020). By not performing most of the rituals celebrated at present-day misa kuani, Gabriela and Jonathan had a P'urhépecha wedding like those described in *La Relacion de Michoacán*, in which the wedding centers on the priest or the person who shares their words of wisdom, the Diosïri uandarhi (Alcalá [1541] 2000). While I doubt that Gabriela and Jonathan intentionally organized their wedding so it would be like those described in *La Relación de Michoacán*, it further highlights the importance of the kamataru niani as a clear continuation of preconquest P'urhépecha practices. By underscoring the kamataru niani, Gabriela and Jonathan's wedding also demonstrated that most of the rituals performed during the wedding are not necessary for a successful tembuchakua. In many ways, Gabriela and Jonathan's wedding reflected the previous relationship between their families. Most families in Angahuan maintain their distance and respect unless they are embedded in certain forms of reciprocity influenced by confianza. Therefore, organizing an elaborate misa kuani with all of the rituals will help a family create or negotiate new social networks based on the practice of reciprocity. In Gabriela and Jonathan's wedding, the performance of certain rituals may have been superfluous (and therefore they were left out); for other families, those rituals are key to the formation of social networks. Judging by each family's joy and happiness on that day, Gabriela and Jonathan created, curated, and performed their wedding based on their needs and preferences. By defying expectations, they demonstrated the agency people have over their cultural practices, underscored the importance of certain rituals during the misa kuani, and highlighted the transformation of the misa kuani, thereby protecting its continuity.

Chucha and José's Wedding: The Sivil Kuambuni-Misa Kuani Modality

Paulina and Mateo's wedding in January 2010 was the first one I knew of that performed the sivil kuambuni and the misa kuani on the same day. This was uncommon but not unknown. My host family and I were relatives of Paulina, so our responsibilities during the tembuchakua were limited, and, despite being ring godmother, I participated in and documented very few events. So I will describe Chucha and José's wedding instead of Paulina and Mateo's.

In July 2010, Chucha, the fourth daughter in my host family, eloped with her boyfriend, José (as described in chap. 3). Chucha and José originally wanted to have the sivil kuambuni and the misa kuani separately, but during the planning stages, the families decided that both celebrations should occur on the same day. One reason for combining all the rituals into one day was to save money, but Chucha and José also wanted to be married as soon as possible because, after the potpinsani, Chucha had been returned to her house, and they could not be together until they celebrated the misa kuani. The organization of the wedding was a relatively relaxed affair in which both families worked together to create a wonderful celebration. As both José and Chucha belong to large social networks of family and friends, their wedding was an almost community-wide affair with hundreds of guests.

The wedding was organized quickly and celebrated in mid-October 2010. After several days of preparatory activities, all the rituals that were to take place before the day of the wedding were celebrated the night before the wedding (as described in chap. 4). Weddings that combine both the sivil kuambuni and the misa kuani tend to begin with the religious mass and then continue with the civil service.[11] Chucha and her family got up at 5:00 a.m. to finish the arrangements for the celebrations and prepare Chucha for the mass at 9:00 a.m. Meanwhile, the groom's family accompanied the wind band to Chucha's house and then, in a procession, took Chucha to the church. For the mass, they hired the "Cantoras," a famous female group from the community that specializes in Spanish and P'urhépecha religious music. If the bride marries in a white gown, the Cantoras tend to sing in Spanish; if she marries in a traditional dress, they sing in P'urhépecha. For Chucha and José's wedding mass, however, they sang in P'urhépecha, even though Chucha wore a white gown.

After the mass, the newlyweds walked outside the church where their families and friends waited. They were showered with confetti, received hugs and blessings, and took photographs with their relatives.[12] After the greetings and blessings, the procession was organized and everyone walked to José's home where they had breakfast. After that, the sivil kuambuni took place (fig. 6.6).

A table was set up at José's house where a judge from Uruapan conducted the civil ceremony. After Chucha and José, their parents, and their wedding godparents had signed the civil marriage documents, José's family served lunch: birria. After the birria, the rituals of the white/mestizo wedding began: the toast, the waltz, the cake, throwing the bouquet, and la víbora. After these wedding rituals were finished, the P'urhépecha rituals began. Because it was already early afternoon, the wedding party had to move quickly between rituals. While Chucha and her godparents were accompanied to their respective homes, José's relatives brought the food gifts for the churipo and korunda (meat, corn, salt, onions, etc.), thus combining two of the rituals in movement.

At home, Chucha changed into the traditional dress. Just as Cayetana, Chucha's older sister, finished braiding Chucha's hair, José's young relatives arrived with the ribbons to make Chucha's colorful floor-length braids. José's relatives prepared Chucha for the kamataru niani, after which she rested before the kamataru niani (described in chap. 5). After completing the ritual, the wedding party went to José's home for dinner: churipo and korunda. José and his relatives stayed at his house, and the godparents took Chucha and her relatives back to her home.

While Chucha and José were at the kamataru niani, their young relatives participated in the uarhantsani. Because Chucha's siblings and cousins wanted

194   CREATING CULTURE, PERFORMING COMMUNITY

to dance, and they could not dance with the groom's relatives, everybody contributed money to hire a wind band to play for four hours, enough time to dance through the streets of Angahuan. So, while José's relatives danced, Chucha's did too.

Not long after Chucha had returned home and the uarhantsani had concluded, the papu arrived. After the papu's dance, the kanarperakua began (fig. 6.7). Both Chucha and José had been told that if anybody tried to carry or throw them, they should not resist or start a fight but play along. However, some of Chucha's cousins were rough with José, and a small fight ensued. The fight was quickly stopped, and the kanarperakua resumed peacefully. After that, Chucha and José gave thanks to their older relatives (the blessings and thank-you's). Chucha and José were instructed to thank only their older relatives and their uncles and aunts. Then they were crowned with the kanakua, after which they were accompanied to their bedroom. With that, the wedding celebrations concluded.

To perform all of the different wedding rituals in one day, José and Chucha had to decide which ones to include. Most of the sivil kuambuni rituals were not performed or were merged with the misa kuani. One aspect of Chucha and José's wedding that differed from the misa kuani—and has a clear connection to the sivil kuambuni—was the birria lunch offered after the civil ceremony. In the expected format of the misa kuani (even if the white/mestizo wedding is also celebrated), guests are only given breakfast and not lunch. In those cases where lunch is provided (at Joel and Daniela's wedding, for example), it is not offered to everybody.

If families celebrate the sivil kuambuni and the misa kuani separately, they must decide which rituals are performed at which wedding. For example, the night before Joel and Daniela's misa kuani, the bathing of the bride and the gifting of the ocotes were not celebrated, as both rituals had already been performed for the sivil kuambuni. Rituals that occur in both the sivil kuambuni and the misa kuani are not repeated if the weddings are separate unless the families want to celebrate everything twice, which would cost more money. However, at weddings such as Chucha and José's, families might decide to celebrate all of the different rituals that are part of the three-day tembuchakua celebrations. At other weddings that combine the sivil kuambuni and misa kuani, families might decide to celebrate the most important aspects of the misa kuani and forgo the rituals of the sivil kuambuni. Chucha and José's tembuchakua was organized to include most if not all of the rituals of both the sivil kuambuni and the misa kuani.

One of the main reasons for combining the sivil kuambuni and the misa kuani is the cost involved. During the 2008–2009 US economic recession and

Fig. 6.7 Chucha and José before the kanarperakua. October 2010. Photo provided by Gómez Santacruz family.

the war on drugs, Angahuan's economy suffered. In 2009–2010, some families had to limit their daily spending and cut down on special celebrations. During my research stay in 2009–2010, people in the community were tailoring many traditional practices to their economic realities. However, according to my collaborator Agustín, people may celebrate the sivil kuambuni and the misa kuani on the same day so that the couple can marry as soon as possible to avoid gossip and friction among the extended family and other community members (described in chap. 3). Another possible reason for combining these two ceremonies is the fact that couples do not want to spend too much time apart before the misa kuani. In the case of Chucha and José, they wanted to celebrate their misa kuani quickly so they could live together. Families may also decide to have a double wedding because the wedding season is about to end. For example, if Chucha and José had decided to celebrate their misa kuani and

196   CREATING CULTURE, PERFORMING COMMUNITY

their sivil kuambuni separately, they would have had to wait until December to celebrate their misa kuani if they had done the sivil kuambuni in October or September. Javier, a first cousin of my host sisters, got married in February 2012. As Lent was fast approaching and the young couple and their families did not want to wait until after Holy Week to celebrate the misa kuani, they celebrated the sivil kuambuni and the misa kuani on the same day.

At least three factors contribute to the misa kuani-sivil kuambuni format: the families' financial constraints, the desire to prevent gossip, and the young couple's wishes to be together as soon as possible. Most weddings today combine features of the sivil kuambuni and the misa kuani. This further demonstrates the flexibility of the tembuchakua and Angahuan's traditional practices in general, as families choose which rituals to celebrate and how. This wedding modality highlights cultural transformations as the simultaneous process of continuity and change in action.

Traditionalizing the Misa Kuani

When I returned to Angahuan in the summer of 2011, my research collaborators told me about a recent wedding trend in Angahuan at that time: a movement to rescue the most traditional elements of the misa kuani. Contrasted with the sivil kuambuni-misa kuani format, which aims to reduce the costs of celebrating a tembuchakua, this return to the traditional form is much more expensive and, to some degree, more exclusive. It applies only to the misa kuani. According to some of my research collaborators, one of the principal characteristics of this new modality is to reject modernity and return to the way the misa kuani was celebrated in the past.[13] According to Agustín in 2011, less than 10 percent of Angahuan families plan a traditional misa kuani; it is typically done at the insistence of the couple's parents. One reason for this low participation rate is that a traditional misa kuani costs too much. It features more ritual events, and it is more expensive to acquire some of the necessary elements for the rituals.

The format of the traditional misa kuani is the same as the present-day one: many of the rituals are the same but with some variations. If the families involved want to celebrate the misa kuani in the traditional way, after the potpinsani or the uarhipini (see chap. 3), every Sunday until the misa kuani, the groom's family must take a basket of fruit, breads, and presents to the bride and her family. This means that each week, the groom's family must spend between $300 and $500 MXN (or $30–$50 USD) on gifts for the bride and her family, and even more during special events.

As described in chapter 4, the night before the misa kuani, the groom's female relatives bathe the bride, and the groom's male relatives take ocotes to the bride's home. Currently, the groom's young male relatives take ocotes in their pickup trucks and SUVs. In the traditional version, the groom's family hires horses and donkeys to take the ocotes. Thirty years ago, most people in Angahuan had horses and donkeys; now, only the tourist guides and some community members have them. Hiring horses and donkeys can be very expensive. According to my host sisters, for Javier's wedding (the one celebrated in February 2012), his family hired horses and donkeys to go to the forest to look for the wood that was supposed to be taken to the bride's house. In that way, Javier's wedding was a sivil kuambuni-misa kuani with elements of the traditional misa kuani.

In a traditional misa kuani, the bride wears her P'urhépecha dress, which means that only the rituals of the P'urhépecha wedding will be performed. While variability depends on each family, all the rituals must be performed (i.e., rituals in movement, relationship-formalization rituals, and rituals of controlled violence). Another ritual in the traditional modality is the iuinskua, which is performed the day after the wedding. On that day, the groom's cousins, accompanied by a wind band, must take wood, chickens, corn, and other ingredients to the bride's parents' house—this is done to make sure that the bride can cook.

During my 2009–2010 stay, I had heard about the iuinskua but was told that it had been many years since it was celebrated during a misa kuani. According to Agustín, the last time was in 2002 in the house of Dr. Simón Rivera (QEPD). As Agustín told me in 2011, he had heard of a family who wanted to have a traditional wedding. Agustín talked to the groom's father, as he was interested in filming the wedding for a documentary he wanted to make. The groom's father explained to him that while he wanted to do the wedding the traditional way, they could not do so; he had another son, and the traditional misa kuani, especially the iuinskua, can only be performed in the last son's wedding. In this sense, the iuinskua is a type of closure ritual, a way to conclude the weddings of all the male children in a family.

Despite the expense, this traditional modality is becoming more popular, especially the use of horses and donkeys for the wood and ocotes. On my last day in Angahuan in the summer of 2011, Lourdes, one of my research collaborators, told me that another family had celebrated the traditional misa kuani, but she was unsure of which rituals were performed. She was not close to the families involved in the misa kuani and had not participated in it. However, she did remember seeing a group of the groom's young relatives taking the wood and ocotes on horses and donkeys.

Some people in Angahuan want to return to the traditional modality so they can remove the elements they view as modern in current cultural practices. This process of traditionalization, of performing the traditional way of celebrating events, is not exclusive to weddings. Some cargueros in the church and in the Iurhixu, together with the priest and other communal officials, are advocating for a return to the traditional and simpler ways of celebrating special events in the community—in part to control the excessive spending. Interestingly, however, celebrating the traditional misa kuani is more expensive than celebrating it in the nontraditional way. I believe that this movement to perform rituals "as they were done before" is tied to current communal and regional social movements that focus on political, economic, and cultural autonomy (as described in chap. 1). The traditional misa kuani, therefore, is an example of both traditionalization and innovation and further supports my main argument: that people in Angahuan create, curate, perform, and transform their cultural practices so they can better reflect their values, needs, expectations, and interests, and, by doing so, they perform what it means to be a member of their P'urhépecha community.

Transforming the Tembuchakua: Creating Culture, Performing Community

The different tembuchakua modalities presented here—white/mestizo wedding, breaking with expectations, sivil kuambuni-misa kuani modality, and traditionalizing the misa kuani—are not mutually exclusive, tightly bound, or defined. Families have control over which ritual elements to perform and how. Even though families adapt the different modalities of the tembuchakua to fit their needs and expectations, they follow a particular template that provides a cultural logic to the transformation that allows them to perform their belonging to Angahuan and their P'urhépecha culture.

In this chapter, I discussed how the tembuchakua is transformed by two simultaneous processes—customization and traditionalization—and how those processes are also influenced by ideas of innovation and expectations. Foreign elements are customized into the wedding, and local elements are traditionalized. While the inclusion of the civil wedding can be considered one of the first customization acts in the last sixty to seventy years (as described in chap. 4), the most recent one in Angahuan, the white/mestizo wedding, is a clear example of cultural agency. While the civil wedding was an imposition from the state, the white/mestizo wedding was a choice. However, the customization of both cultural practices (civil wedding and white/mestizo wedding) increased the participation of young people in the tembuchakua in general. In this regard, young people have been the driving force behind transformations in the wedding as well as other foreign cultural practices in the community that have been customized, such as graduations and even quinceañeras.[14]

As a reaction to the rapid growth, and cultural, social, and economic changes in the community, some people are arguing for a return to the traditional way of celebrating vernacular cultural practices. In some instances, this return to the traditional way of celebrating, while not necessarily an invention, is a creation and re-creation of how people engage in and understand their culture. The current traditional modality of the misa kuani allows people to transform their culture based on their understanding of it. Families also respond to expectations, and people expect to see certain ritual practices during a particular event. Families, such as Gabriela and Jonathan's, however, organize the wedding based on their needs and preferences, not others' expectations. Another way in which people in Angahuan transform the misa kuani is by defying certain stereotypes. For some, the idea of female purity plays an important part in how the tembuchakua will be organized and performed. Recently, however, couples who had not celebrated their misa kuani and had been living together for many years, have been financing and celebrating their weddings, which was unthinkable some years ago.[15]

Even when it seems that the tembuchakua has a clear and delimited structure, people in Angahuan adapt and transform it. The tembuchakua is always in a process of transformation influenced by ideas of innovation and expectations. Over time, more elements have been incorporated into the tembuchakua, showcasing P'urhépecha creativity and aesthetics. But the roots, which highlight the main P'urhépecha cultural values, are still there. As Agustín told me (and as I quoted in the intro.), "Se está agrandando, pero a la vez se está respetando lo que ya había" ("It is growing, but at the same time, we are respecting what was already there"). The tembuchakua, as the quintessential P'urhépecha cultural event, provides a template that allows for these transformations and the continuation of P'urhépecha cultures in Angahuan. I look forward to seeing how new generations continue to transform weddings and other cultural practices so that their P'urhépecha culture continues to be relevant and alive for future generations.

Notes

1. My work departs from conceptualizations of continuity and change that argue that change is a step closer to acculturation or assimilation (Beals [1945] 1992; Carrasco 1952; Foster [1967] 1988).

200   CREATING CULTURE, PERFORMING COMMUNITY

2. This phenomenon of expectation is not unique or new to Angahuan. Beals ([1945] 1992) reported that while doing research in Cherán, people would constantly describe how events were supposed to happen, but what Beals and his team of researchers witnessed was different than what was explained to them beforehand.

3. In the interlude, I described Joel and Daniela's P'urhépecha wedding, which happened after the white/mestizo portion of their ceremony. To clarify the order of events, after the mass, the whole procession walked to Joel's house, where the white/mestizo wedding took place; after that, Daniela and her godparents were taken to their respective homes as the rituals tied to the P'urhépecha wedding began.

4. I was later told by my host sisters that this gift-giving ritual is optional: the bride's and groom's families and their baptism and confirmation godparents all must agree to perform this ritual. Since this was Joel's home, only his baptism and confirmation godparents brought gifts. If Daniela's godparents also wanted to bring gifts, they had to present them in her home. As my research collaborators explained, some baptism, confirmation, or first communion godparents feel that after their godchild has married, they no longer have any responsibility to him or her. In this sense, the gift exchange at Joel and Daniela's wedding could have at least two meanings. The first is that his baptism and confirmation godparents wanted to reinforce their godparenthood by their continual participation in the practice of reciprocity. The second meaning could be that the gifts symbolized their last act as godparents, which therefore severed the ties of reciprocity. I never saw this event again, nor did I hear of it taking place elsewhere in the community.

5. See n. 8 of the introduction for a description of the víbora de la mar.

6. The biting of the cake and being pushed into it is a widespread cultural practice in México.

7. By unusual, I mean different. My intention is not to make a moral judgment or to criticize but to highlight how different this wedding was compared to my other experiences so far in Angahuan.

8. In all my time in Angahuan, I attended only celebrations in which my host family was required to participate, and I was directed on what to do and how to behave. In this case, I was not sure how to behave or what I should do, so I felt lost. In conversations with Chucha, she confessed that she also felt lost because she is also not used to attending celebrations where it's not her turn to participate or help.

9. Store-bought tortillas are expensive, especially compared to what it costs to make ichuskuta by hand.

10. I could argue, however, that the reason they made me cake godmother was because they knew I would not complain about having to pay for the cake even though she had not celebrated the white/mestizo wedding.

11. Although I am sure that the order of the religious and civil rituals could be reversed; if the mass is not celebrated first, it would be difficult to perform all the rituals of both types of wedding on the same day.

12. Because I could not attend the wedding, I became the video godmother: I sent money so they could hire someone to record the wedding. They saved a copy of the recording for me.

13. The way modernity is understood in this context has to do with technology, as represented by cars, clothing, and music.

14. A quinceañera is a coming-of-age ritual for young women on their fifteenth birthday, celebrated throughout Latin America, in US-Latinx communities, and is incredibly popular in México. Quinceañeras are not common in Angahuan, but some families have organized them for their daughters.

15. In 2011, Inés, one of my host sisters, told me that some years ago, a couple with children celebrated their misa kuani with all the rituals. Their children even participated in some of the rituals, including the uarhantsani.

Fig. 7.1 Takichani for Daniela and Joel's wedding godmother. October 2009.

Conclusion

Getting Married in Angahuan, Revisited

Chucha, Pela, and I woke up late on the day after the main celebrations of Joel and Daniela's misa kuani (see interlude). My feet hurt from walking and dancing all over the community, and my lower back and waist were bruised from the weight and tightness of the traditional dress. Na Juana and Ta Emiliano, despite their exhaustion, had to return to Ta Sergio and Na Antonia's house to help celebrate the final rituals of the tembuchakua. During this last day of wedding celebrations, smaller ritual acts are performed but only by those whose turn it is (les toca)—in this case, the parents' and godparents' generation. Chucha, Pela, and I stayed home to clean, prepare the day's meals (we were making mole, as it was Pancho's saint day), and recuperate from the two days of rituals and celebrations.

As I was told, the day after their wedding, the bride and groom, after spending the night at the bride's parents' house, must wake up early to prepare kamata to take to the groom's parents' house and to their new wedding godparents. At each house, the newlyweds must make sure their parents and godparents are doing well (recovering from the celebrations and drinking) and help clean the houses. After that, they return to the bride's house. In some cases, as Agustín informed me, the newlyweds' families decide to celebrate the iuinskua (described in chap. 6).

As explained by my host family, the celebration that must occur the day after the wedding is the takichani, the taking of the children. This event is celebrated at the godparents' house and is only attended by close relatives of the newlyweds' parents. Months before the wedding, close relatives of the groom and bride must prepare two dolls that represent the wedding godparents. The female doll is dressed as the godmother (in Angahuan's traditional female attire), and the male doll is dressed similarly to how the godfather dresses and with the utensils of his trade (e.g., if the godfather is a carpenter, the doll will have a hammer). My host sisters told me that for one of the weddings in which Na Juana and Ta Emiliano were godparents, the dolls were beautifully dressed and decorated. At the time of that wedding, Ta Emiliano worked as a tourist guide taking people to the Paricutín. His doll was dressed as he usually dresses (jeans, plaid shirt, and boots) and had the identification card that some of the tourist guides from the community wear while working.

At Joel and Daniela's wedding, Na Juana oversaw the godmother's doll (fig. 7.1). Several months before the wedding, she began embroidering the pieces for the uanengo and tatchukua and bought the cloth for the sïtakua and saco. The morning after the wedding, Na Juana and Ta Emiliano left for Joel's home, where they stayed before going for dinner at the godparents' house. Na Juana left with the doll that she had prepared for the occasion. At the godparents' house, they continued celebrating the compadrazgo and the new social network and family created with this marriage. This concluded the celebration of Joel and Daniela's tembuchakua.

Getting Married during COVID-19

As we near the end of our journey, I would like to briefly describe some recent changes to the tembuchakua. During the 2009 H1N1 flu epidemic, cultural events continued in Angahuan. But when the COVID-19 pandemic began in March 2020, all celebrations were canceled. By May 2020, the Mexican government had instituted strict health guidelines to begin opening services to the public. In most places in México, the Catholic Church was unable to hold open masses, but in Angahuan, they gradually began to celebrate masses outside in the church's atrium. During the celebrations of Santo Santiago in July 2020, the community closed the roads into the community and did not allow outsiders to join the celebrations. Through Facebook posts and WhatsApp messages with acquaintances and relatives in Angahuan, I could see how people were adjusting to these restrictions. People were spread far apart and wearing masks during processions, which were done as quickly as possible to limit exposure time. As soon as people could safely congregate, the calendar of events in Angahuan was again packed with celebrations and rituals.

During the pandemic, the wedding calendar was completely disrupted. The Catholic Church did not officially allow public masses or the celebration of sacraments until the summer of 2021.[1] Therefore, people in Angahuan started celebrating weddings in July 2021, a month when weddings are not

CONCLUSION

normally celebrated. That July 2021, my host family organized and celebrated the wedding of their youngest daughter, Leti, which was supposed to happen in April 2020.[2]

As travel between the United States and México resumed, migrants returned to Angahuan to participate in community-wide celebrations or to get married. The daughter of relatives of Na Juana and Ta Emiliano, who was born and raised in the United States, returned to Angahuan in March 2022 to get married. Her new husband is not from Angahuan, so their wedding was different: they did not travel to and from the three main homes (the groom's, bride's, and god-parents') where the rituals and celebrations would be organized. The wedding was held in the Mirador, the main communal tourism spot, where they hung huge tents and organized three areas that symbolized the houses. The bride got married in a white dress and was accompanied by bridesmaids (something that I had not seen in Angahuan). They celebrated the different rituals of the white wedding, and she later changed to a traditional P'urhépecha dress. To imitate the movements among the houses, the wedding guests moved through the venue between the three designated areas. The bride's hair was decorated with the colorful, floor-length braids, but I am not sure if the compadrazgo ritual was celebrated or whether other rituals associated with the P'urhépecha wedding were performed. Based on the pictures and videos, it was a grand wedding, accompanied by mariachis and Los Rayos del Sol, Angahuan's principal pirekua group.

As more people get vaccinated and COVID-19 cases and deaths decline, weddings and other cultural events in Angahuan are resuming. Based on Facebook posts and pictures shared by my host family, people are investing more money and making sure that the events are more elaborate than before.

Creating Culture, Performing Community:
Some Parting, but Hopefully Not Final, Words

Throughout this book, and through a careful analysis of wedding rituals, I proposed three interwoven arguments / axes / points of encounter: by negotiating processes that are influenced by ideas of aesthetics, people in Angahuan create their culture; through the performance of rituals, people in Angahuan learn and practice some of their core values and hence signal their belonging to their community; and by understanding cultural transformations as the simultaneous process of continuity and change that are influenced by ideas of innovation and expectations, the tembuchakua serves as a cultural template that allows for the continuity of P'urhépecha culture in Angahuan. To help support and understand these interwoven arguments/stories, I described how society is divided by age, gender, and social status; how people learn to behave and perform based on the idea of te toca; how some of the main P'urhépecha cultural values and worldviews are created and performed during ritual; and how people creatively engage with their cultural practices to accommodate them to new circumstances and situations.

Since I began conducting research in Angahuan almost twenty years ago, the tembuchakua has been continuously transformed; young people's actions and agency in communal life are more visible, and they have taken the lead in the current transformations of the wedding and other cultural vernacular practices. Moreover, one of the results of Angahuan's fight for autonomy (see chap. 1) is that many people are favoring the "traditional" way of celebrating events (the idea of traditionalization as explained in chap. 6), which influences how people celebrate weddings and other life cycle events. In this way, people in Angahuan are challenging limited and limiting understandings of Indigenous identity and experience. Despite stereotypical and narrow understandings of Indigenous vernacular cultural practices that depict them as unchanging, "traditional," or needing to be removed from "modernity" to be "authentic," weddings in Angahuan provide the perfect space to understand how people in P'urhépecha communities negotiate, create, curate, and perform their cultural practices based on their cultural values and worldviews. And because Angahuan is recognized as an enclave for P'urhépecha culture, it is an ideal space to analyze the processes of cultural transformation.

Scholars have documented weddings in other P'urhépecha communities and highlighted their importance (see Martínez-Rivera 2020 for a detailed analysis of those works), so I feel confident in stating that the tembuchakua is the quintessential cultural event in P'urhépecha communities. In May 2022, during the Grupo Kw'aniskuyarhani's bimonthly meeting, which focused on the pirekua, one of the presenters mentioned that in the community of Tarecuato, when a young man dies before he gets married, during his funeral and his first Days of the Dead, young women organize a type of wedding ceremony for the young deceased by taking flowers and other mementos to his grave. The pirekua group Los Gorriones de Tarecuato has a song called "Locoia Urhapiti" that describes this practice. On November 2, 2021, eleven young men (between fourteen and thirty-four) from Tarecuato were killed by narcos while they looked for beehives as part of their celebrations of Days of the Dead. During the funerary service for the slain young men, female relatives performed the wedding-funerary rituals, and the pirekua by Los Gorriones was played. This heartbreaking event

CONCLUSION

highlights the importance of wedding practices in P'urhépecha communities, but more than anything, it stresses how P'urhépecha people find strength and solace through ritual in moments of extreme violence and death.

In this book, I tried to avoid offering definitive interpretations of weddings, P'urhépecha culture, or even Angahuan because I wanted to emphasize the multiplicity and variability of cultural practices and experiences. My analysis stems from my experience and position in the community. One thing I did not discuss is how a wedding is performed when the bride, groom, or godparents are not from Angahuan. According to Padre Nacho, most couples who get married in Angahuan are from the community. During his tenure in Angahuan, he officiated at only seven weddings where either the bride or the groom was not from Angahuan. Since Padre Nacho's time in the community (ending in 2008), Angahuan's demographics have changed. Some of the young men are returning from the United States with their turisï girlfriends or wives. Therefore, another area of research opportunity is how weddings are planned when one or more of the three main families involved are not from the community. Since I last conducted active fieldwork in Angahuan in 2016, new styles of performing the tembuchakua have been developed. The sivil kuambuni-misa kuani modality has become more common, and families are also combining different traditional practices. I have not fully developed the impact of the drug war on weddings or on P'urhépecha culture in general; however, this topic is worth further investigation. Another important area of research and activism is documenting and supporting same-sex weddings and marriages. In February 2022, Humberto and Florencio, two young men from Ihuatzio (a P'urhépecha community in the Lake of Pátzcuaro region) celebrated the first Boda Igualitaria P'urhépecha (same-sex P'urhépecha wedding). Mario A. Gómez Zamora (n.d.) documented this wedding as part of their dissertation research, "Queerness and Gender Performance in Indigenous P'urhépecha Communities in Michoacán and the United States."

This book is the foundation of my lifelong project: reconceptualizing Indigeneity. And while I do not directly focus on Indigenous identity politics, this element has been present in my analytical goal: to understand Indigenous experience through everyday practices. Each chapter contributes to my overarching argument that Indigenous cultures are constantly in a process of transformation and that Indigenous people are responsible for the creation of their cultural practices. In future projects, I will expand the focus to other areas of youth culture and young adult participation in the sociocultural life in Angahuan. I am mainly interested in how young people create their own spaces

Fig. 7.2 Thank-you basket with breads. July 2009.

inside the community through traditional games and sports, music, and other aspects of expressive culture. By analyzing youth participation in the creation, negotiation, and performance of their culture, we can begin to break away from the limiting expectations of what it means to be Indigenous and understand Indigeneity as an ever-changing experience and identity.

Two metaphors that guided and inspired me while I wrote this book were those of walking and movement and of weaving. These two ideas may seem contradictory, as walking may imply impermanence, and weaving, permanence, but I saw how both complemented each other, as they both are tied in/with stories. Moreover, and as illustrated throughout this book, movement is a central component of P'urhépecha cultural practices, as most of my research occurred while walking through the community and participating in events that me tocaba. In those moments, I was surrounded by stories and discussions about how to organize, prepare, and celebrate an event. Additionally, by walking alongside my family and friends in Angahuan, I saw how they created new or different paths and transformed their vernacular cultural practices to fit their needs and interests. And now, as I witness my Angahuan niblings and how they are learning, adapting, creating, curating, and performing their cultural practices, I am filled with hope and excitement for the future of P'urhépecha cultures.

CONCLUSION

Notes

1. Vaccinations against COVID-19 began in México in March 2021, focusing first on the older and vulnerable populations. By the summer of 2021, people over fifty had received at least a first dose, so the government began to allow smaller events if people were masked and socially distanced.

2. I did not attend this wedding, as I was unable to travel to Angahuan during the pandemic. However, I did enjoy the wedding through videos, pictures, and posts shared on Facebook and WhatsApp.

References

Acosta, Aidé. 2011. "Celebrating *Las Posadas* in the Heartland: Creating Home in New Destinations." *Anthropology News* (February) 52 (2): 36–37.

Alcalá, Jerónimo de. (1541) 2000. *Relación de Michoacán o, Relación de las Ceremonias y Ritos y Gobernacion de los Indios de la Provincia de Michoacán.* Edition with studies and appendixes coordinated by Moisés Franco Mendoza. Zamora: El Colegio de Michoacán.

Alcaraz, Ángela. 1925. "Las Canacuas." *Mexican Folkways* 6 (3): 117–128.

Amézcua Luna, Jarco, and Gerardo Sánchez Díaz. 2015. *P'urhépecha.* Pueblos Indígenas de México del Siglo XXI. México City: Comisión Nacional para el Desarrollo de los Pueblos Indígenas.

Archibal, Jo-ann, Q'um Q'um Xiiem, Jenny Bol Jun Lee-Morgan, and Jason De Santolo, eds. 2019. *Decolonizing Research: Indigenous Storywork as Methodology.* London: Zed Scholar.

Astorga, Luis. 2012. *El Siglo de las drogas. El narcotráfico, del porfiriato al Nuevo milenio.* Mexico City: Editorial Grijalbo.

Barragán, René, and Luis Arturo González Bonilla. 1940. "Vida Actual de los Tarascos." In *Los Tarascos: Monografía Histórica, Etnográfica y Económica,* edited by Lucio Mendieta y Nuñez, 127–176. Mexico: Imprenta Universitaria, Universidad Nacional Autónoma de Mexico Instituto de Investigaciónes Sociales.

Bauman, Richard. 1977. *Verbal Art as Performance.* Prospect Heights, IL: Waveland.

Beals, Ralph Larson. (1945) 1992. *Cherán un pueblo al pie de la sierra Tarasca.* Translated by Agustín Jacinto Zavala. Zamora: El Colegio de Michoacán.

Behar, Ruth. 1996. *The Vulnerable Observer: Anthropology That Breaks Your Heart.* Boston: Beacon.

REFERENCES

Bello Maldonado, Álvaro. 2008. "Los espacios de la juventud indígena. Territorio y migración en una comunida purépecha de Michoacán, México." In *Jóvenes Indígenas y Globalizacion en America Latina*, edited by Maya Lorena Pérez Ruiz, 161–179, Colección Científica. Mexico City: Instituto Nacional de Antropología e Historia.

Berglund, Jeff, Jan Johnson, and Kimberli Lee, eds. 2016. *Indigenous Pop: Native American Music from Jazz to Hip Hop*. Tucson: University of Arizona Press.

Berry, Maya J., Claudia Chávez Argüelles, Shanya Cordis, Sarah Ihmoud, and Elizabeth Velásquez Estrada. 2017. "Toward a Fugitive Anthropology: Gender, Race, and Violence in the Field." *Cultural Anthropology* 32 (4): 537–565.

Bishop, Joyce Mildred. 1977. "El Corazón del Pueblo: A Study of Religious Cargo System of San Juan Nuevo Parangaricutiro, Michoacán, México." PhD diss., University of California, Berkeley.

Bonfil Batalla, Guillermo. (1987) 2005. *México Profundo: Una Civilización Negada*. Mexico City: DeBolsillo.

Brandes, Stanley. 1988. *Power and Persuasion: Fiestas and Social Control in Rural Mexico*. Philadelphia: University of Pennsylvania Press.

Briggs, Charles L. 1996. "The Politics of Discursive Authority in Research on the 'Invention of Tradition.'" *Cultural Anthropology* 11 (4): 435–469.

Bucholtz, Mary. 2002. "Youth and Cultural Practice." *Annual Review of Anthropology* 31:525–552.

Cárdenas Fernández, Blanca. 2006. "Ch'anantskua (Juego de la Madurez)." *America sin nombre* 8:100–105.

Carrasco, Pedro, 1952. *Tarascan Folk Religion. An Analysis of Economic, Social, and Religious Interactions*. New Orleans: Middle American Research Institute.

Cerano, Pedro Dante, dir. 1999. *Ch'anantskua*. Documentary. Morelia: Centro de Video Indígena de Michoacán.

Chamoreau, Claudine. 2009. *Hablemos p'urhépecha. Wantee juchari anapu*, Morelia: UIIM/IIH–UMSNH/IRD/Ambassade France au Mexique/CCC–IFAL /Grupo Kw'aniskuyarhani.

Chávez, Xóchitl. 2021. "'La Sierra Juárez in Riverside': The Inaugural Oaxacan Philharmonic Bands Audition on a University Campus." In *Theorizing Folklore from the Margins: Critical and Ethical Approaches*, edited by Solimar Otero and Mintzi A. Martínez-Rivera, 274–292. Bloomington: Indiana University Press.

Chilisa, Bagele. 2012. *Indigenous Research Methodologies*. Thousand Oaks, CA: Sage.

Clifford, James. 2001. "Indigenous Articulations." *Contemporary Pacific* 13 (2): 468–490.

Cohen, Abner. 1993. *Masquerade Politics: Explorations in the Structure of Urban Cultural Movements*. Berkeley: University of California Press.

REFERENCES

Comunidad de Angahuan. 1999. *Estatuto Comunal, Comunidad P'urhépecha de Angahuan*. Resolución Presidencial No. 4700, R.AN. No DCCCLXXV. Municipio de Uruapan, Michoacán, México.

Cortés Máximo, Juan Carlos, ed. 2019. *Marhuatspeni: El servir sagrado entre los P'urhépecha*. Morelia: Instituto de Investigaciónes Históricas-Universidad Michoacana de San Nicolás de Hidalgo, El Colegio de Michoacán.

Dass, Rhonda. 2021. "Behaving Like Relatives: Or, We Don't Sit around and Talk Politics with Strangers." In *Theorizing Folklore from the Margins: Critical and Ethical Approaches*, edited by Solimar Otero and Mintzi A. Martínez-Rivera, 103–112. Bloomington: Indiana University Press.

Deloria, Philip J. 2004. *Indians in Unexpected Places*. Lawrence: University Press of Kansas.

Dominguez, Francisco. 1925a. "Danza Antigua de Guaris." *Mexican Folkways* 6 (13): 110–116.

———. 1925b. "La Música de las Canacuas." *Mexican Folkways* 6 (13): 119–128.

Durkheim, Emile. (1915) 1965. *The Elementary Forms of the Religious Life*. New York: Free Press.

Eggler, Willis A. 1948. "Plant Communities in the Vicinity of the Volcano el Parícutin, México after Two and a Half Years of Eruption." *Ecology* 29 (4): 415–436.

Flores Mercado, Georgina. 2017. *La pirekua como Patrimonio Cultural Inmaterial de la Humanidad. Efectos del nuevo paradigma patrimonial*. Mexico City: National Autonomous University of Mexico, Instituto de Investigaciónes Sociales.

———. 2020. *Un futuro posible para la pirekua: políticas patrimoniales, música tradicional e identidad p'urhépecha*. Mexico City: Universidad Nacional Autónoma de México, Instituto de Investigaciónes Sociales, Escuela Nacional de Estudios Superiores-Morelia.

Forte, Maximilian C., ed. 2010. *Indigenous Cosmopolitans. Transnational and Transcultural Indigeneity in the Twenty-First Century*. New York: Peter Lang.

Foshag, William F., and Jenaro Gonzalez R. 1956. *Birth and Development of Paricutin Volcano, México*. Geological Investigations in the Paricutin Area, México. Geological Survey Bulletin 965-D. United States Department of Interior and Geological Survey. United States Government Printing Office, Washington, DC.

Foster, George M. (1967) 1988. *Tzintzuntzan: Mexican Peasants in a Changing World*. New York: Waveland Press.

Franco Mendoza, Moisés. 1997. *La Ley y La Costumbre en la Cañada de los Once Pueblos*. Zamora: El Colegio de Michoacán.

Fuentes Díaz, Antonio. 2015. "Narcotráfico y autodefensa comunitaria en 'Tierra Caliente,' Michoacán, México." *Ciencia UAT* 10 (1): 68–82.

REFERENCES

Fuentes Díaz, Antonio, and Guillermo Paleta Pérez. 2015. "Violencia y autodefensas comunitarias en Michoacán, México." *Íconos. Revista de Ciencias Sociales* 53:171–186.

Gaillard, Jean-Christophe. 2007. "Resilience of Traditional Societies in Facing Natural Hazards." *Disaster Prevention and Management* 16 (4): 522–544.

Garrido Izaguirre, Eva Maria. 2020. *Donde el diablo mete la cola: Antropología del arte y estética indígena.* Morelia: Escuela Nacional de Estudios Superiores, Unidad Morelia.

Gilberti, Maturino. (1559) 1997. *Vocabulario en Lengua de Mechuacan.* Zamora: El Colegio de Michoacán.

———. (1558) 2004. *Arte de la Lengua de Michoacán.* Transcription, edition, and notes by Cristina Monzón. Zamora: El Colegio de Michoacán, Fideicomiso Teixidor.

Gómez Bravo, Lucas, Benjamin Pérez González, and Irineo Rojas Hernández. 2001. *Uandakua Uenakua P'urhépecha Jimbo: Introducción al Idioma P'urhépecha.* Morelia: Universidad Michoacana de San Nicolás de Hidalgo-Centro de Investigación de la Cultura P'urhépecha.

Gómez Zamora, Mario A., ed. 2017. *Entre el Recuerdo y la Memoria: Historias de Patamban.* Morelia: Instituto de Investigaciones Históricas, Universidad Michoacana de San Nicolás de Hidalgo.

———. n.d. "Queerness and Gender Performance in Indigenous P'urhépecha Communities in Michoacán and the United States." PhD diss., University of California, Santa Cruz.

Gonzalez, Francisco E. 2009. "Mexico's Drug War Gets Brutal." *Current History* 108:72–76.

González, Rachel Valentina. 2019. *Quinceañera Style: Social Belonging and Latinx Consumer Identities.* Austin: University of Texas Press.

González-Martin, Rachel V., Mintzi A. Martínez-Rivera, and Solimar Otero. 2022. "Redirecting Currents: Theoretical Wayfinding with Latinx Folkloristics and Women of Color Transnational Feminisms." Special issue, *Journal of American Folklore* 135 (536). https://muse.jhu.edu/issue/47854.

Goodale, Mark. 2006. "Reclaiming Modernity: Indigenous Cosmopolitanism and the Coming of the Second Revolution in Bolivia." *American Ethnologist* 33 (4): 634–649.

Govers, Cora. 2006. *Performing the Community: Representation, Ritual and Reciprocity in the Totonac Highlands of Mexico.* Berlin: Lit Verlag.

Greene, Shane. 2009. *Customizing Indigeneity: Paths to a Visionary Politics in Peru.* Palo Alto, CA: Stanford University Press.

Grixti, Joe. 2006. "Symbiotic Transformations: Youth, Global Media and Indigenous Culture in Malta." *Media, Culture & Society* 28 (1): 105–122.

REFERENCES

Guerra Manzo, Enrique. 2015. "Las autodefensas de Michoacán: Movimiento social, paramilitarismo y neocaciquismo." *Política y Cultura* 44:7–31.

Gutierrez, Celedonio. 1974–1975. "San Juan Parangaricutiro: Memorias de un Campesino." In *Anales del INAH*, introduction and notes by Mary Lee Nolan, 7 (5): 85–120.

Heaven, Cara, and Matthew Tubridy. 2003. "Global Youth Culture and Youth Identity." In *Highly Affected, Rarely Considered: International Youth Parliament Commission Report on the Impact of Globalisation on Young People*, edited by James Arvanitakis, 149–160. Surry Hills, NSW: International Youth Parliament (IYP); Oxfam Community Aid Abroad.

Hellier-Tinoco, Ruth. 2011. *Embodying México: Tourism, Nationalism & Performance*. Oxford: Oxford University Press.

Hernández Dimas, Guadalupe. 2004. *La mujer p'urhépecha: una mirada desde la pobreza de las comunidades*. Morelia: Instituto Michoacano de la Mujer-Secretaría de Desarrollo Social de Michoacán, México.

Hernández Dimas, Guadalupe, and Luis Sereno Coló, eds. 2005. *Mujeres p'urhépecha. Caminando entre piedras / Uárhiti p'urhépecha. Tsakapendu Xanara- ni*. Morelia: Instituto Michoacano de la Mujer-Secretaría de Desarrollo Social de Michoacán, México.

Huacuz Elías, María Guadalupe. 2009. "Encuentros y desencuentros en torno al género en las comunidades purépechas." Presentation at the Grupo Kw'aniskuyarhani meeting on November 28, 2009 in Pátzcuaro, Michoacán.

Human Rights Watch. 2015. "Mexico: Police Killings in Michoacán. Evidence of Extrajudicial Executions in Apatzingan and Tanhuato." https://www.hrw.org/news/2015/10/28/mexico-police-killings-michoacan.

Hutchinson, Sydney. 2007. *From Quebradita to Duranguense: Dance in Mexican American Youth Culture*. Tucson: University of Arizona Press.

Ibrahim, Awad. 2014. "Introduction." In *Critical Youth Studies Reader*, edited by Awad Ibrahim and Shirley R. Steinberg, XV–XX. New York: Peter Lang.

Ibrahim, Awad, and Shirley R. Steinberg, eds. 2014. *Critical Youth Studies Reader*. New York: Peter Lang.

Jacinto Zavala, Agustín. 1995. "El Costumbre' como modelo de Formación Histórico-Social." In *Estudios Michoacanos* VI, edited by Victor Gabriel Muro González, 23–40. Zamora: El Colegio de Michoacán.

———. (1983) 1997. "La Japingua en la Mitología Purépecha." In *Sabiduría Popular*, 2nd ed., edited by Arturo Chamorro, 275–288. Zamora: El Colegio de Michoacán.

Jackson, Jason Baird. 2008. "Traditionalization in Ceremonial Ground Oratory: Native American Speechmaking in Eastern Oklahoma." *Midwestern Folklore* 34 (2): 3–16.

REFERENCES

Jackson, Jean E., and Kay B. Warren. 2005. "Indigenous Movements in Latin America, 1992–2004: Controversies, Ironies, New Directions." *Annual Review of Anthropology* 34:549–573.

Jiménez, Ernesto. 2024. "AMLO superó a Calderón: cierra su sexenio con más crímenes de Estado que durante la 'guerra contra el narco.'" *Infobae*, September 29, 2024. https://www.infobae.com/mexico/2024/09/29/amlo-supero-a-calderon-cierra-su-sexenio-con-mas-crimenes-de-estado-que-durante-la-guerra-contra-el-narco/.

Kearney, Michael. 1986. "From the Invisible Hand to Visible Feet: Anthropological Studies of Migration and Development." *Annual Review of Anthropology* 15:331–361.

Kemper, Robert V. 1979. "Compadrazgo in City and Countryside: A Comparison of Tzintzuntzan Migrants and Villagers." *Kroeber Anthropological Society Papers* 55–56:25–44.

———. 2011. "Estado y antropología en México y Estados Unidos: Reflexiones sobre los proyectos Tarascos." *Relaciones: Estudios de Historia y Sociedad* 32 (128): 209–241.

Kemper, Robert V., and Julie Adkins. 2004. "De la 'moderna área tarasca' a la 'tierra natal P'urhépecha': conceptos cambiantes de identidad étnica y regional." *Relaciones* 100:227–278.

Kertzer, David I. 1988. *Ritual, Politics and Power*. New Haven, CT: Yale University Press.

Kovach, Margaret. 2009. *Indigenous Methodologies: Characteristics, Conversations, and Contexts*. Toronto: University of Toronto Press.

———. 2010. "Conversational Method in Indigenous Research." *First Peoples Child & Family Review* 5 (1): 40–48.

———. 2018. "Doing Indigenous Methodologies: A Letter to a Research Class." In *The SAGE Handbook of Qualitative Research*. 5th ed., edited by Norman K. Denzin and Yvonna S. Lincoln, 214–234. Thousand Oaks, CA: Sage.

Leco Tomás, Casimiro. 2017. "Jaripeos Purépechas en Wendell, Carolina del Norte, Estados Unidos." *Acta Universitaria* 27 (2): 83–92.

León, Nicolás. (1889) 1982. "El Matrimonio entre los Tarascos Precolombianos y sus Actuales Usos." *Revista Nueva Antropología* 5 (18): 69–78.

Liffman, Paul M. 2005. "Fuegos, Guías y Raíces: Estructuras Cosmológicas y Procesos Históricos en la Territorialidad Huichol." *Relaciones* 101:53–79.

———. 2011. *Huichol Territory and the Mexican Nation: Indigenous Ritual, Land Conflict and Sovereignty Claims*. Tucson: University of Arizona Press.

Lumholtz, Carl. 1904. *El México Desconocido: Cinco años de exploración entre las tribus de la Siera Madre Occidental; en la Sierra Caliente de Tepic y Jalisco, y entre los Tarascos de Michoacán*. Translated by Balbino Dávalos. New York: Charles Scribner's Sons.

REFERENCES

Magaña, Maurice Rafael. 2020. *Cartographies of Youth Resistance: Hip-Hop, Punk, and Urban Autonomy in Mexico.* Berkeley: University of California Press.

Maldonado Aranda, Salvador. 2013. "Stories of Drug Trafficking in Rural Mexico: Territories, Drugs and Cartels in Michoacán." *European Review of Latin American and Caribbean Studies* 94:43–66.

Malinowski, Bronislaw. (1922) 1953. *Argonauts of the Western Pacific: An Account of Native Enterprise and Adventure in the Archipelagoes of Melanesian New Guinea.* New York: E. P. Dutton.

Márquez Joaquín, Pedro, ed. 2007. *¿Tarascos o P'urhépecha? Voces sobre antiguas y nuevas discusiones en torno al gentilicio michoacano.* Morelia: Universidad Michoacana de San Nicolás de Hidalgo, Instituto de Investigaciónes Históricas, El Colegio de Michoacán, Gobierno del Estado de Michoacán, Universidad Intercultural Indígena de Michoacán, Grupo Kw'anískuyarhani de Estiosos del Pueblo Purépecha, Fondo Editorial Morevallado.

———. 2014. *Pirekua: canto poco conocido.* Zamora: El Colegio de Michoacán, Consejo para el Arte y la Cultura de la Región P'urhepecha.

———. 2023. *Juramukua, gobernanza p'urhépecha.* Zamora: El Colegio de Michoacán.

Martínez-Rivera, Mintzi A. 2014. "'De El Costumbre al Rock': Rock Indígena and Being Indigenous in 21st Century Mexico." *Journal of Latin American and Caribbean Ethnic Studies* 9 (3): 272–292.

———. 2018. "(Re)Imagining Indigenous Popular Culture." In *Race and Cultural Practice in Popular Culture*, edited by Domino Renee Perez and Rachel V. González-Martin, 91–109. New Brunswick, NJ: Rutgers University Press.

———. 2020. "Misa Kuani: la boda p'urhépecha y sus transformaciones históricas. Un análisis etnohistórico y etnográfico." *Relaciones Estudios de Historia y Sociedad* 41 (163): 97–118.

———. 2021. "'No One Would Believe Us:' An Auto-Ethnography of Conducting Fieldwork in a Conflict Zone." In *Theorizing Folklore from the Margins: Critical and Ethical Approaches*, edited by Solimar Otero and Mintzi A. Martínez-Rivera, 257–273. Bloomington: Indiana University Press.

———. 2022. "Field/Campo. Doing Research of/from/at Home: Fieldwork Research Ethics in Latinx Contexts." In special volume "Redirecting Currents: Theoretical Wayfinding with Latinx Folkloristics and Women of Color Transnational Feminisms," edited by Rachel V. González-Martin, Mintzi A. Martínez-Rivera, and Solimar Otero, *Journal of American Folklore* 135 (536): 180–189.

———. 2023. "Following the Kurpiticha Trail." In *Dancing with Life: Recontextualizing Mexican Masks.* Museum Catalogue and Exhibit, edited and curated by Pavel Shlossberg for the American Indian Collection at the Northwest Museum of Arts and Culture (MAC), Spokane, WA, 42–45. Austin: University of Texas Press.

———. Forthcoming. "The Legend of Mintzita or When La Llorona Is Your *Tocaya.*" In *Weeping Women: The Haunting Presence of La Llorona in Mexican and Chicanx Lore*, edited by Kathleen Alcalá and Norma Elia Cantú. San Antonio: Trinity University Press.

———. Forthcoming. "What Do We Mean by Decolonizing (Folklore) Methods? Some Stories, Suggestions, and Strategies from Someone in the Middle of the Journey." In *Decolonizing Folklore*, edited by Tim Frandy, Selina Morales, and Phillys May-Machunda. Madison: University of Wisconsin Press.

Mathews, Holly F. 1985. "'We Are Mayordomo': A Reinterpretation of Women's Roles in the Mexican Cargo System." *American Ethnologists* 12 (2): 285–301.

Mauss, Marcel. (1954) 1967. *The Gift: Forms and Function of Exchange in Archaic Society*. New York: Norton.

Mayer, Enrique. 2002. *The Articulated Peasant: Household Economies in the Andes*. Boulder, CO: Westview.

McDowell, John Holmes. 2002. *Poetry and Violence: The Ballad Tradition of Mexico's Costa Chica*. Urbana: University of Illinois Press.

Mead, Margaret. 1928. *Coming of Age in Samoa*. New York: HarperCollins.

Medina Pérez, Alberto. 2006. *Guía Lingüística del Idioma P'urhépecha*. Morelia: Universidad Michoacana de San Nicolás de Hidalgo.

Mendieta y Núñez, Lucio, ed. 1940. *Los Tarascos: Monografía Histórica, Etnográfica y Económica*. Mexico City: Imprenta Universitaria, Universidad Nacional Autónoma de Mexico Instituto de Investigaciónes Sociales.

Mendoza Valentín, Rafael. 1994. *50 Aniversario del pueblo que se negó a morir: San Juan Nuevo Parangaricutiro Michoacán, México*. Nuevo San Juan Parangaricutiro: H. Ayuntamiento de Nuevo San Juan Parangaricutiro.

———. 1995. *Yo ví nacer un volcán*. León: Coloristas y Asociados.

———. n.d. *Historia Chiquita, Volcán Grandote. Relatos ilustrados de San Juan Nuevo Parangaricutiro, Michoacán*. Nuevo San Juan Parangaricutiro: H. Ayuntamiento de Nuevo San Juan Parangaricutiro.

Mendoza, Zoila. 2010. "La fuerza de los caminos sonoros: caminata y música en Qoyllurit'i." *Anthropologica* 28 (28): 15–38.

Mignolo, Walter, and Catherine E. Walsh. 2018. *On Decoloniality: Concepts, Analysis, Praxis*. Durham, NC: Duke University Press.

Mintz, Sidney W., and Eric R. Wolf. 1950. "An Analysis of Ritual Co-Parenthood (Compadrazgo)." *Southwestern Journal of Anthropology* 6 (4): 341–368.

Monzón García, Cristina. 2004. *Los morfemas espaciales del p'urhépecha*. Zamora: El Colegio de Michoacán.

Mora, Mariana. 2017. *Kuxlejal Politics: Indigenous Autonomy, Race, and Decolonizing Research in Zapatista Communities*. Austin: University of Texas Press.

Myerhoff, Barbara G. 1974. *Peyote Hunt: The Sacred Journey of the Huichol Indians*. Ithaca, NY: Cornell University Press.

REFERENCES

Narayan, Kirin. 1993. "How 'Native' Is a Native Anthropologist?" *American Anthropologist* 95 (3): 671–686.

Noel, Andrea. 2015. "Where Mexico's Drug War Was Born: Timeline of the Security Crisis in Michoacán." Vice News: Americas Section. https://news.vice.com/article/where-mexicos-drug-war-was-born-a-timeline-of-the-security-crisis-in-michoacan.

Nolan, Mary Lee. 1979. "Impact of Paricutin in Five Communities." In *Volcanic Activity and Human Ecology,* edited by Payson D. Sheets and Donald Grayson, 293–305. New York: Academic Press.

Noyes, Dorothy. 2003. *Fire in the Plaça: Catalan Festival Politics after Franco.* Philadelphia: University of Pennsylvania Press.

Ojeda Dávila, Lorena. 2006. *Fiestas y Ceremonias Tradicionales P'urhépecha.* Morelia: Secretaria de Cultura de Michoacán.

———. 2015. "Cherán: el poder del concenso y las políticas comunitarias." *Política Común* 7. https://doi.org/10.3998/pc.12322227.0007.007.

———, ed. 2018. *Pioneros de la antropología en Michoacán. Mexicanos y estadounidenses en la región tarasca/purépecha.* Morelia: Universidad Michoacana de San Nicolás de Hidalgo, Conacyt, El Colegio de Michoacán.

Otero, Solimar. 2020. *Archives of Conjure: Stories of the Dead in Afrolatinx Cultures.* New York: Columbia University Press.

Otero, Solimar, and Mintzi A. Martínez-Rivera. 2017. "Poder y Cultura: Latino/a Folklore and Popular Culture." Special issue, *Chiricú Journal: Latina/o Literatures, Arts, and Cultures* 2:1.

———. 2021. *Theorizing Folklore from the Margins: Critical and Ethical Approaches.* Bloomington: Indiana University Press.

Padilla Pineda, Mario. 2000. *Ciclo Festivo y Orden Ceremonial: El Sistema de Cargo Religiosos en San Pedro Ocumicho.* Zamora: El Colegio de Michoacán.

Paleta Peréz, Guillermo, and Antonio Fuentes Díaz. 2013. "Territorios, inseguridad y autodefensas comunitarias en localidades de la Meseta Purépecha de Michoacán, México." *Revista Márgenes* 13 (10): 62–68.

Pardo Veiras, José Luis, and Íñigo Arredondo. 2021. "Una guerra inventada y 350,000 muertos en México" *The Washington Post,* June 14, 2021. https://www.washingtonpost.com/es/post-opinion/2021/06/14/mexico-guerra-narcotrafico-calderon-homicidios-desaparecidos/.

Paredes Martínez, Carlos Salvador. 2017. *Al tañer de las campanas. Los pueblos indígenas del antiguo Michoacán en la época colonial.* Historia de los pueblos indígenas de México. Mexico City: Centro de Investigaciónes y Estudios Superiores en Antropología Social y Comisión Nacional para el Desarrollo de los Pueblos Indígenas.

Perez, Domino Renee. 2023. *Fatherhood in the Borderlands: A Daughter's Slow Approach.* Austin: University of Texas Press.

220 REFERENCES

Pérez Caballero, Jesús. 2015. "Autodefensas Michoacanas, variante regional de la 'guerra al narcotráfico' en México." *Revista CIDOB d' Afers Internacionals* 110:165–187.

Pérez Ruiz, Maya Lorena, ed. 2008. *Jóvenes indígenas y globalización en América Latina.* Mexico City: Instituto Nacional de Antropología e Historia.

———. 2011a. "Retos para la investigación de los jóvenes indígenas." *Alteridades* 21 (42): 65–75.

———. 2011b. "Ser joven entre los mayas de Yucatán. Diferencia y desigualdad en la globalización." *Sociedad y Discurso* 20:79–102/124.

———. 2014. "Los jóvenes indígenas vistos por la antropología en México. Una ventana a la etnografía del siglo XX." In *Temas de la antropología Mexicana, vol. 2,* edited by José Luis Vera Cortés, 233–259. Mexico City: Academia Mexicana de Ciencias. Antropológicas A.C.

———. 2015. *Ser joven y ser maya en un mundo globalizado.* Mexico City: Instituto Nacional de Antropología e Historia.

Pitarch, Pedro, and Gemma Orobitg, eds. 2012. *Modernidades Indígenas.* Madrid: Iberoamericana and Vervuert.

Plá, Rosa. 1988. *Los Días del Volcán Paricutín.* Morelia: Instituto Michoacano de Cultura, Carrasquilla Editores, S.A. de C.V.

———. 1989. "Leyendas y Tradición Oral en San Juan Parangaricutiro: Pueblo Nuevo." *Estudios Michoacanos III,* 3:269–287.

Próspero Maldonado, Rocio, 2000. *Kurpiticha (Los Curpitres): Herencia Tradicional de San Juan Parangaricutiro, Michoacán.* Nuevo San Juan Parangaricutiro: H. Ayuntamiento de Nuevo San Juan Parangaricutiro.

Ramirez Garayzar, Amalia. 2014. *Tejiendo la identidad. El rebozo entre las mujeres purépechas de Michoacán.* Mexico City: Consejo Nacional para la Cultura y las Artes, Direccion General de Culturas Populares.

Rappaport, Roy A. 1992. "Ritual." In *Folklore, Cultural Performance and Popular Entertainments: A Communications-Centered Handbook,* edited by Richard Bauman, 249–260. New York: Oxford University Press.

Reed, John D. 1970. "Paricutin Revisited: A Review of a Man's Attempt to Adapt to Ecological Changes Resulting from Volcanic Catastrophe." *Geoforum* 4:7–25.

Rhode, Francisco José. 1946. "Angahuan." *Anales del Instituto de Investigaciones Estéticas* 4 (14): 5–18.

Richards-Greeves, Gillian. 2013. "Going Home: The Native Ethnographer's Baggage and the Crisis of Representation." *Anthropology News* 54:11–12, 15–16.

Rincón García, Luis A. 2007. *Comunicación y Cultura en Zinacantán. Un acercamiento a los procesos comunicacionales.* San Cristobal de las Casas: Centro Estatal de Lenguas, Arte y Literatura.

Rivera Cusicanqui, Silvia. 2014. *Un mundo ch'ixi es posible: ensayos desde un presente en crisis.* Buenos Aires: Tinta Limón Ediciones.

REFERENCES

Rodríguez, Roberto Cintli. 2014. *Our Sacred Maíz Is Our Mother: Indigeneity and Belonging in the Americas*. Tucson: University of Arizona Press.

romero, fabian. 2023. "Insurgent Kinship: Queer P'urhépecha Migrations and Kinship." PhD diss., University of Washington-Seattle.

Rosado-May, Francisco J., Luis Urrieta Jr., Andrew Dayton, and Barbara Rogoff. 2020. "Innovation as a Key Feature of Indigenous Ways of Learning: Individual and Communities Generating Knowledge." In *Handbook of the Cultural Foundations of Learning*, edited by N. S. Nasir, C. D. Lee, R. Pea, and M. McKinney de Royston, 79–96. New York: Routledge.

Roth-Seneff, Andrew, and Robert Kemper. 1983. "Tarascans." In *The Handbook of North American Indians, Vol. 10 Southwest*, edited by Alfonso Ortiz, 243–247. Washington, DC: Smithsonian Institution.

Roth-Seneff, Andrew, and Manuel Sosa. 2003. "Tradiciones del Estado, usos y costumbres y desarrollo communal: el caso del astillador de Angahuan, Michoacán." *Estudios Michoacanos* 10:117–139.

Ruiz, Isidro. 2020. "Luchan por la necesaria reinvidicación de los pueblos originarios." *El Sol de Zamora*, July 27, 2020. https://www.elsoldezamora .com.mx/local/luchan-por-la-necesaria-reivindicacion-de-los-pueblos -originarios-5028820.html.

Saavedra, R. 1925. "En Tierra de Tarascos." *Magazine de Geografía Nacional* 1 (2): 1–33.

Santana, Daniel. 2019. "Indigenous Masculinities and the Tarascan Borderlands in Sixteenth-Century Michoacán." PhD diss., University of Texas at El Paso.

Savage, Jon. 2008. *Teenage: The Prehistory of Youth Culture: 1875–1945*. New York: Penguin Books.

Schechner, Richard. 1985. *Between Theater and Anthropology*. Philadelphia: University of Pennsylvania Press.

Schieffelin, Edward L. 1985. "Performance and the Cultural Construction of Reality." *American Ethnologist* 12:707–724.

———. 1998. "Problematizing Performance." In *Ritual, Performance and Media*, edited by Felicia Hughes-Freeland, 194–207. New York: Routledge.

Shlossberg, Pavel. 2015. *Crafting Identity: Transnational Indian Arts and the Politics of Race in Central México*. Tucson: University of Arizona Press.

———. ed. 2023. *Dancing with Life: Recontextualizing Mexican Masks*. Museum Catalogue and Exhibit, American Indian Collection at the Northwest Museum of Arts and Culture (MAC), Spokane, WA. Austin: University of Texas Press.

Schütze, Stephanie. 2014. "Purhépechas in Tarecuato and Chicago: Shifts in Local Power Structures through Transnational Negotiations." *Latin American Perspectives* 41 (3): 75–89.

Segato, Rita Laura. 2013. *La crítica de la colonialidad en ocho ensayos y una antropología por demanda*. Bueno Aires: Prometeo Libros.

Siegal, David. 2023. *The Interlude in Academe: Reclaiming Time and Space for Intellectual Life*. Lanham, MD: Lexington Books.

Shorter, David Delgado. 2009. *We Will Dance Our Truth: Yaqui History in Yoeme Performances*. Lincoln: University of Nebraska Press.

Smith, Linda Tuhiwai. 1999. *Decolonizing Methodologies: Research and Indigenous Peoples*. London: Zed Books.

Soto Bravo, Valente. 1982. *Propuesta de un anteproyecto de Educación Purépecha. Estudio comparativo de la educación confesional, oficial, familiar y comunitaria en Angahuan, Michoacán*. Pátzcuaro: Programa de Formación Profesional de Etnolingüistas SEP-INI-CIESAS.

Spears-Rico, Gabriela. 2015. "Consuming the Native Other: Mestiza/o Melancholia and the Performance of Indigeneity in Michoacan." PhD diss., University of California, Berkeley.

———. 2019. "In the Time of War and Hashtags: Rehumanizing Indigeneity in the Digital Landscape." In *Indigenous Interfaces: Spaces, Technology, and Social Networks in México and Central America*. Critical Issues in Indigenous Studies, edited by Gloria E. Chacon and Jennifer Menjivar Gomez, 180–200. Tucson: University of Arizona Press.

Steinberg, Shirley R., and Awad Ibrahim, eds. 2015. *Critically Researching Youth*. New York: Peter Lang.

Storm, Marian. 1945. *A Book for Travelers in Michoacán: Enjoying Uruapan, México*. México City: Editorial Bolivar.

Sutton-Smith, Brian. 1999. *Children's Folklore: A Source Book*. Denver, CO: University Press of Colorado.

Toor, Frances. 1925. "Una nota sobre las Canacuas." *Mexican Folkways* 6 (3): 108–109.

Tortorici, Seb. 2007. "'Heran Todos Putos': Sodomitical Subcultures and Disordered Desires in Early Colonial Mexico." *Ethnohistory* 54 (1): 35–64.

Toussaint, Manuel. 1945–1946. "Angahua." *Journal of the Society of Architectural Historians*. 5:24–26.

Trask, Parker D. 1943. "The Mexican Volcano Paricutin." *Science* 98 (2554): 501–505.

Troutman, John W. 2009. *Indian Blues: American Indians and the Politics of Music 1879–1934*. Norman: University of Oklahoma Press.

Turner, Victor. 1967. *The Forest of Symbols: Aspects of Ndembu Ritual*. Ithaca, NY: Cornell University Press.

———. (1969) 1977. *The Ritual Process: Structure and Anti-Structure*. Ithaca, NY: Cornell University Press.

———. 1982. *From Ritual to Theater. The Human Seriousness of Play*. New York: PAJ.

Urrieta, Luis. Jr. 2012. "Las identidades también lloran/Identities Also Cry: Exploring the Human Side of Latina/o Indigenous Identities." In *Comparative Indigeneities of the Americas: Toward a Hemispheric Approach*, edited by A. Aldama, M. B. Castellanos, and L. Gutiérrez Nájera, 321–335. Tucson: University of Arizona Press.

———. 2017. "Identity, Violence, and Authenticity: Challenging Static Conceptions of Indigeneity." *Latino Studies* 15 (2): 254–261.

van Gennep, Arnold. 1960. *The Rites of Passage*. Translated by Monika B. Vizedom and Gabrielle L. Caffee. Chicago: University of Chicago Press.

Velasco Ortiz, Laura, and Margot Olavarria. 2014. "Transnational Ethnic Processes: Indigenous Mexican Migrations to the United States." *Latin American Perspectives* 41 (3): 54–74.

Virtanen, Pirjo Kristiina. 2012. *Indigenous Youth in Brazilian Amazonia: Changing Lived Worlds*. New York: Palgrave Macmillan.

Warren, Benedict J. 1984. *The Conquest of Michoacán: The Spanish Domination of the Tarascan Kingdom in Western México, 1521–1530*. Norman: University of Oklahoma Press.

Works, Martha A., and Keith S. Hadley. 2000. "Hace Cincuenta Años: Repeat Photography and Landscape Change in the Sierra Purépecha of Michoacán, México." *Yearbook, Conference of Latin Americanist Geographers* 26:139–155.

Zúñiga Bravo, Federico Gerardo. 2019. "Espacio turístico y turismo cultural a través de la ruta Don Vasco en Michoacán, México." *Revista Geográfica de América Central* 63 (2):75–100.

Index

Page numbers in italics indicate illustrations.

aguadora (Holy Week ritual), 79–80, 86n30
Alcalá, Jerónimo de, 94–95
anchikuarhua (serving family and community), 147, 165
Angahuan, 11–16, 33–34; barrios of, 70, 73; community life in, 16–21; economy of, 39, 41, 43–46, 55n18; growing up in, 65–66; maps of, 37, 156; during Mexican Revolution, 39; mountains of, 10, 32, 37–38, 38; preconquest artifacts of, 39; public library of, 49; schools of, 42; social organization of, 109; youth culture of, 67–69, 84n8
arras (gold-painted coins), 129n1
Assumption of the Virgin, 79–80, 86n30; cargueros of, 48, 57n32, 160, 170; fiesta of, 6, 17, 61, 83n1
Aureoles Conejo, Silvano, 57n38
Aztec Empire, 39

Bakhtin, Mikhail, 163–64
baptism, 175; godparents of, 101, 167, 169–70, 200
bathing the bride (bañar a la novia), 6, 88, 89–90, 114–17, 194
Bauman, Richard, 178
Beals, Ralph Larson, 84n15, 200n2
Beca Oportunidades program, 46

Berry, Maya J., 24
Brandes, Stanley, 159
bridesmaids, 205
Briggs, Charles, 177
Bucholtz, Mary, 63–64

Caballeros Templarios (narcos), 22, 23
Cabildo de Ancianos, 38, 46–48
Calderón, Felipe, 21–22
Cárdenas Fernández, Blanca, 67
cargo system, 3, 28n6, 93, 147, 170; advancement in, 47–48; civil, 46–47, 49, 56n29, 57n31; compadrazgo and, 66, 69, 83n7; religious, 46–48, 57n37; same-sex couples and, 84n15
Carnival, 67. See also Lent
carrying the bride (kamandini), 160–63, 161, 185
Cartel Jalisco Nueva Generación (narcos), 22
Carvajal, Antonio de, 39, 54n13
casarse de blanco (white wedding), 5–6, 134, 135, 174, 183–84, 205. See also mestizo weddings
Cerano, Pedro, 67
Ch'anantskua (Juego de la Madurez), 67
Cherán, 14, 42, 84n15, 200n2; economy of, 35–36; self-defense movement of, 23, 30n31, 48

226　　INDEX

civil wedding. *See* sivil kuambuni
Clifford, James, 111, 124
clothing: of brides, 5–6, 120, 123, 134–35, 139,
　184, 197; of married women, 102
Comisariado de Bienes Comunales, 47,
　57n32
Comisión para el Desarrollo de los Pueblos
　Indígenas (CDI), 35, 36, 53n4
compadrazgo ritual, 50–51, 140, 166–69, 204;
　cargo system and, 66, 69, 83n7. *See also*
　godparents
confianza, 94, 101, 192. *See also* te toca
　obligations
Consejo de Govierno Comunal, 49
Consejo de Vigilancia, 47
Consejo Supremo Indígena de
　Michoacán, 48
Cortés Máximo, Juan Carlos, 147
Costumbre (form of government), 23, 30n31
Council of Elders, 38, 46–48
courtship rituals, 61–65, 69–82, 71, 74, 76
COVID-19 pandemic, 24, 48, 204–5
Cristero revolts (1926–1929), 42
Critical Indigenous Studies, 64
Critical Native American and Indigenous
　Studies, 8
Critical Race and Ethnic Studies, 8, 19, 64
Critical Youth Studies, 8, 19, 64–65
cultural borrowing, 64
customization, 110–11, 117, 124, 176, 177,
　184–86, 198–99

Danza de los Viejitos, 36, 73, 85n25
Days of the Dead, 6, 22, 66, 187, 188, 206
Deloria, Phillip J., 111
desaparecidos, 23
Diosïri uandarhi (person who speaks of
　God), 50, 140, 165–66, 169; misa kuani
　and, 191; origins of, 171nn10–12
domestic violence, 104nn10–11, 163
drug war violence, 21–24, 30n30, 48, 57n38,
　195, 206–7

elopement (ueakuarhini), 6, 67, 77, 80, 89;
　engagement versus, 90–92, 94–98, 102,
　103; misa kuani after, 100, 102; reasons for,
　98–100; "stealing the bride" as, 104n8

embroidery, 15, 27n3, 45, 46
engagement. *See* uarhipini
Epiphany, 6, 17, 73
ethnographic research. *See* research
　methods

Familia Michoacana (narcos), 22
first communions, 50–51,
　101, 200
forgiveness, asking for (potpinsani), 98–103,
　109, 192, 196
Foster, George, 114
Fox, Vicente, 21, 54n5

Garrido Izaguirre, Eva María, 109, 111–12,
　123–24
gender equality, 58n43, 166
gender norms, 49–50, 84n13; educational
　opportunities and, 55n17; LGBTQ+
　and, 57n40, 58n43, 84n15, 207; marital
　status and, 102–3; of pastorelas, 72–73,
　76; social position and, 90–91, 94; in
　Tarascan Empire, 58nn41–42; of women
　entrepreneurs, 46
Gender Studies, 64
Gilberti, Maturino, 36
godparents, 50–52, 107–9, 117–22, 129n1,
　165–69; baptism, 101, 167, 169–70, 200;
　compadrazgo ritual of, 50–51, 69, 83n7,
　140; first communion, 50–51, 101, 200;
　graduation, 52; selection of, 118–19, 122;
　takichani for, 202, 203–4; types of, 129n1,
　175; of wedding cake, 108, 167, 175, 182,
　187, 189, 200n10; of wedding ring,
　175, 192
Gómez Bravo, Lucas, 13–14, 26, 36
Gómez Santacruz family, 16, 20; home of,
　14–15, 37, 38; members of, 14
Gómez Zamora, Mario A., 9, 58n43
González, Rachel V., 7
Greene, Shane, 84n9, 110–11,
　124, 177
Grixti, Joe, 64

Heaven, Cara, 64
Hernández Dimas, Guadalupe, 58n43
Hñähñu communities, 35

Holy Week, 77, 97; aguadora ritual of, 79–80, 86n30; Uiítakua during, *68, 70*

Hummel, Agatha, 46

Ibrahim, Awad, 64–65

identity politics, 111

Indigenous identity, 4, 28n7, 53n4, 129n2, 206–8; cargo system and, 56n29; cultural transformation and, 10–11; "customizing" of, 84n9; knowledge systems and, 178

Indigenous rock music, 111

Indigenous teacher movement, 96

in-laws, 100, 104nn10–11

Instituto Nacional Indigenista (INI), 54n5

iuinskua, 197, 203

Iurhixu convent, 39, 44, 45; cargueros of, 77, 198; Uiítakua and, 70

Jacinto Zavala, Agustín, 93–94

Jackson, Jason, 177

jakajkukua (following rules of nature), 147, 160, 164, 165

jaripeo (rodeo), 42, 61, 80, 171n8

Jefe de Tenencia, 47, 49, 57n32

kamandini (carrying the bride), 160–63, *161*, 185

kamataru niani wedding ritual, 130n11, 152, 165–67, 189–92

kanakuecha (bread crowns and necklaces), *60*, 61–63, 66, 83n3, *168*, 168–69, 172nn17–18, 194

kanarperakua gift-giving ritual, *141*, 141–42, 159–63, 170, 194

kashumbikua (behaving honorably), 147, 152, 165

Kertzer, David I., 159

kuanindikuecha (embroidered shawls), 27n3, 45, 46

kurpiti dance, 70, 73–75, *74*, 79, 85n19, 170

Latinx, 19

Lent, 6, 67, 97, 196

León, Nicolás, 172n17

levantamientos, 66, 84n16, 175

LGBTQ+, 57n40, 58n43, 84n15, 207. *See also* gender norms

López Obrador, Andrés Manuel, 30n30, 54n5

luchpani (wrestling), 160–63, 185

Magaña, Maurice Rafael, 65

Manchineri communities, 121

marhuatspeni (serving the people), 147–48

marriage license, 114

Martínez Chávez family, 21

Mauss, Marcel, 92

Mazahua communities, 35

McDowell, John H., 159–60

Mendoza, Zoila, 149

mestizo weddings, 135, 176–77, 180–86, *181, 183, 186*; clothing for, 1–2, 6; cultural transformation of, 187–93.198–199; godparents of, 129n1; misa kuani of, 175, 184, 194. *See also* casarse de blanco

Mexican Revolution (1910–1920), 39, 114

microloans, 46

migrant workers, 43–44, 46, 55n19, 180; remittances from, 43; return of, 3, 67–69, 81–83

misa kuani (Catholic wedding ceremony), 5–7, 27n4, 66, 133–42, 192; creating of, 117–22; Days of the Dead and, 187, 188; Dioïri uandarhi and, 191; elopement and, 100, 102; engagement and, 97, 98, 102, 104n7; eve of, 128–29; framework of, 149–69; invitations to, 121, 127; kamataru niani, 190; mestizo wedding with, 175, 184, 194; preparations for, *106*, 117, *124*, 124–27, *127*; sivil kuambuni with, 98, 113–14, 126–27, 176, 192–96, 207; traditionalizing of, 196–98; variations of, 146, 149, 176, 190

Mora, Mariana, 8

mothers-in-law, 100, 104nn10–11

Mudejar art, 45, 56n25

Museo Comunitario Kutsïkua Arhákucha, 54n12

Nahua communities, 35

narco groups, 22–23. *See also* drug war violence

Noyes, Dorothy, 152

Obama immigration policies, 56n21

ocotes (torches), *113*, 114, 116, 127, 194, 197

INDEX

Ojeda Dávila, Lorena, 170n3
Otero, Solimar, 7

padrinu arhip'eni niani (godparent request),
  118–19
papu, 140, *153*, 154, 157, *158*, 194
Parakata-Tzintzun Working Group, 58n43
Paricutín volcano, 2, *12*, 18, 32, 38, 41, 44–45
pastorela dance, 70–73, *71*, 75–76,
  79, 170
Patum, 152
Pátzcuaro, 11, 24
Pérez Ruiz, Maya Lorena, 8
Pimu Akuri, 77
pirekua (song), 13, 36, 80–81, 120, 205, 206
Pirinda communities, 35
Población Indígena Estimada (PIE), 53n4
Pomacanchi community, 158
posadas (Christmas parties), 19, 30n27
potpinsani (asking forgiveness), 98–103, 109,
  192, 196
p'urhekujkua (warrior spirit), 147, 160, 164
P'urhépecha communities, 3, 13, 33–36, 53n4;
  aesthetics of, 109, 112, 123–24; cuisine of,
  29n19, 36, 129n6; language of, 13, 24–25, 36;
  music of, 13, 36, 111, 205; values of, 146–48,
  155, 166, 169
P'urhépecha Empire. *See* Tarascan Empire
P'urhépecha Studies, 8–9, 17

quinceañeras, 199, 201n14

Rappaport, Roy A., 148
reciprocity, 92–94, 101, 160, 163. *See also* te
  toca obligations
relationship-formalization rituals, 148, 149,
  164–69
religious cargo system, 46–48, 57n37
religious wedding ceremony. *See* misa kuani
research methods, 3–4, 128; in conflict zone,
  21–24; decolonial, 7–8, 19–20, 24, 64;
  fieldwork, 16–17, 19
Resurrección cargueros, 48, *68*, 69–70, 79, 82
Rhode, Francisco José, 45
rites of passage, 9, 63, 67, 69
rituals, 148, 197; of controlled violence,
  148, 149, 158–64, 185; definition of, 10;

in movement, 148–58, *150–53*, *156*, *158*;
  relationship-formalization, 148, 149,
  164–69
Rivera, Simón, 197
Rivera Cusicanqui, Silvia, 8
robo de la novia (stealing the bride), 104n8.
  See also elopement
rodeo. *See* jaripeo
Rodríguez, Roberto Cintli, 7
romero, fabian, 9
Rosado-May, Francisco J., 178
Ruta de Don Vasco (tour route), 44

Saavedra, R., 172n17
San Isidro fiesta, 80, 145
San Juan Parangaricutiro church, 41, 44,
  56n23
Santa Cecilia fiesta, 80
Santana, Daniel, 58n42
Santo Santiago Church, *37, 39*–41, *40*, 44, 45;
  fiesta of, 6, 13, 17, 47, 80, 204
Schechner, Richard, 130n13
Schlossberg, Pavel, 9
Seminario de la Cultura P'urhépecha
  (SECUPU), 147, 170n1
Shorter, David Delgado, 128
Siegal, David J., 128
sivil kuambuni (civil wedding ceremony),
  5–7, 28n9, *191*; history of, 129n5; misa
  kuani with, 113–14, 126–27, 176, 192–96,
  207; tembuchakua and, *113*, 113–17
social networks, 148; definition of, 84n11;
  reciprocity of, 92–94, 101, 163; uarhansani
  dance and, 157
Sosa, Manuel, 18, 37–38, 165
Soto Bravo, Valente, 171n13
Spears-Rico, Gabriela, 9
Steinberg, Shirley R., 64–65

takichani, *202*, 203–4
Tarascan Empire, 11, 27n5, 35, 39, 58nn41–42,
  171n10
Tarasco Project, 8, 29n13
tatchukua (embroidered petticoat), 27n3,
  72, 204
tembuchakua, 3, 5–11, 103; conceptualizing
  of, 7–11; creating culture as, 123–24, 128;

INDEX

229

cultural transformation of, 18, 117, 170, 175–92, 198–99; final rituals of, 203–4; misa kuani and, 194; organizing of, 103, 107–10, 119–22; as rite of passage, 9, 17; same-sex, 84n15, 207; sivil kuambuni and, *113*, 113–17

Templarios (narcos), 22, 23

te toca obligations, 7, 17, 52, 66; life events of, 90, 92; as performative act, 92, 94, 128; reciprocity of, 92–94, 160, 163; during wedding ceremonies, 100–101, 189–90

Three Kings Day, 6, 17, 73

tourism, 36, 41, 43, 44

Toussaint, Manuel, 45

traditionalization, 177, 196–98

traditional medicine, 147

trojes (log cabins), 2–3, 14, 15

Trump immigration policies, 56n21

Tubridy, Matthew, 64

Turner, Victor, 148, 159

Tzintzuntzan community, 159

uanengo (embroidered blouse), 27n3, 45, 204

uarhantsani dance, 139–40, *150*, *151*, *152*–57, *156*

uarhipini (engagement), 90–92, 95–98, 102, 103, 104n7. *See also* elopement

uarhota (courtship ritual), 61, *76*, 76–79, 86n28

uarhukua (stickball game), 13, 67

ueakuarhini. *See* elopement

Uiítakua (Carreras de Santos), *68*, *69–70*

UNESCO, 36, 54n10

Universidad Michoacana de San Nicolás de Hidalgo, 42–43

Urrieta, Luis, Jr., 9

Vázquez León, Luis, 29n23

Viagras (narcos), 22

víbora de la mar game, 6, 28n8, 182, *183*, *184*–86

Victoriano Cruz, Pedro, 147

Viejitos. *See* Danza de los Viejitos

Virgin Mary. *See* Assumption of the Virgin

Virgin of Guadalupe, 6, 86n30; cargueros of, 48, 57n32, 170, 179–80

Virtanen, Pirjo Kristiina, 121

war on drugs. *See* drug war violence

Warren, Benedict J., 54n13

Wixárika people, 149

women's rights, 58n43, 166. *See also* gender equality

Zamora, 35

Zetas (narcos), 22. *See also* drug war violence

Mintzi Auanda Martínez-Rivera is Assistant Professor of English (Folklore) and Latinx Studies at The Ohio State University. She is editor with Solimar Otero of *Theorizing Folklore from the Margins: Critical and Ethical Approaches* (IUP, 2021).

For Indiana University Press

Allison Chaplin, Acquisitions Editor

Anna Garnai, Production Coordinator

Sophia Hebert, Assistant Acquisitions Editor

Samantha Heffner, Marketing and Publicity Manager

Katie Huggins, Production Manager

Darja Malcolm-Clarke, Project Manager/Editor

Dan Pyle, Online Publishing Manager

Michael Regoli, Director of Publishing Operations

Pamela Rude, Senior Artist and Book Designer